English

Literary Criticism:

ROMANTIC

AND

VICTORIAN

GOLDENTREE BOOKS

R. C. BALD, SAMUEL H. BEER & WILLIAM C. DEVANE
Series Editors

THOMAS E. CONNOLLY, Editor
Joyce's "Portrait": Criticisms & Critiques

C. DAY LEWIS, Editor
English Lyric Poems, 1500–1900

O. B. HARDISON, JR., Editor
Modern Continental Literary Criticism

O. B. HARDISON, JR., Editor
English Literary Criticism: The Renaissance

SAMUEL HYNES, Editor
English Literary Criticism: Restoration and 18th Century

DANIEL G. HOFFMAN and SAMUEL HYNES, Editors
English Literary Criticism: Romantic and Victorian

KATHERINE LEVER
The Novel and the Reader

MILTON MARX
The Enjoyment of Drama, 2nd Edition

WILLIAM MATTHEWS
Later Medieval English Prose

HAROLD OREL, Editor
The World of Victorian Humor

ROBERT L. PETERS, Editor
Victorians on Literature & Art

EDWARD STONE, Editor
Henry James: Seven Stories and Studies

DANIEL G. HOFFMAN AND SAMUEL HYNES

University of
Pennsylvania

Swarthmore
College

EDITORS

English
Literary Criticism:
ROMANTIC
AND
VICTORIAN

New York

APPLETON-CENTURY-CROFTS

Division of Meredith Publishing Company

PREFACE

THIS BOOK CONCLUDES THE Goldentree series of anthologies of English literary criticism. Together these collections cover three broad periods of literature: the Renaissance, the neo-classical period, and the nineteenth century. Literary historians are accustomed to divide the nineteenth century into two distinct periods, the Romantic Movement and the Victorian Era. With respect to literary criticism and the assumptions on which it is based, however, it is more accurate to consider the century as a single "post-classical" period, enriched by the continuing claims of two basic conceptions of literature. Indeed these divided and intermingling streams are with us yet. We may call them Art-as-Vision and Art-as-Morality.

These conceptions may be discerned in Blake, Wordsworth, and Coleridge, the first three critics in this book. Blake conceives of Art as Vision, the self-transcending discovery of truths, not to be found by reason alone, which unify the world and give spiritual significance to life and to art. At the very inception of the Romantic Movement Blake's opposition to empiricism is extreme: he would overthrow the Rule of Reason, avow the primacy of the self against conformity to society, seek truth in symbols, and make a religion of his revelations. Revolting in their turn against the same dominant rationalism, Shelley, Keats, Mill, Pater, and Yeats held similar doctrines. Most of these writers regard the poet as a prophet or seer, are concerned with the psychology of creation, and assert the autonomy of the imagination.

But it is Coleridge who gives the sanction of a firm intellectual position to the primacy of the visionary imagination. Basing his view on theories of being and of knowledge developed from English neoplatonism and from the German Idealist philosophers then current, he defines the imagination as "a repetition in the finite mind of the eternal act of creation in the infinite." The immediate aim of poetry is to provide not truth but pleasure, a pleasure inseparable from the harmonious interaction of its parts. The poet "brings the whole soul of man into activity," for the imagination "dissolves, diffuses, dissipates" our impressions and memories of the sensory world in order to "re-create," or at the least, "to struggle to idealize and unify." Thus the pleasure at which art aims derives from the poet's creation of an ideal order. Hazlitt is Coleridge's most immediate English disciple. Abroad, he strongly influenced Poe, who took the extreme position that the pleasure which is the end of poetry excludes the truth and the morality of life; Poe's thought in turn brought Baudelaire's theories to fruition. By the end of the century Arthur Symons had translated the French symbolists and preached their doctrines to W. B. Yeats, who was already steeped in the views of Blake and Shelley. By then Henry James, defending the novel against didactic moralism, argued for the inseparability of form, content, and treatment on grounds that resemble Coleridge's affirmation of the integrity and autonomy of the poem. Coleridge has proved the germinal aesthetician for both the Symbolist movement in poetry and the formalist movement in criticism.

Although Wordsworth to some degree shared the concerns of his friend Coleridge, his critical position is based upon a view of Nature as deified, numinous, exemplifying a revealed moral order. Art, he says, must shed or shun artifice to place the soul directly in touch with the sublime underlying order of things. His emphasis upon the moral suasion of art, it will be seen, accommodates to the new Romantic psychology a conviction of neoclassical criticism. And it points toward a different line of later critical thought from that of the aesthetics of Vision.

Romantic poetry had characteristically presented man on isolation, seeking communion with eternal and transcendent values. By the middle of the century, however, the apocalyptic impulses inspired by the French Revolution gave way to increasing concern with man as a social being and with literature as a reflection of society. The great critics of this period are Ruskin and Arnold, who seek in literature the values and ideals not of individual Visionaries but of the life of which that literature is a record and, in Arnold's famous phrase, a criticism. At the same time the novel of manners, depicting society, rather than Nature or the soul, as the source and subject of individual aspirations, began to displace the poem as the form in which major statements would be made. It seemed that the morality in a work could once again, as in the neo-classical period, be measured by prevailing mores and its intentions be more or less didactically prescribed. The claims morality makes upon art were taken up by such practicing novelists as George Eliot and Meredith and, as has been suggested, modified by Henry James.

As will be seen, many of the century's critics are influenced by both traditions. Romanticism began as a reaction against the rationalism of the preceding age; it was, among other things, a movement to restore and exalt the personal, the emotional, the visionary elements in poetry for which Augustan criticism had made no dispensation. But this new emphasis was not in itself a rejection of the moral or even the didactic function of literature. It was rather a new way of considering the poetic act, by which the moral function of poetry might better be performed. When, however, moralizing critics undertook to dominate the creative artist, dictating subject matter and denying the writer access to realms of experience his own view of truth compelled him to treat, the reaction produced a series of movements more extreme than the original Romantic theories.

Aestheticism, Decadence, and Symbolism all went further than had the Romantics in asserting the view of art as vision without reference to any moral or social values, indeed often in opposition to such values. But here again the reaction was not complete. The Victorian emphasis was not swept away. At the same time that Yeats and Arthur Symons were propounding Symbolism, their contemporaries Edmund Gosse and George Saintsbury continued to be Victorian moralists. Later still, T. S. Eliot was to build upon Arnold's theory his view of the responsibilities of literature to society, taking from Coleridge and the Symbolists assumptions about the autonomy of the creative work, while Henry James's conviction of the moral integrity of artistic freedom has set the tone for the discussion of the novel in our time.

The selections in this book are based on the most authoritative sources and are complete unless otherwise indicated. A headnote to each selection offers brief biographical and critical information and a selected bibliography of works which deal with the author in his capacity as critic. For further information the following general works will be useful: *The Cambridge Bibliography of English Literature,* 5 vols. (Cambridge, 1940–57); George Saintsbury, *A History of Criticism and Literary Taste in Europe,* 3 vols. (Edinburgh, 1900–04); René Wellek, *A History of Modern Criticism 1750–1950,* 4 vols. (New Haven, 1955–[in progress]); William K. Wimsatt, Jr., and Cleanth Brooks, *Literary Criticism: A Short History* (New York, 1957).

Also: M. H. Abrams, *The Mirror and the Lamp* (New York, 1953); Walter J. Bate, *From Classic to Romantic* (Cambridge, Mass., 1946), and *Prefaces to Criticism* (Garden City, N. Y., 1959); Alba Warren, Jr., *English Poetic Theory, 1825–65* (Princeton, 1950).

For further bibliographical data see: P. F. Baum, *et al., The Victorian Poets, A Guide to Research* (Cambridge, Mass., 1956); Carolyn and Lawrence Houtchens, eds., *The English Romantic Poets and Essayists, A Review of Research and Criticism* (New York, 1957); and Thomas M. Raysor, ed., *The English Romantic Poets, A Review of Research* (New York, 1956).

D.G.H.
S.H.

Swarthmore, Pennsylvania

CONTENTS

English

Literary Criticism:

ROMANTIC

AND

VICTORIAN

William Blake

[1787–1827]

❦

BLAKE WAS BORN IN LONDON and lived in the heart of the city almost all his life. He was never sent to school but was apprenticed at 14 to an engraver from whom he learned the craft by which he earned his living. His first book of poems was published with the financial assistance of friends; all his later works Blake engraved and printed by hand. During his lifetime Blake received very little recognition, either as a painter or as a poet, and only in his last years did he gather a circle of admirers around him. But neither his confidence in his vision nor his artistic gifts failed him; he completed his greatest series of engravings, those for the Book of Job, when he was almost 70, and he was at work on his illustrations of Dante when he died.

Blake has two claims to his place at the beginning of this volume: as an antagonist of the dominant eighteenth-century critical doctrines, and as a proponent of contrary views that became standard in the following century. His attitude toward neo-classicism is made dramatically clear in his annotations to Reynolds' *Discourses.* Reynolds was one of the most orthodox (and best) of neo-classical theorists; Blake furiously rejects Reynolds' principles, and even his terminology —Inspiration, Vision, and Imagination—replace Reynolds' Reason, Rules, and General Nature.

As this new critical vocabulary suggests, Blake's opinions anticipated many commonplace Romantic theories: the primacy of Imagination, the personal origins of creative power, the organic nature of artistic form, the truth of the child's vision, the revolutionary power of art— all turn up in later critical writing. In many ways Blake is peculiarly close to the twentieth century: his view of the relation of politics and art is not unlike that held by W. H. Auden and other poets of the Thirties, and his defence of obscurity in art ("that which can be made Explicit is not worth my care") might have been uttered by Joyce's Stephen Dedalus. But above all it is his recognition of the power of symbols to express meanings hidden from the senses that links him to

1

modern poets like Yeats (a connection which Yeats acknowledged in both his criticism and his verse).

It is well to remember that Blake was only an occasional, amateur critic. The examples included here demonstrate this point clearly enough—a personal letter, and some marginal jottings in a book. His remarks are neither systematic nor general (Blake deeply distrusted generalization as a method); they are rather the insights and opinions of a unique mind intent upon justifying its own creations.

BIBLIOGRAPHY. *Complete Writings of William Blake,* ed. Geoffrey Keynes (London and New York, 1957); *Letters,* ed. Keynes (New York, 1956).

S. Foster Damon, *William Blake: His Philosophy and Symbols* (Boston and New York, 1924); Northrop Frye, *Fearful Symmetry: A Study of William Blake* (Princeton, 1947); Mark Schorer, *William Blake: The Politics of Vision* (New York, 1946); William Butler Yeats, *Essays and Introductions* (New York, 1961).

TEXT. *Complete Writings,* ed. Keynes (London and New York, The Nonesuch Press, 1957).

LETTER TO THE REVD DR. TRUSLER [1]

[1799]

REVD SIR,

I really am sorry that you are fall'n out with the Spiritual World, Especially if I should have to answer for it. I feel very sorry that your Ideas & Mine on Moral Painting differ so much as to have made you angry with my method of Study. If I am wrong, I am wrong in good company. I had hoped your plan comprehended All Species of this Art, & Expecially that you would not regret that Species which gives Existence to Every other, namely, Visions of Eternity. You say that I want somebody to Elucidate my Ideas. But you ought to know that What is Grand is necessarily obscure to Weak men. That which can be made Explicit to the Idiot is not worth my care. The wisest of the

---

[1] Dr. John Trusler (1735–1820), an eccentric clergyman-author, had been introduced to Blake as a possible patron, but nothing came of the venture.

Ancients consider'd what is not too Explicit as the fittest for Instruction, because it rouzes the faculties to act. I name Moses, Solomon, Esop, Homer, Plato.

But as you have favor'd me with your remarks on my Design, permit me in return to defend it against a mistaken one, which is, That I have supposed Malevolence without a Cause. Is not Merit in one a Cause of Envy in another, & Serenity & Happiness & Beauty a Cause of Malevolence? But Want of Money & the Distress of A Thief can never be alledged as the Cause of this Thieving, for many honest people endure greater hardships with Fortitude. We must therefore seek the Cause elsewhere than in want of Money, for that is the Miser's passion, not the Thief's.

I have therefore proved your Reasonings Ill proportion'd, which you can never prove my figures to be; they are those of Michael Angelo, Rafael & the Antique, & of the best living Models. I percieve that your Eye is perverted by Caricature Prints, which ought not to abound so much as they do. Fun I love, but too much Fun is of all things the most loathsom. Mirth is better than Fun, & Happiness is better than Mirth. I feel that a Man may be happy in This World. And I know that This World Is a World of Imagination & Vision. I see Every thing I paint In This World, but Every body does not see alike. To the Eyes of a Miser a Guinea is more beautiful than the Sun, & a bag worn with the use of Money has more beautiful proportions than a Vine filled with Grapes. The tree which moves some to tears of joy is in the Eyes of others only a Green thing that stands in the way. Some see Nature all Ridicule & Deformity, & by these I shall not regulate my proportions; & Some Scarce see Nature at all. But to the Eyes of the Man of Imagination, Nature is Imagination itself. As a man is, So he Sees. As the Eye is formed, such are its Powers. You certainly Mistake, when you say that the Visions of Fancy are not to be found in This World. To Me This World is all One continued Vision of Fancy or Imagination, & I feel Flatter'd when I am told so. What is it sets Homer, Virgil & Milton in so high a rank of Art? Why is the Bible more Entertaining & Instructive than any other book? Is it not because they are addressed to the Imagination, which is Spiritual Sensation, & but mediately to the Understanding or Reason? Such is True Painting, and such was alone valued by the Greeks & the best modern Artists. Consider what Lord Bacon says: "Sense sends over to Imagination before Reason have judged, & Reason sends over to Imagination before the Decree can be acted." See Advancemt of Learning, Part 2, P. 47 of first Edition.

But I am happy to find a Great Majority of Fellow Mortals who can Elucidate My Visions, & Particularly they have been Elucidated by Children, who have taken a greater delight in contemplating my Pictures than I even hoped. Neither Youth nor Childhood is Folly or Incapacity. Some Children are Fools & so are some Old Men. But There is a vast Majority on the side of Imagination or Spiritual Sensation.

To Engrave after another Painter is infinitely more laborious than to Engrave one's own Inventions. And of the size you require my price has been Thirty Guineas, & I cannot afford to do it for less. I had Twelve for the Head I sent you as a Specimen; but after my own designs I could do at least Six times the quantity of labour in the same time, which will account for the difference of price as also that Chalk Engraving is at least six times as laborious as Aqua tinta. I have no objection to Engraving after another Artist. Engraving is the profession I was apprenticed to, & should never have attempted to live by any thing else, If orders had not come in for my Designs & Paintings, which I have the pleasure to tell you are Increasing Every Day. Thus If I am a Painter it is not to be attributed to Seeking after. But I am contented whether I live by Painting or Engraving.

I am, Revd. Sir, your very obedient servant,

WILLIAM BLAKE.

13 Hercules Buildings
    Lambeth
August 23. 1799

from

ANNOTATIONS TO SIR JOSHUA REYNOLDS' DISCOURSES

[1808]

[We have indicated to which Discourse notes refer, but have not included Reynolds' remarks—Eds.]

This Man was Hired to Depress Art.

This is the Opinion of Will Blake: my Proofs of this Opinion are given in the following Notes.

> Advice of the Popes who succeeded the Age of Rafael
> Degrade first the Arts if you'd Mankind Degrade.
> Hire Idiots to Paint with cold light & hot shade:
> Give high Price for the worst, leave the best in disgrace,
> And with Labours of Ignorance fill every place.

Having spent the Vigour of my Youth & Genius under the Opression of Sr Joshua & his Gang of Cunning Hired Knaves Without Employment & as much as could possibly be Without Bread, The Reader must Expect to Read in all my Remarks on these Books Nothing but Indignation & Resentment. While Sr Joshua was rolling in Riches, Barry was Poor & Unemploy'd except by his own Energy; Mortimer was call'd a Madman, & only Portrait Painting applauded & rewarded by the Rich & Great. Reynolds & Gainsborough Blotted & Blurred one against the other & Divided all the English World between them. Fuseli, Indignant, almost hid himself. I am hid.

The Arts & Sciences are the Destruction of Tyrannies or Bad Governments. Why should A Good Government endeavour to Depress what is its Chief & only Support?

The Foundation of Empire is Art & Science. Remove them or Degrade them, & the Empire is No More. Empire follows Art & Not Vice Versa as Englishmen suppose . . .[2]

[2] The above remarks are written on the title page and preliminary pages.

Invention depends Altogether upon Execution or Organization;
as that is right or wrong so is the Invention perfect or imperfect. Whoever is set to Undermine the Execution of Art is set
to Destroy Art. Michael Angelo's Art depends on Michael Angelo's
Execution Altogether . . .

To Generalize is to be an Idiot. To Particularize is the Alone
Distinction of Merit. General Knowledges are those Knowledges
that Idiots possess . . .

> When Sr Joshua Reynolds died
> All Nature was degraded;
> The King drop'd a tear into the Queen's Ear,
> And all his Pictures Faded.[3]

DISCOURSE I

I consider Reynold's Discourses to the Royal Academy as the
Simulations of the Hypocrite who smiles particularly where he
means to Betray. His Praise of Rafael is like the Hysteric Smile of
Revenge. His Softness & Candour, the hidden trap & the poisoned
feast. He praises Michel Angelo for Qualities which Michel Angelo
abhorr'd, & He blames Rafael for the only Qualities which Rafael
Valued. Whether Reynolds knew what he was doing is nothing to
me: the Mischief is just the same whether a Man does it Ignorantly
or Knowingly. I always consider'd True Art & True Artists to be
particularly Insulted & Degraded by the Reputation of these
Discourses, As much as they were Degraded by the Reputation
of Reynolds's Paintings, & that Such Artists as Reynolds are at all
times Hired by the Satans for the Depression of Art—A Pretence
of Art, To destroy Art.

The Neglect of Fuseli's Milton in a Country pretending to the
Encouragement of Art is a Sufficient Apology for My Vigorous
Indignation, if indeed the Neglect of My own Powers had not
been. Ought not the Employers of Fools to be Execrated in
future Ages? They Will and Shall! Foolish Men, your own real
Greatness depends on your Encouragement of the Arts, & your
Fall will depend on their Neglect & Depression. What you Fear is
your true Interest. Leo X was advised not to Encourage the Arts;
he was too Wise to take this Advice.

[3] These remarks are written in the margins of the introductory matter.

The Rich Men of England form themselves into a Society to Sell & Not to Buy Pictures. The Artist who does not throw his Contempt on such Trading Exhibitions, does not know either his own Interest or his Duty.

> When Nations grow Old, The Arts grow Cold
> And Commerce settles on every Tree,
> And the Poor & the Old can live upon Gold,
> For all are Born Poor, Aged Sixty three.

Reynolds's Opinion was that Genius May be Taught & that all Pretence to Inspiration is a Lie & a Deceit, to say the least of it. For if it is a Deceit, the whole Bible is Madness. This Opinion originates in the Greeks' calling the Muses Daughters of Memory.

The Enquiry in England is not whether a Man has Talents & Genius, But whether he is Passive & Polite & a Virtuous Ass & obedient to Noblemen's Opinions in Art & Science. If he is, he is a Good Man. If Not, he must be Starved. . .

Minute Discrimination is Not Accidental. All Sublimity is founded on Minute Discrimination.

I do not believe that Rafael taught Mich. Angelo, or that Mich. Angelo taught Rafael, any more than I believe that the Rose teaches the Lilly how to grow, or the Apple tree teaches the Pear tree how to bear Fruit. I do not believe the tales of Anecdote writers when they militate against Individual Character.

Imitation is Criticism.

. . . Are we to understand him to mean that Facility in Composing is a Frivolous pursuit? A Facility in Composing is the Greatest Power of Art, & Belongs to None but the Greatest Artists, the Most Minutely Discriminating & Determinate.

Mechanical Excellence is the Only Vehicle of Genius . . .

Execution is the Chariot of Genius.

DISCOURSE II

. . . The Man who asserts that there is no such Thing as Softness in Art, & that every thing in Art is Definite & Determinate, has not been told this by Practise, but by Inspiration & Vision, because Vision is Determinate & Perfect, & he Copies That without

Fatigue, Every thing being Definite & determinate. Softness is Produced alone by Comparative Strength & Weakness in the Marking out of the Forms. I say These Principles could never be found out by the Study of Nature with Con—, or Innate, Science.

DISCOURSE III

A work of Genius is a Work "Not to be obtain'd by the Invocation of Memory & her Syren Daughters, but by Devout prayer to that Eternal Spirit, who can enrich with all utterance & knowledge & sends out his Seraphim with the hallowed fire of his Altar to touch & purify the lips of whom he pleases." MILTON.

The following Discourse is particularly Interesting to Block heads, as it endeavours to prove That there is No such thing as Inspiration & that any Man of a plain Understanding may by Thieving from Others become a Mich. Angelo.

Without Minute Neatness of Execution The Sublime cannot Exist! Grandeur of Ideas is founded on Precision of Ideas . . .

The Man who on Examining his own Mind finds nothing of Inspiration ought not to dare to be an Artist; he is a Fool & a Cunning Knave suited to the Purposes of Evil Demons.

The Man who never in his Mind & Thoughts travel'd to Heaven Is No Artist.

Artists who are above a plain Understanding are Mock'd & Destroy'd by this President of Fools.

It is Evident that Reynolds Wish'd none but Fools to be in the Arts & in order to this, he calls all others Vague Enthusiasts or Madmen.

What has Reasoning to do with the Art of Painting? . . .

Knowledge of Ideal Beauty is Not to be Acquired. It is Born with us. Innate Ideas are in Every Man, Born with him; they are truly Himself. The Man who says that we have No Innate Ideas must be a Fool & Knave, Having No Con-Science or Innate Science.

One Central Form composed of all other Forms being Granted, it does not therefore follow that all other Forms are Deformity.

All Forms are Perfect in the Poet's Mind, but these are not

Abstracted nor compounded from Nature, but are from Imagination.

The Great Bacon—he is Call'd: I call him the Little Bacon—says that Every thing must be done by Experiment; his first principle is Unbelief, and yet here he says that Art must be produc'd Without such Method. He is Like Sr Joshua, full of Self-Contradiction & Knavery.

What is General Nature? is there Such a Thing? what is General Knowledge? is there such a Thing? Strictly Speaking All Knowledge is Particular . . .

Distinct General Form Cannot Exist. Distinctness is Particular, Not General . . .

DISCOURSE IV

The Two Following Discourses are Particularly Calculated for the Setting Ignorant & Vulgar Artists as Models of Execution in Art. Let him who will, follow such advice. I will not. I know that The Man's Execution is as his Conception & No better . . .

DISCOURSE VI

How ridiculous it would be to see the Sheep Endeavouring to walk like the Dog, or the Ox striving to trot like the Horse; just as Ridiculous it is to see One Man Striving to Imitate Another. Man varies from Man more than Animal from Animal of different Species . . .

If Art was Progressive We should have had Mich. Angelos & Rafaels to Succeed & to Improve upon each other. But it is not so. Genius dies with its Possessor & Comes not again till Another is Born with It.

Identities or Things are Neither Cause nor Effect. They are Eternal.

Reynolds Thinks that Man Learns all that he knows. I say on the Contrary that Man Brings All that he has or can have Into the World with him. Man is Born Like a Garden ready Planted & Sown. This World is too poor to produce one Seed.

Reynolds: The mind is but a barren soil; a soil which is soon exhausted, and will produce no crop, . . .

The mind that could have produced this Sentence must have

been a Pitiful, a Pitiful Imbecillity. I always thought that the Human Mind was the most Prolific of All Things & Inexhaustible. I certainly do Thank God that I am not like Reynolds . . .

He who can be bound down is No Genius. Genius cannot be Bound; it may be Render'd Indignant & Outrageous.
"Opression makes the Wise Man Mad."

SOLOMON.

DISCOURSE VII

The Purpose of the following discourse is to Prove That Taste & Genius are not of Heavenly Origin & that all who have supposed that they Are so, are to be Consider'd as Weak headed Fanatics.

The Obligations Reynolds has laid on Bad Artists of all Classes will at all times make them his Admirers, but most especially for this discourse, in which it is proved that the Stupid are born with Faculties Equal to other Men, Only they have not Cultivated them because they thought it not worth the trouble.

Obscurity is Neither the Source of the Sublime nor of any Thing Else . . .

The Ancients did not mean to Impose when they affirm'd their belief in Vision & Revelation. Plato was in Earnest: Milton was in Earnest. They believ'd that God did Visit Man Really & Truly & not as Reynolds pretends . . .

DISCOURSE VIII

Burke's Treatise on the Sublime & Beautiful is founded on the Opinions of Newton & Locke; on this Treatise Reynolds has grounded many of his assertions in all his Discourses. I read Burke's Treatise when very Young; at the same time I read Locke on Human Understanding & Bacon's Advancement of Learning; on Every one of these Books I wrote my Opinions, & on looking them over find that my Notes on Reynolds in this Book are exactly Similar. I felt the Same Contempt & Abhorrence then that I do now. They mock Inspiration & Vision. Inspiration & Vision was then, & now is, & I hope will always Remain, my Element, my Eternal Dwelling place; how can I then hear it Contemned without returning Scorn for Scorn? . . .

William Wordsworth

[1770–1850]

WORDSWORTH WAS BORN IN THE Lake District of England and lived there until he went to Cambridge in 1787. In 1791–2 he spent a year in France and became briefly a supporter of the French revolutionary cause. After his return to England he settled in the country with his sister, Dorothy, and later also with Coleridge; these, he said, were the two people to whom his intellect owed most.

In 1798 Wordsworth and Coleridge together published *Lyrical Ballads,* a collection of poems embodying their theories of poetry at that time. Wordsworth's *Preface,* which spells out his version of those theories, was written for the second edition (1800); Coleridge's version appears in his *Biographia Literaria* (see below, pp. 42–92).

The foundation of Wordsworth's critical principles is in the meaning which he gives to the word *nature.* Nature, for Wordsworth, means all those aspects of the physical world—the elements, the seasons, rural life—through which the truth of universal harmony and order is given beautiful and permanent form. Human nature instinctively responds to those forms; therefore the best human condition is one in which man is most directly exposed to the beneficent powers of nature, and freed of artificial intellectual and social barriers to natural feeling.

From these assumptions follow the two principal theories of the *Preface*: a theory of poetic language, and a theory of poetic creation. Wordsworth's theory of language distinguishes between "poetic diction" and "the language really spoken by men"; poetic diction, by which he means the artificial language of much eighteenth-century poetry, is bad because it implies that a poem is an intellectually constructed thing, different in kind from ordinary human experience. Being artificial and sophisticated, it stands between the reader and the direct experience of natural truth, which is best expressed in the simplest and thus most permanent language of common speech heightened by passion.

For Wordsworth, as for most Romantic theorists, the creative process is immediate and emotional, "the spontaneous overflow of powerful feelings"; Wordsworth is typically Romantic in concentrating his critical attention on the psychology of creation, and not, as eighteenth-century critics tended to do, on the psychology of communication—*i.e.* on the artist, not on the reader. But Wordsworth is not a pure "self-expressionist"; he recognizes that the initial poetic emotion may be "recollected in tranquillity," thus allowing for the operation of judgment and meditation as well as spontaneity; and he maintains a strong moral bias. "Every poet," he wrote in a letter, "is a teacher"; he teaches by enlightening the understanding and purifying the affections of his readers. This is accomplished by bringing the reader as directly as possible into contact with the beautiful and permanent forms of nature.

Wordsworth's criticism is neither entirely original nor entirely consistent. His idea of the emotional nature of poetry, his concern for general truth and for moral purpose have their roots in eighteenth-century theory. His various remarks about "the language really used by men" leave his standards of classification unclear—is it to be rustic speech, or speech purified of artificial constructions, or speech proven by long common usage? And in his own practice he often employed the very "poetic" locutions that he condemns in theory. On this point, as well as on others, Coleridge, a more systematic and sophisticated critic, found it easy to poke holes in Wordsworth's arguments; but these inconsistencies seem less damaging if we remember that Wordsworth was writing not a *Defence of Poetry*, but a self-defence, a formulation of the theoretical assumptions behind his own poetic greatness.

BIBLIOGRAPHY. *Wordsworth's Literary Criticism*, ed. Nowell C. Smith (London, 1905).

Marjorie L. Barstow, *Wordsworth's Theory of Poetic Diction* (New Haven, 1917); Joseph W. Beach, *Concept of Nature in Nineteenth-Century English Poetry* (New York, 1936); Arthur Beatty, *William Wordsworth. His Doctrine and Art in Their Historical Relations* (Madison, Wisc., 1922); John Jones, *The Egotistical Sublime: A History of Wordsworth's Imagination* (London, 1954); Markham L. Peacock, Jr., *Critical Opinions of William Wordsworth* (Baltimore, 1950); J. C. Smith, *Study of Wordsworth* (Edinburgh, 1944).

TEXT. *Poetical Works* (London, 1850), vol. V.

preface to

LYRICAL BALLADS

[1800]

THE FIRST VOLUME of these Poems has already been submitted to general perusal. It was published, as an experiment, which, I hoped, might be of some use to ascertain how far, by fitting to metrical arrangement a selection of the real language of men in a state of vivid sensation, that sort of pleasure and that quantity of pleasure may be imparted, which a Poet may rationally endeavour to impart.

I had formed no very inaccurate estimate of the probable effect of those Poems: I flattered myself that they who should be pleased with them would read them with more than common pleasure: and, on the other hand, I was well aware, that by those who should dislike them they would be read with more than common dislike. The result has differed from my expectation in this only, that a greater number have been pleased than I ventured to hope I should please.

Several of my Friends are anxious for the success of these Poems, from a belief that, if the views with which they were composed were indeed realised, a class of Poetry would be produced, well adapted to interest mankind permanently, and not unimportant in the quality, and in the multiplicity of its moral relations: and on this account they have advised me to prefix a systematic defence of the theory upon which the Poems were written. But I was unwilling to undertake the task, knowing that on this occasion the Reader would look coldly upon my arguments, since I might be suspected of having been principally influenced by the selfish and foolish hope of *reasoning* him into an approbation of these particular Poems: and I was still more unwilling to undertake the task, because, adequately to display the opinions, and fully to enforce the arguments, would require a space wholly disproportionate to a preface. For, to treat the subject with the clearness and coherence of which it is susceptible, it would be necessary to give a full account of the present state of the public taste in this country, and to determine how far this taste is healthy or depraved; which, again, could not be determined without pointing out in what manner language and the human mind act and re-act on each other, and without retracing the revolutions, not of literature alone, but likewise of society itself. I have therefore altogether declined to enter regularly upon this defence; yet I am sensible that there would be something like impropriety in abruptly obtruding upon the Public, without a few words of introduction, Poems so materially different from those upon which general approbation is at present bestowed.

It is supposed, that by the act of writing in verse an Author makes a formal engagement that he will gratify certain known habits of association; that he not only thus apprises the Reader that certain classes of ideas and expressions will be found in his book, but that others will be carefully excluded. This exponent or symbol held forth by metrical language must in different eras of literature have excited very different expectations: for example, in the age of Catullus, Terence, and Lucretius, and that of Statius or Claudian; and in our own country, in the age of Shakespeare and Beaumont and Fletcher, and that of Donne and Cowley, or Dryden, or Pope. I will not take upon me to determine the exact import of the promise which, by the act of writing in verse, an Author in the present day makes to his reader: but it will undoubtedly appear to many persons that I have not fulfilled the terms of an engagement thus voluntarily contracted. They who have been accustomed to the gaudiness and inane phraseology of many modern writers, if they persist in reading this book to its conclusion, will, no doubt, frequently have to struggle with feelings of strangeness and awkwardness: they will look round for poetry, and will be induced to inquire by what species of courtesy these attempts can be permitted to assume that title. I hope therefore the reader will not censure me for attempting to state what I have proposed to myself to perform; and also (as far as the limits of a preface will permit) to explain some of the chief reasons which have determined me in the choice of my purpose: that at least he may be spared any unpleasant feeling of disappointment, and that I myself may be protected from one of the most dishonourable accusations which can be brought against an Author; namely, that of an indolence which prevents him from endeavouring to ascertain what is his duty, or, when his duty is ascertained, prevents him from performing it.

The principal object, then, proposed in these Poems was to choose incidents and situations from common life, and to relate or describe them, throughout, as far as was possible, in a selection of language really used by men, and, at the same time, to throw over them a certain colouring of imagination, whereby ordinary things should be presented to the mind in an unusual aspect; and further, and above all, to make these incidents and situations interesting by tracing in them, truly though not ostentatiously, the primary laws of our nature: chiefly, as far as regards the manner in which we associate ideas in a state of excitement. Humble and rustic life was generally chosen, because, in that condition, the essential passions of the heart find a better soil in which they can attain their maturity, are less under restraint, and speak a plainer and more emphatic language; because in that condition of life our elementary feelings co-exist in a state of greater simplicity, and, consequently, may be more accurately contemplated, and more forcibly communicated; because the manners of rural life germinate from those elementary feelings, and, from the necessary character of rural occupations, are more easily comprehended, and are more durable; and, lastly, because in that condition the passions of men are incorporated with the beautiful and permanent forms of nature. The language, too, of these men has been adopted (purified indeed from what appear to be its real defects, from all lasting and rational causes of dislike or disgust) because such men hourly communicate with the best objects from which the best part of language is originally derived; and because, from their rank in society and the sameness and narrow circle of their intercourse, being less under the influence of social vanity, they convey their feelings and notions in simple and unelaborated expressions. Accordingly, such a language, arising out of repeated experience and regular feelings, is a more permanent, and a far more philosophical language than that which is frequently substituted for it by poets, who think that they are conferring honor upon themselves and their art, in proportion as they separate themselves from the sympathies of men, and indulge in arbitrary and capricious habits of expression, in order to furnish food for fickle tastes, and fickle appetites, of their own creation.[1]

I cannot, however, be insensible to the present outcry against the triviality and meanness, both of thought and language, which some of my contemporaries have occasionally introduced into their metrical compositions; and I acknowledge that this defect, where it exists, is more dishonorable to the writer's own character than false refinement or arbitrary innovation, though I should contend at the same time it is far less pernicious in the sum of its consequences. From such verses the poems in these volumes will be found distinguished at least by one mark of difference, that each of them has a worthy *purpose*. Not that I always began to write with a distinct purpose formally conceived; but habits of meditation have, I trust, so prompted and regulated my feelings, that my descriptions of such objects as strongly excite those feelings will be found to carry along with them a *purpose*. If this opinion be erroneous, I can have little right to the name of a poet. For all good poetry is the spontaneous overflow of powerful feelings: and though this be true, poems to which any value can be attached were never produced on any variety of subjects but by a man who, being possessed of more than usual organic sensibility, had also thought long and deeply. For our continued influxes of feeling are modified and directed by our thoughts, which are indeed the representatives of all our past feelings; and, as by contemplating the relation of these general representatives to each other, we discover what is really important to men, so, by the repetition and continuance of this act, our feelings will be connected with important subjects, till at length, if we be originally possessed of much sensibility, such habits of mind will be produced that, by obeying blindly and mechanically the impulses of those habits, we shall describe objects, and utter sentiments, of such a nature, and in such connection with each other, that the understanding of the reader must necessarily be in some degree enlightened, and his affections strengthened and purified.

---

[1] It is worth while here to observe that the affecting parts of Chaucer are almost always expressed in language pure and universally intelligible even to this day. [Wordsworth's note.]

It has been said that each of these poems has a purpose. Another circumstance must be mentioned which distinguishes these poems from the popular poetry of the day; it is this, that the feeling therein developed gives importance to the action and situation, and not the action and situation to the feeling.

A sense of false modesty shall not prevent me from asserting that the reader's attention is pointed to this mark of distinction, far less for the sake of these particular poems than from the general importance of the subject. The subject is indeed important! For the human mind is capable of being excited without the application of gross and violent stimulants; and he must have a very faint perception of its beauty and dignity who does not know this, and who does not further know that one being is elevated above another in proportion as he possesses this capability. It has therefore appeared to me that to endeavor to produce or enlarge this capability is one of the best services in which, at any period, a writer can be engaged; but this service, excellent at all times, is especially so at the present day. For a multitude of causes, unknown to former times, are now acting with a combined force to blunt the discriminating powers of the mind, and, unfitting it for all voluntary exertion, to reduce it to a state of almost savage torpor. The most effective of these causes are the great national events which are daily taking place, and the increasing accumulation of men in cities, where the uniformity of their occupations produces a craving for extraordinary incident, which the rapid communication of intelligence hourly gratifies. To this tendency of life and manners the literature and theatrical exhibitions of the country have conformed themselves. The invaluable works of our elder writers, I had almost said the works of Shakespeare and Milton, are driven into neglect by frantic novels, sickly and stupid German tragedies, and deluges of idle and extravagant stories in verse.—When I think upon this degrading thirst after outrageous stimulation, I am almost ashamed to have spoken of the feeble endeavor made in these volumes to counteract it; and, reflecting upon the magnitude of the general evil, I should be oppressed with no dishonorable melancholy, had I not a deep impression of certain inherent and indestructible qualities of the human mind, and likewise of certain powers in the great and permanent objects that act upon it, which are equally inherent and indestructible; and were there not added to this impression a belief that the time is approaching when the evil will be systematically opposed, by men of greater powers, and with far more distinguished success.

Having dwelt thus long on the subjects and aim of these poems, I shall request the reader's permission to apprise him of a few circumstances relating to their *style*, in order, among other reasons, that he may not censure me for not having performed what I never attempted. The reader will find that personifications of abstract ideas rarely occur in these volumes, and are utterly rejected, as an ordinary device to elevate the style, and raise it above prose. My purpose was to imitate, and, as far as possible, to adopt the very language of men; and assuredly such personifications do not make any natural or regular part of that language. They are, indeed, a figure of speech occasionally prompted by passion, and I have made use of them as such; but have endeavored utterly to reject them as a mechanical device of style, or as a family language which writers in meter seem to lay claim to by prescription. I have wished to keep the reader in the company of flesh and blood, persuaded that by so doing I shall interest him. Others who pursue a different track will interest him likewise; I do not interfere with their claim, but wish to prefer a claim of my own. There will also be found in these volumes little of what is usually called poetic diction; as much pains has been taken to avoid it as is ordinarily taken to produce it; this has been done for the reason already alleged, to bring my language near to the language of men; and further, because the pleasure which I have proposed to myself to impart is of a kind very different from that which is supposed by many persons to be the proper object of poetry. Without being culpably particular, I do not know how to give my reader a more exact notion of the style in which it was my wish and intention to write, than by informing him that I have at all times endeavored to look steadily at my subject; consequently there is, I hope, in these poems little falsehood of description, and my ideas are expressed in language fitted to their respective importance. Something must have been gained by this practice, as it is friendly to one property of all good poetry, namely, good sense: but it has necessarily cut me off from a large portion of phrases and figures of speech which from father to son have long been regarded as the common inheritance of poets. I have also thought it expedient to restrict myself still further, having abstained from the use of many expressions, in themselves proper and beautiful, but which have been foolishly repeated by bad poets, till such feelings of disgust are connected with them as it is scarcely possible by any art of association to overpower.

If in a poem there should be found a series of lines, or even a single line, in which the language, though naturally arranged, and according to the strict laws of meter, does not differ from that of prose, there is a numerous class of critics, who, when they stumble upon these prosaisms, as they call them, imagine that they have made a notable discovery, and exult over the poet as over a man ignorant of his own profession. Now these men would establish a canon of criticism which the reader will conclude he must utterly reject, if he wishes to be pleased with these volumes. And it would be a most easy task to prove to him that not only the language of a large portion of every good poem, even of the most elevated character, must necessarily, except with reference to the meter, in no respect differ from that of good prose, but likewise that some of the most interesting parts of the best poems will be found to be strictly the language of prose when prose is well written. The truth of this assertion might be demonstrated by innumerable passages from almost all the poetical writings, even of Milton himself. To illustrate the subject in a general manner, I will here adduce a short composition of Gray, who was at the head of those who, by their reasonings, have attempted to widen the space of separation betwixt prose and metrical composition, and was more than any other man curiously elaborate in the structure of his own poetic diction.

> In vain to me the smiling mornings shine,
> And reddening Phoebus lifts his golden fire:
> The birds in vain their amorous descant join,
> Or cheerful fields resume their green attire.
> These ears, alas! for other notes repine;
> *A different object do these eyes require;*
> *My lonely anguish melts no heart but mine;*
> *And in my breast the imperfect joys expire;*

> Yet morning smiles the busy race to cheer,
> And new-born pleasure brings to happier men;
> The fields to all their wonted tribute bear;
> To warm their little loves the birds complain.
> *I fruitless mourn to him that cannot hear,*
> *And weep the more because I weep in vain.*[2]

It will easily be perceived, that the only part of this sonnet which is of any value is the lines printed in italics; it is equally obvious that, except in the rhyme, and in the use of the single word "fruitless" for fruitlessly, which is so far a defect, the language of these lines does in no respect differ from that of prose.

By the foregoing quotation it has been shown that the language of prose may yet be well adapted to poetry; and it was previously asserted that a large portion of the language of every good poem can in no respect differ from that of good prose. We will go further. It may be safely affirmed that there neither is, nor can be, any *essential* difference between the language of prose and metrical composition. We are fond of tracing the resemblance between poetry and painting, and, accordingly, we call them sisters: but where shall we find bonds of connection sufficiently strict to typify the affinity betwixt metrical and prose composition? They both speak by and to the same organs; the bodies in which both of them are clothed may be said to be of the same substance, their affections are kindred, and almost identical, not necessarily differing even in degree; poetry [3] sheds no tears "such as angels weep," but natural and human tears; she can boast of no celestial ichor that distinguishes her vital juices from those of prose; the same human blood circulates through the veins of them both.

If it be affirmed that rhyme and metrical arrangement of

2 "Sonnet on the Death of Richard West."
3 I here use the word "poetry" (though against my own judgment) as opposed to the word "prose," and synonymous with metrical composition. But much confusion has been introduced into criticism by this contradistinction of poetry and prose, instead of the more philosophical one of poetry and matter of fact, or science. The only strict antithesis to prose is metre; nor is this, in truth, a *strict* antithesis, because lines and passages of metre so naturally occur in writing prose, that it would be scarcely possible to avoid them, even were it desirable [Wordsworth's note].

themselves constitute a distinction which overturns what has just
been said on the strict affinity of metrical language with that of
prose, and paves the way for other artificial distinctions which the
mind voluntarily admits, I answer that the language of such
poetry as is here recommended is, as far as is possible, a selection
of the language really spoken by men; that this selection, where-
ever it is made with true taste and feeling, will of itself form a
distinction far greater than would at first be imagined, and will
entirely separate the composition from the vulgarity and meanness of ordinary life; and, if meter be superadded thereto, I
believe that a dissimilitude will be produced altogether sufficient
for the gratification of a rational mind. What other distinction
would we have? Whence is it to come? And where is it to exist?
Not, surely, where the poet speaks through the mouths of his
characters: it cannot be necessary here, either for elevation of
style, or any of its supposed ornaments: for, if the poet's subject
be judiciously chosen, it will naturally, and upon fit occasion,
lead him to passions the language of which, if selected truly and
judiciously, must necessarily be dignified and variegated, and
alive with metaphors and figures. I forbear to speak of an incongruity which would shock the intelligent reader, should the
poet interweave any foreign splendor of his own with that which
the passion naturally suggests: it is sufficient to say that such
addition is unnecessary. And surely it is more probable that those
passages which with propriety abound with metaphors and
figures will have their due effect, if, upon other occasions where
the passions are of a milder character, the style also be subdued
and temperate.

But as the pleasure which I hope to give by the poems now
presented to the reader must depend entirely on just notions
upon this subject, and as it is in itself of high importance to our
taste and moral feelings, I cannot content myself with these detached remarks. And if, in what I am about to say, it shall appear
to some that my labor is unnecessary, and that I am like a man
fighting a battle without enemies, such persons may be reminded
that, whatever be the language outwardly holden by men, a
practical faith in the opinions which I am wishing to establish
is almost unknown. If my conclusions are admitted, and carried
as far as they must be carried if admitted at all, our judgments

concerning the works of the greatest poets both ancient and modern will be far different from what they are at present, both when we praise, and when we censure; and our moral feelings influencing and influenced by these judgments will, I believe, be corrected and purified.

Taking up the subject, then, upon general grounds, let me ask, what is meant by the word Poet? What is a poet? To whom does he address himself? And what language is to be expected from him?—He is a man speaking to men: a man, it is true, endowed with more lively sensibility, more enthusiasm and tenderness, who has a greater knowledge of human nature, and a more comprehensive soul, than are supposed to be common among mankind; a man pleased with his own passions and volitions, and who rejoices more than other men in the spirit of life that is in him; delighting to contemplate similar volitions and passions as manifested in the goings-on of the universe, and habitually impelled to create them where he does not find them. To these qualities he has added a disposition to be affected more than other men by absent things as if they were present; an ability of conjuring up in himself passions which are indeed far from being the same as those produced by real events, yet (especially in those parts of the general sympathy which are pleasing and delightful) do more nearly resemble the passions produced by real events than anything which, from the motions of their own minds merely, other men are accustomed to feel in themselves:—whence, and from practice, he has acquired a greater readiness and power in expressing what he thinks and feels, and especially those thoughts and feelings which, by his own choice, or from the structure of his own mind, arise in him without immediate external excitement.

But whatever portion of this faculty we may suppose even the greatest poet to possess, there cannot be a doubt that the language which it will suggest to him must often, in liveliness and truth, fall short of that which is uttered by men in real life under the actual pressure of those passions, certain shadows of which the poet thus produces, or feels to be produced, in himself.

However exalted a notion we would wish to cherish of the character of a poet, it is obvious that while he describes and imitates passions, his employment is in some degree mechanical, compared with the freedom and power of real and substantial action and suffering. So that it will be the wish of the poet to bring his feelings near to those of the persons whose feelings he describes,—nay, for short spaces of time, perhaps, to let himself slip into an entire delusion, and even confound and identify his own feelings with theirs; modifying only the language which is thus suggested to him by a consideration that he describes for a particular purpose, that of giving pleasure. Here, then, he will apply the principle of selection which has been already insisted upon. He will depend upon this for removing what would otherwise be painful or disgusting in the passion; he will feel that there is no necessity to trick out or to elevate nature: and, the more industriously he applies this principle, the deeper will be his faith that no words which *his* fancy or imagination can suggest will be to be compared with those which are the emanations of reality and truth.

But it may be said by those who do not object to the general spirit of these remarks, that, as it is impossible for the poet to produce upon all occasions language as exquisitely fitted for the passion as that which the real passion itself suggests, it is proper that he should consider himself as in the situation of a translator, who does not scruple to substitute excellencies of another kind for those which are unattainable by him, and endeavors occasionally to surpass his original, in order to make some amends for the general inferiority to which he feels that he must submit. But this would be to encourage idleness and unmanly despair. Further, it is the language of men who speak of what they do not understand; who talk of poetry as of a matter of amusement and idle pleasure; who will converse with us as gravely about a *taste* for poetry, as they express it, as if it were a thing as indifferent as a taste for rope-dancing, or Frontiniac or Sherry. Aristotle, I have been told, has said that poetry is the most philosophic of all writing: it is so: its object is truth, not individual and local, but general, and operative; not standing upon external testimony, but carried alive into the heart by passion; truth which is its own testimony, which gives competence and confidence to the tribunal to which it appeals, and receives them from the same tribunal. Poetry is the image of man and nature. The obstacles which stand in the way of the fidelity of the biographer and historian, and of their consequent utility, are incalculably greater than those which are to be encountered by the poet who comprehends the dignity of his art. The poet writes under one restriction only, namely, the necessity of giving immediate pleasure to a human being possessed of that information which may be expected from him, not as a lawyer, a physician, a mariner, an astronomer, or a natural philosopher, but as a man. Except this one restriction, there is no object standing between the poet and the image of things; between this, and the biographer and historian, there are a thousand.

Nor let this necessity of producing immediate pleasure be considered as a degradation of the poet's art. It is far otherwise. It is an acknowledgement of the beauty of the universe, an acknowledgment the more sincere, because not formal, but indirect; it is a task light and easy to him who looks at the world in the spirit of love: further, it is a homage paid to the native and naked dignity of man, to the grand elementary principle of pleasure, by which he knows, and feels, and lives, and moves. We have no sympathy but what is propagated by pleasure: I would not be misunderstood; but wherever we sympathize with pain, it will be found that the sympathy is produced and carried on by subtle combinations with pleasure. We have no knowledge, that is, no general principles drawn from the contemplation of particular facts, but what has been built up by pleasure, and exists in us by pleasure alone. The man of science, the chemist and mathematician, whatever difficulties and disgusts they may have had to struggle with, know and feel this. However painful may be the objects with which the anatomist's knowledge is connected, he feels that his knowledge is pleasure; and where he has no pleasure he has no knowledge. What then does the poet? He considers man and the objects that surround him as acting and reacting upon each other, so as to produce an infinite complexity of pain and pleasure; he considers man in his own nature and in his ordinary life as contemplating this with a certain quantity of immediate knowledge, with certain convictions, intuitions, and deductions, which from habit acquire the quality of intuitions; he considers him as looking upon this complex scene of ideas and sensations, and finding everywhere objects that immediately excite in him sympathies which, from the necessities of his nature, are accompanied by an over-balance of enjoyment.

To this knowledge which all men carry about with them, and to these sympathies in which, without any other discipline than that of our daily life, we are fitted to take delight, the poet principally directs his attention. He considers man and nature as essentially adapted to each other, and the mind of man as naturally the mirror of the fairest and most interesting properties of nature. And thus the poet, prompted by this feeling of pleasure, which accompanies him through the whole course of his studies, converses with general nature, with affections akin to those which, through labor and length of time, the man of science has raised up in himself, by conversing with those particular parts of nature which are the objects of his studies. The knowledge both of the poet and the man of science is pleasure; but the knowledge of the one cleaves to us as a necessary part of our existence, our natural and unalienable inheritance; the other is a personal and individual acquisition, slow to come to us, and by no habitual and direct sympathy connecting us with our fellow-beings. The man of science seeks truth as a remote and unknown benefactor; he cherishes and loves it in his solitude: the poet, singing a song in which all human beings join with him, rejoices in the presence of truth as our visible friend and hourly companion. Poetry is the breath and finer spirit of all knowledge; it is the impassioned expression which is in the countenance of all science. Emphatically may it be said of the poet, as Shakespeare hath said of man, "that he looks before and after." He is the rock of defence for human nature; an upholder and preserver, carrying everywhere with him relationship and love. In spite of difference of soil and climate, of language and manners, of laws and customs: in spite of things silently gone out of mind, and things violently destroyed; the poet binds together by passion and knowledge the vast empire of human society, as it is spread over the whole earth, and over all time. The objects of the poet's thoughts are everywhere; though the eyes and senses of man are, it is true, his favorite guides, yet he will follow wheresoever he can find an atmosphere of sensation in which to move his wings. Poetry is the first and last of all knowledge—it is as immortal as the heart of man. If the labors of men of science should ever create any material revolution, direct or indirect, in our condition, and in the impressions which we habitually receive, the poet will sleep then no more than at present; he will be ready to follow the steps of the man of science, not only in those general indirect effects, but he will be at his side, carrying sensation into the midst of the objects of the science itself. The remotest discoveries of the chemist, the botanist, or mineralogist, will be as proper objects of the poet's art as any upon which it can be employed, if the time should ever come when these things shall be familiar to us, and the relations under which they are contemplated by the followers of these respective sciences shall be manifestly and palpably material to us as enjoying and suffering beings. If the time should ever come when what is now called science, thus familiarized to men, shall be ready to put on, as it were, a form of flesh and blood, the poet will lend his divine spirit to aid the transfiguration, and will welcome the being thus produced, as a dear and genuine inmate of the household of man. —It is not, then, to be supposed that any one who holds that sublime notion of poetry which I have attempted to convey, will break in upon the sanctity and truth of his pictures by transitory and accidental ornaments, and endeavor to excite admiration of himself by arts the necessity of which must manifestly depend upon the assumed meanness of his subject.

What has been thus far said applies to poetry in general, but especially to those parts of composition where the poet speaks through the mouths of his characters; and upon this point it appears to authorize the conclusion that there are few persons of good sense who would not allow that the dramatic parts of composition are defective, in proportion as they deviate from the real language of nature, and are colored by a diction of the poet's own, either peculiar to him as an individual poet or belonging simply to poets in general; to a body of men who, from the circumstance of their compositions being in meter, it is expected will employ a particular language.

It is not, then, in the dramatic parts of composition that we look for this distinction of language; but still it may be proper and necessary where the poet speaks to us in his own person and character. To this I answer by referring the reader to the description before given of a poet. Among the qualities there enumerated as principally conducing to form a poet, is implied nothing differing in kind from other men, but only in degree. The sum of what was said is, that the poet is chiefly distinguished from other men by a greater promptness to think and feel without immediate external excitement, and a greater power in expressing such thoughts and feelings as are produced in him in that manner. But these passions and thoughts and feelings are the general passions and thoughts and feelings of men. And with what are they connected? Undoubtedly with our moral sentiments and animal sensations, and with the causes which excite these; with the operations of the elements, and the appearances of the visible universe; with storm and sunshine, with the revolutions of the seasons, with cold and heat, with loss of friends and kindred, with injuries and resentments, gratitude and hope, with fear and sorrow. These, and the like, are the sensations and objects which the poet describes, as they are the sensations of other men, and the objects which interest them. The poet thinks and feels in the spirit of human passions. How, then, can his language differ in any material degree from that of all other men who feel vividly and see clearly? It might be *proved* that it is impossible. But supposing that this were not the case, the poet might then be allowed to use a peculiar language when expressing his feelings for his own gratification, or that of men like himself. But poets do not write for poets alone, but for men. Unless, therefore, we are advocates for that admiration which subsists upon ignorance, and that pleasure which arises from hearing what we do not understand, the poet must descend from this supposed height; and, in order to excite rational sympathy, he must express himself as other men express themselves. To this it may be added that while he is only selecting from the real language of men, or, which amounts to the same thing, composing accurately in the spirit of such selection, he is treading upon safe ground, and we know what we are to expect from him. Our feelings are the same with respect to meter; for, as it may be proper to remind the reader, the distinction of meter is regular and uniform, and not, like that which is produced by what is usually called POETIC DICTION, arbitrary, and subject to infinite caprices upon which no calculation whatever can be made. In the one case, the reader is utterly at the mercy of the poet, respecting what imagery or diction he may choose to connect with the passion; whereas in the other, the meter obeys certain laws, to which the poet and reader both willingly submit because they are certain, and because no interference is made by them with the passion, but such as the concurring testimony of ages has shown to heighten and improve the pleasure which co-exists with it.

It will now be proper to answer an obvious question, namely, Why, professing these opinions, have I written in verse? To this, in addition to such answer as is included in what has been already said, I reply, in the first place, Because, however I may have restricted myself, there is still left open to me what confessedly constitutes the most valuable object of all writing, whether in prose or verse—the great and universal passions of men, the most general and interesting of their occupations, and the entire world of nature before me—to supply endless combinations of forms and imagery. Now, supposing for a moment that whatever is interesting in these objects may be as vividly described in prose, why should I be condemned for attempting to superadd to such description the charm which, by the consent of all nations, is acknowledged to exist in metrical language? To this, by such as are yet unconvinced, it may be answered that a very small part of the pleasure given by poetry depends upon the meter, and that it is injudicious to write in meter, unless it be accompanied with the other artificial distinctions of style with which meter is usually accompanied, and that, by such deviation, more will be lost from the shock which will thereby be given to the reader's associations than will be counterbalanced by any pleasure which he can derive from the general power of numbers. In answer to those who still contend for the necessity of accompanying meter with certain appropriate colors of style in order to the accomplishment of its appropriate end, and who also, in my opinion, greatly underrate the power of meter in itself, it might, perhaps, as far as relates to these volumes, have been almost sufficient to observe that poems are extant, written upon more humble subjects, and in a still more naked and simple style, which have continued to give pleasure from generation to generation. Now if nakedness and simplicity be a defect, the fact here mentioned affords a strong presumption that poems somewhat less naked and simple are capable of affording pleasure at the present day; and what I wished *chiefly* to attempt, at present, was to justify myself for having written under the impression of this belief.

But various causes might be pointed out why, when the style is manly, and the subject of some importance, words metrically arranged will long continue to impart such a pleasure to mankind as he who proves the extent of that pleasure will be desirous to impart. The end of poetry is to produce excitement in co-existence with an overbalance of pleasure; but, by the supposition, excitement is an unusual and irregular state of the mind; ideas and feelings do not, in that state, succeed each other in accustomed order. If the words, however, by which this excitement is produced be in themselves powerful, or the images and feelings have an undue proportion of pain connected with them, there is some danger that the excitement may be carried beyond its proper bounds. Now the co-presence of something regular, something to which the mind has been accustomed in various moods and in a less excited state, cannot but have great efficacy in tempering and restraining the passion by an intertexture of ordinary feeling, and of feeling not strictly and necessarily connected with the passion. This is unquestionably true; and hence, though the opinion will at first appear paradoxical, from the tendency of meter to divest language, in a certain degree, of its reality, and thus to throw a sort of half-consciousness of unsubstantial existence over the whole composition, there can be little doubt but that more pathetic situations and sentiments, that is, those which have a greater proportion of pain connected with them, may be endured in metrical composition, especially in rhyme, than in prose. The meter of the old ballads is very artless, yet they contain many passages which would illustrate this opinion; and, I hope, if the following poems be attentively perused, similar instances will be found in them. This opinion may be further illustrated by appealing to the reader's own experience of the reluctance with which he comes to the reperusal of the distressful parts of *Clarissa Harlowe,* or *The Gamester,*[4]

---

[4] *Clarissa, or the History of a Young Lady,* a pathetic novel by Samuel Richardson (1748); *The Gamester,* a domestic tragedy by Edward Moore (1753).

while Shakespeare's writings, in the most pathetic scenes, never act upon us, as pathetic, beyond the bounds of pleasure—an effect which, in a much greater degree than might at first be imagined, is to be ascribed to small but continual and regular impulses of pleasurable surprise from the metrical arrangement.—On the other hand (what it must be allowed will much more frequently happen) if the poet's words should be incommensurate with the passion, and inadequate to raise the reader to a height of desirable excitement, then (unless the poet's choice of his meter has been grossly injudicious) in the feelings of pleasure which the reader has been accustomed to connect with meter in general, and in the feeling, whether cheerful or melancholy, which he has been accustomed to connect with that particular movement of meter, there will be found something which will greatly contribute to impart passion to the words, and to effect the complex end which the poet proposes to himself.

If I had undertaken a SYSTEMATIC defence of the theory here maintained, it would have been my duty to develop the various causes upon which the pleasure received from metrical language depends. Among the chief of these causes is to be reckoned a principle which must be well known to those who have made any of the arts the object of accurate reflection; namely, the pleasure which the mind derives from the perception of similitude in dissimilitude. This principle is the great spring of the activity of our minds, and their chief feeder. From this principle the direction of the sexual appetite, and all the passions connected with it, take their origin: it is the life of our ordinary conversation; and upon the accuracy with which similitude in dissimilitude, and dissimilitude in similitude are perceived, depend our taste and our moral feelings. It would not be a useless employment to apply this principle to the consideration of meter, and to show that meter is hence enabled to afford much pleasure, and to point out in what manner that pleasure is produced. But my limits will not permit me to enter upon this subject, and I must content myself with a general summary.

I have said that poetry is the spontaneous overflow of powerful feelings; it takes its origin from emotion recollected in tranquillity: the emotion is contemplated till, by a species of re–action, the tranquillity gradually disappears, and an emotion, kindred to that which was before the subject of contemplation, is gradually produced, and does itself actually exist in the mind. In this mood successful composition generally begins, and in a mood similar to this it is carried on; but the emotion, of whatever kind, and in whatever degree, from various causes, is qualified by various pleasures, so that in describing any passions whatsoever, which are voluntarily described, the mind will, upon the whole, be in a state of enjoyment. If Nature be thus cautious to preserve in a state of enjoyment a being so employed, the poet ought to profit by the lesson held forth to him, and ought especially to take care that, whatever passions he communicates to his reader, those passions, if his reader's mind be sound and vigorous, should always be accompanied with an over-balance of pleasure. Now the music of harmonious metrical language, the sense of difficulty overcome, and the blind association of pleasure which has been previously received from works of rhyme or meter of the same or similar construction, an indistinct perception perpetually re-newed of language closely resembling that of real life, and yet, in the circumstance of meter, differing from it so widely—all these imperceptibly make up a complex feeling of delight, which is of the most important use in tempering the painful feeling always found intermingled with powerful descriptions of the deeper passions. This effect is always produced in pathetic and im-passioned poetry; while in lighter compositions the ease and gracefulness with which the poet manages his numbers are them-selves confessedly a principal source of the gratification of the reader. All that it is *necessary* to say, however, upon this subject, may be effected by affirming, what few persons will deny, that of two descriptions, either of passions, manners, or characters each of them equally well executed, the one in prose and the other in verse, the verse will be read a hundred times where the prose is read once.

Having thus explained a few of my reasons for writing in verse, and why I have chosen subjects from common life, and endeavored to bring my language near to the real language of men, if I have been too minute in pleading my own cause, I have at the same time been treating a subject of general interest; and for this reason a few words shall be added with reference solely to these particular poems, and to some defects which will prob-ably be found in them. I am sensible that my associations must have sometimes been particular instead of general, and that, con-

sequently, giving to things a false importance, I may have sometimes written upon unworthy subjects; but I am less apprehen-
sive on this account, than that my language may frequently have
suffered from those arbitrary connections of feelings and ideas
with particular words and phrases, from which no man can altogether protect himself. Hence I have no doubt that, in some
instances, feelings, even of the ludicrous, may be given to my
readers by expressions which appeared to me tender and pathetic.
Such faulty expressions, were I convinced they were faulty at
present, and that they must necessarily continue to be so, I
would willingly take all reasonable pains to correct. But it is
dangerous to make these alterations on the simple authority of a
few individuals, or even of certain classes of men; for where
the understanding of an author is not convinced, or his feelings
altered, this cannot be done without great injury to himself: for
his own feelings are his stay and support; and, if he set them
aside in one instance, he may be induced to repeat this act till
his mind shall lose all confidence in itself, and become utterly
debilitated. To this it may be added that the critic ought never
to forget that he is himself exposed to the same errors as the
poet, and perhaps in a much greater degree: for there can be no
presumption in saying of most readers that it is not probable they
will be so well acquainted with the various stages of meaning
through which words have passed, or with the fickleness or
stability of the relations of particular ideas to each other; and,
above all, since they are so much less interested in the subject,
they may decide lightly and carelessly.

Long as the reader has been detained, I hope he will permit
me to caution him against a mode of false criticism which has
been applied to poetry, in which the language closely resembles
that of life and nature. Such verses have been triumphed over in
parodies, of which Dr. Johnson's stanza is a fair specimen:—

> I put my hat upon my head
> And walked into the Strand,
> And there I met another man
> Whose hat was in his hand.[5]

[5] A parody of *The Hermit of Warkworth*, by Thomas Percy. See *The
Poems of Samuel Johnson*, ed. Smith and McAdam (Oxford, 1941), pp.
156–8.

Immediately under these lines let us place one of the most justly admired stanzas of the "Babes in the Woods."

These pretty babes with hand in hand
Went wandering up and down;
But never more they saw the man
Approaching from the town.[6]

In both these stanzas the words, and the order of the words, in no respect differ from the most unimpassioned conversation. There are words in both, for example, "the Strand," and "the town," connected with none but the most familiar ideas; yet the one stanza we admit as admirable, and the other as a fair example of the superlatively contemptible. Whence arises this difference? Not from the meter, not from the language, not from the order of the words; but the *matter* expressed in Dr. Johnson's stanza is contemptible. The proper method of treating trivial and simple verses to which Dr. Johnson's stanza would be a fair parallelism, is not to say, This is a bad kind of poetry, or This is not poetry; but, This wants sense; it is neither interesting in itself, nor can *lead* to anything interesting; the images neither originate in that sane state of feeling which arises out of thought, nor can excite thought or feeling in the reader. This is the only sensible manner of dealing with such verses. Why trouble yourself about the species till you have previously decided upon the genus? Why take pains to prove that an ape is not a Newton, when it is self-evident that he is not a man?

One request I must make of my reader, which is, that in judging these poems he would decide by his own feelings genuinely, and not by reflection upon what will probably be the judgment of others. How common is it to hear a person say, I myself do not object to this style of composition, or this or that expression, but to such and such classes of people it will appear mean or ludicrous! This mode of criticism, so destructive of all sound unadulterated judgment, is almost universal: let the reader then abide, independently, by his own feelings, and, if he finds

6 From the anonymous ballad, "The Children in the Wood," stanza XV. See *Oxford Book of Ballads,* ed. Arthur Quiller-Couch (Oxford, 1910), p. 858.

himself affected, let him not suffer such conjectures to interfere with his pleasure.

If an author, by any single composition, has impressed us with respect for his talents, it is useful to consider this as affording a presumption that on other occasions, where we have been displeased, he nevertheless may not have written ill or absurdly; and further, to give him so much credit for this one composition as may induce us to review what has displeased us with more care than we should otherwise have bestowed upon it. This is not only an act of justice, but, in our decisions upon poetry especially, may conduce in a high degree to the improvement of our own taste; for an *accurate* taste in poetry, and in all the other arts, as Sir Joshua Reynolds has observed, is an *acquired* talent, which can only be produced by thought and a long-continued intercourse with the best models of composition. This is mentioned, not with so ridiculous a purpose as to prevent the most inexperienced reader from judging for himself (I have already said that I wish him to judge for himself), but merely to temper the rashness of decision, and to suggest that, if poetry be a subject on which much time has not been bestowed, the judgment may be erroneous; and that, in many cases, it necessarily will be so.

Nothing would, I know, have so effectually contributed to further the end which I have in view, as to have shown of what kind the pleasure is, and how that pleasure is produced, which is confessedly produced by metrical composition essentially different from that which I have here endeavored to recommend: for the reader will say that he has been pleased by such composition; and what more can be done for him? The power of any art is limited; and he will suspect that, if it be proposed to furnish him with new friends, that can be only upon condition of his abandoning his old friends. Besides, as I have said, the reader is himself conscious of the pleasure which he has received from such composition, composition to which he has peculiarly attached the endearing name of poetry; and all men feel an habitual gratitude, and something of an honorable bigotry, for the objects which have long continued to please them: we not only wish to be pleased, but to be pleased in that particular way in which we have been accustomed to be pleased. There is in these feelings enough to resist a host of arguments; and I should be the less able to combat them successfully, as I am willing to allow that, in order entirely to enjoy the poetry which I am recommending, it would be necessary to give up much of what is ordinarily enjoyed. But, would my limits have permitted me to point out how this pleasure is produced, many obstacles might have been removed, and the reader assisted in perceiving that the powers of language are not so limited as he may suppose; and that it is possible for poetry to give other enjoyments, of a purer, more lasting, and more exquisite nature. This part of the subject has not been altogether neglected, but it has not been so much my present aim to prove that the interest excited by some other kinds of poetry is less vivid, and less worthy of the nobler powers of the mind, as to offer reasons for presuming that, if my purpose were fulfilled, a species of poetry would be produced which is genuine poetry, in its nature well adapted to interest mankind permanently, and likewise important in the multiplicity and quality of its moral relations.

From what has been said, and from a perusal of the poems, the reader will be able clearly to perceive the object which I had in view: he will determine how far it has been attained; and, what is a much more important question, whether it be worth attaining: and upon the decision of these two questions will rest my claim to the approbation of the public.

APPENDIX TO THE PREFACE

[1802]

PERHAPS, AS I HAVE no right to expect that attentive perusal, without which, confined, as I have been, to the narrow limits of a preface, my meaning cannot be thoroughly understood, I am anxious to give an exact notion of the sense in which the phrase poetic diction has been used; and for this purpose, a few words shall here be added, concerning the origin and characteristics of the phraseology, which I have condemned under that name.

The earliest poets of all nations generally wrote from passion excited by real events; they wrote naturally, and as men: feeling powerfully as they did, their language was daring, and figurative. In succeeding times, Poets, and Men ambitious of the fame of Poets, perceiving the influence of such language, and desirous of producing the same effect without being animated by the same passion, set themselves to a mechanical adoption of these figures of speech, and made use of them, sometimes with propriety, but much more frequently applied them to feelings and thoughts with which they had no natural connection whatsoever. A language was thus insensibly produced, differing materially from the real language of men in *any situation*. The Reader or Hearer of this distorted language found himself in a perturbed and unusual state of mind: when affected by the genuine language of passion he had been in a perturbed and unusual state of mind also: in both cases he was willing that his common judgment and understanding should be laid asleep, and he had no instinctive and infallible perception of the true to make him reject the false; the one served as a passport for the other. The emotion was in both cases delightful, and no wonder if he confounded the one with the other, and believed them both to be produced by the same, or similar causes. Besides, the Poet spake to him in the character of a man to be looked up to, a man of genius and authority. Thus, and from a variety of other causes, this distorted language was received with admiration; and Poets, it is probable, who had before contented themselves for the most part with misapplying only expressions which at first had been dictated by real passion, carried the abuse still further, and introduced phrases composed apparently in the spirit of the original figurative language of passion, yet altogether of their own invention, and characterised by various degrees of wanton deviation from good sense and nature.

It is indeed true, that the language of the earliest Poets was felt to differ materially from ordinary language, because it was the language of extraordinary occasions; but it was really spoken by men, language which the Poet himself had uttered when he had been affected by the events which he described, or which he had heard uttered by those around him. To this language it is probable that metre of some sort or other was early superadded. This separated the genuine language of Poetry still further from common life, so that whoever read or heard the poems of these earliest Poets felt himself moved in a way in which he had not been accustomed to be moved in real life, and by causes manifestly different from whose which acted upon him in real life. This was the great temptation to all the corruptions which have followed: under the protection of this feeling succeeding Poets constructed a phraseology which had one thing, it is true, in common with the genuine language of poetry, namely, that it was not heard in ordinary conversation; that it was unusual. But the first Poets, as I have said, spake a language which, though unusual, was still the language of men. This circumstance, however, was disregarded by their successors; they found that they could please by easier means: they became proud of modes of expression which they themselves had invented, and which were uttered only by themselves. In process of time metre became a symbol or promise of this unusual language, and whoever took upon him to write in metre, according as he possessed more or less of true poetic genius, introduced less or more of this adulterated phraseology into his compositions, and the true and the false were inseparably interwoven until, the taste of men becoming gradually perverted, this language was received as a natural language: and at length, by the influence of books upon men, did to a certain degree really become so. Abuses of this kind were imported from one nation to another, and with the progress of refinement this diction became daily more and more corrupt, thrusting out of sight the plain humanities of nature by a motley masquerade of tricks, quaintnesses, hieroglyphics, and enigmas.

It would not be uninteresting to point out the causes of the pleasure given by this extravagant and absurd diction. It depends upon a great variety of causes, but upon none, perhaps, more than its influence in impressing a notion of the peculiarity and exaltation of the Poet's character, and in flattering the Reader's self-love by bringing him nearer to a sympathy with that character; an effect which is accomplished by unsettling ordinary habits of thinking, and thus assisting the Reader to approach to that perturbed and dizzy state of mind in which if he does not find himself, he imagines that he is *balked* of a peculiar enjoyment which poetry can and ought to bestow.

The sonnet quoted from Gray, in the Preface, except the lines printed in Italics, consists of little else but this diction, though

not of the worst kind; and indeed, if one may be permitted to
say so, it is far too common in the best writers both ancient
and modern. Perhaps in no way, by positive example, could more
easily be given a notion of what I mean by the phrase *poetic
diction* than by referring to a comparison between the metrical
paraphrase which we have of passages in the Old and New Testament, and those passages as they exist in our common Translation. See Pope's "Messiah" throughout; Prior's "Did sweeter
sounds adorn my flowing tongue," &c. &c. "Though I speak with
the tongues of men and of angels," &c. &c. 1st Corinthians, chap.
xiii. By way of immediate example take the following of Dr.
Johnson:—

> Turn on the prudent Ant thy heedless eyes,
> Observe her labours, Sluggard, and be wise;
> No stern command, no monitory voice,
> Prescribes her duties, or directs her choice;
> Yet, timely provident, she hastes away
> To snatch the blessings of a plenteous day;
> When fruitful Summer loads the teeming plain,
> She crops the harvest, and she stores the grain.
> How long shall sloth usurp thy useless hours,
> Unnerve thy vigour, and enchain thy powers?
> While artful shades thy downy couch enclose,
> And soft solicitation courts repose,
> Amidst the drowsy charms of dull delight,
> Year chases year with unremitted flight,
> Till Want now following, fraudulent and slow,
> Shall spring to seize thee, like an ambush'd foe.[7]

From this hubbub of words pass to the original. "Go to the Ant,
thou Sluggard, consider her ways, and be wise: which having no
guide, overseer, or ruler, provideth her meat in the summer, and
gathereth her food in the harvest. How long wilt thou sleep, O
Sluggard? when wilt thou arise out of thy sleep? Yet a little
sleep, a little slumber, a little folding of the hands to sleep. So
shall thy poverty come as one that travelleth, and thy want as an
armed man." Proverbs, chap. vi.

[7] "The Ant," *Poems of Samuel Johnson*, ed. Smith and McAdam (Oxford,
1941), pp. 151–2.

One more quotation, and I have done. It is from Cowper's Verses supposed to be written by Alexander Selkirk:—

> Religion! what treasure untold
> Resides in that heavenly word!
> More precious than silver and gold,
> Or all that this earth can afford.
> But the sound of the church-going bell
> These valleys and rocks never heard,
> Ne'er sighed at the sound of a knell,
> Or smiled when a sabbath appeared.
>
> Ye winds, that have made me your sport
> Convey to this desolate shore
> Some cordial endearing report
> Of a land I must visit no more
> My friends, do they now and then send
> A wish or a thought after me?
> O tell me I yet have a friend.
> Though a friend I am never to see.

This passage is quoted as an instance of three different styles of composition. The first four lines are poorly expressed; some Critics would call the language prosaic; the fact is, it would be bad prose, so bad, that it is scarcely worse in metre. The epithet "church-going" applied to a bell, and that by so chaste a writer as Cowper, is an instance of the strange abuses which Poets have introduced into their language, till they and their Readers take them as matters of course, if they do not single them out expressly as objects of admiration. The two lines "Ne'er sighed at the sound," &c., are, in my opinion, an instance of the language of passion wrested from its proper use, and, from the mere circumstance of the composition being in metre, applied upon an occasion that does not justify such violent expressions; and I should condemn the passage, though perhaps few Readers will agree with me, as vicious poetic diction. The last stanza is throughout admirably expressed: it would be equally good whether in prose or verse, except that the Reader has an exquisite pleasure in seeing such natural language so naturally connected with metre. The beauty of this stanza tempts me to conclude with a principle which ought never to be lost sight of, and which has been my chief guide in all I have said,—namely, that in works of *imagination and sentiment*, for of these only have I been treating, in proportion as ideas and feelings are valuable, whether the composition be in prose or in verse, they require and exact one and the same language. Metre is but adventitious to composition, and the phraseology for which that passport is necessary, even where it may be graceful at all, will be little valued by the judicious.

Samuel Taylor Coleridge

[1772–1834]

◄§§►

COLERIDGE WAS BOTH THE most ambitious and the most philosophical of English critics. His poetic career, stimulated by his early and intimate friendship with Wordsworth, was virtually over by the time he was 35; thereafter he turned more and more to those "abstruse researches" by which he attempted to construct a metaphysical system synthesizing his principles of philosophy, psychology, and aesthetics. The vastness of this project no doubt explains in part Coleridge's failure to complete it; other factors were his addiction to opium and his general ill health. He achieved only the fragmentary, often obscure beginnings of his grand design, and of these some parts are more or less direct borrowings from other writers, particularly from German philosophers of his day.

Nevertheless, Coleridge's reputation as a critic is probably higher today than that of any other Englishman. His ideas, unfinished and even contradictory as they sometimes are, remain remarkably current and make him the patriarch of modern criticism. Two theories in particular show his kinship with twentieth-century critical thought: his theory of organic form, and his theory of the imagination. The theory of form is based on the principle that the essence of existence is not matter, but *process;* the work of art is a record of such process, and therefore has the same organic relationships among its parts as has any other vital thing. Thus the work must be judged as a whole, and the parts cannot be arbitrarily separated for criticism. The vital force in the mind which creates a work of art Coleridge called Imagination; it corresponds, in his theory, to the creative process in nature ("the eternal act of creation") by which matter and form are fused and given life. In attributing this primary creative power to the imagination, Coleridge rejected eighteenth-century mechanistic theories of the creative process, and laid the groundwork for modern "ontological" theories of poetry, and for the common view of the poem as an autonomous existence.

Coleridge's most extensive critical work, the *Biographia Literaria,* was begun, Coleridge said, as a defense of Wordsworth, though it quickly expanded, in a characteristically unsystematic way, until it became (in the words of the sub-title) "biographical sketches of my literary life and opinions." The book is full of perceptive and generous appreciations of Wordsworth's poems, but it also includes shrewd criticisms of two points in Wordsworth's preface to the *Lyrical Ballads* (see above, pp. 13 to 35) which Coleridge considered neither critically sound nor truly descriptive of Wordsworth's practice—the theory of poetic diction, and the treatment of meter. Both points had been forced on Wordsworth by his primitivistic view of the relation of man and nature; Coleridge demonstrated that Wordsworth's practice was better than his theory, and formulated his own theories of diction and meter, founded more soundly on the organic theory of poetry.

BIBLIOGRAPHY. *Complete Works,* ed. W. G. T. Shedd, 7 vols. (New York, 1884); *Biographia Literaria,* ed. J. Shawcross, 2 vols. (Oxford, 1907); *Miscellaneous Criticism,* ed. T. M. Raysor (Cambridge, Mass., 1936); *Notebooks,* ed. Kathleen Coburn (London, 1957— [in progress]); *Shakesperian Criticism,* ed. Raysor, 2 vols. (Cambridge, 1930).
M. H. Abrams, *The Mirror and the Lamp* (New York, 1953); W. J. Bate, "Coleridge on the Function of Art," in *Perspectives of Criticism,* ed. Harry Levin (Cambridge, Mass., 1950); J. H. Muirhead, *Coleridge as Philosopher* (London, 1930); I. A. Richards, *Coleridge on Imagination* (New York, 1935).

TEXT. *Biographia Literaria,* ed. Shawcross.

from

BIOGRAPHIA LITERARIA

[1817]

FROM CHAPTER XIII

On the imagination, or esemplastic power.

. . . THE IMAGINATION then, I consider either as primary, or secondary. The primary IMAGINATION I hold to be the living Power and prime Agent of all human Perception, and as a repetition in the finite mind of the eternal act of creation in the infinite I AM. The secondary Imagination I consider as an echo of the former, co-existing with the conscious will, yet still as identical with the primary in the *kind* of its agency, and differing only in *degree,* and in the *mode* of its operation. It dissolves, diffuses, dissipates, in order to re-create; or where this process is rendered impossible, yet still at all events it struggles to idealize and to unify. It is essentially *vital,* even as all objects (*as* objects) are essentially fixed and dead.

FANCY, on the contrary, has no other counters to play with, but fixities and definites. The Fancy is indeed no other than a mode of Memory emancipated from the order of time and space; while it is blended with, and modified by that empirical phenomenon of the will, which we express by the word CHOICE. But equally with the ordinary memory the Fancy must receive all its materials ready made from the law of association.

Whatever more than this, I shall think it fit to declare concerning the powers and privileges of the imagination in the present work, will be found in the critical essay on the uses of the Supernatural in poetry, and the principles that regulate its introduction: which the reader will find prefixed to the poem of *The Ancient Mariner.*[1]

CHAPTER XIV

Occasion of the Lyrical Ballads, and the objects originally proposed— Preface to the second edition—The ensuing controversy, its causes and acrimony—Philosophic definitions of a poem and poetry with scholia.

DURING the first year that Mr. Wordsworth and I were neighbours, our conversations turned frequently on the two cardinal points of poetry, the power of exciting the sympathy of the reader by a faithful adherence to the truth of nature, and the power of giving the interest of novelty by the modifying colors of imagination. The sudden charm, which accidents of light and shade, which moon-light or sun-set diffused over a known and familiar landscape, appeared to represent the practicability of combining both. These are the poetry of nature. The thought suggested itself

---

[1] The essay does not exist, and was probably never written.

(to which of us I do not recollect) that a series of poems might be composed of two sorts. In the one, the incidents and agents were to be, in part at least, supernatural; and the excellence aimed at was to consist in the interesting of the affections by the dramatic truth of such emotions, as would naturally accompany such situations, supposing them real. And real in *this* sense they have been to every human being who, from whatever source of delusion, has at any time believed himself under supernatural agency. For the second class, subjects were to be chosen from ordinary life; the characters and incidents were to be such, as will be found in every village and its vicinity, where there is a meditative and feeling mind to seek after them, or to notice them, when they present themselves.

In this idea originated the plan of the "Lyrical Ballads"; in which it was agreed, that my endeavours should be directed to persons and characters supernatural, or at least romantic; yet so as to transfer from our inward nature a human interest and a semblance of truth sufficient to procure for these shadows of imagination that willing suspension of disbelief for the moment, which constitutes poetic faith. Mr. Wordsworth, on the other hand, was to propose to himself as his object, to give the charm of novelty to things of every day, and to excite a feeling analogous to the supernatural, by awakening the mind's attention from the lethargy of custom, and directing it to the loveliness and the wonders of the world before us; an inexhaustible treasure, but for which, in consequence of the film of familiarity and selfish solicitude we have eyes, yet see not, ears that hear not, and hearts that neither feel nor understand.

With this view I wrote "The Ancient Mariner," and was preparing among other poems, "The Dark Ladie," and the "Christabel," in which I should have more nearly realized my ideal, than I had done in my first attempt. But Mr. Wordsworth's industry had proved so much more successful, and the number of his poems so much greater, that my compositions, instead of forming a balance, appeared rather an interpolation of heterogeneous matter. Mr. Wordsworth added two or three poems written in his own character, in the impassioned, lofty, and sustained diction, which is characteristic of his genius. In this form the "Lyrical Ballads" were published; and were presented by him, as an *experiment,* whether subjects, which from their nature rejected the usual ornaments and extra-colloquial style of poems in general, might not be so managed in the language of ordinary life as to produce the pleasureable interest, which it is the peculiar business of poetry to impart. To the second edition he added a preface of considerable length; in which, notwithstanding some passages of apparently a contrary import, he was understood to contend for the extension of this style to poetry of all kinds, and to reject as vicious and indefensible all phrases and forms of style that were not included in what he (unfortunately, I think, adopting an equivocal expression) called the language of *real* life. From this preface, prefixed to poems in which it was impossible to deny the presence of original genius, however mistaken its direction might be deemed, arose the whole long-continued controversy. For from the conjunction of perceived power with supposed heresy I explain the inveteracy and in some instances, I grieve to say, the acrimonious passions, with which the controversy has been conducted by the assailants.

Had Mr. Wordsworth's poems been the silly, the childish things, which they were for a long time described as being; had they been really distinguished from the compositions of other poets merely by meanness of language and inanity of thought; had they indeed contained nothing more than what is found in the parodies and pretended imitations of them; they must have sunk at once, a dead weight, into the slough of oblivion, and have dragged the preface along with them. But year after year increased the number of Mr. Wordsworth's admirers. They were found too not in the lower classes of the reading public, but chiefly among young men of strong sensibility and meditative minds; and their admiration (inflamed perhaps in some degree by opposition) was distinguished by its intensity, I might almost say, by its *religious* fervor. These facts, and the intellectual energy of the author, which was more or less consciously felt, where it was outwardly and even boisterously denied, meeting with sentiments of aversion to his opinions, and of alarm at their consequences, produced an eddy of criticism, which would of itself have borne up the poems by the violence with which it whirled them round and round. With many parts of this preface, in the sense attributed to them, and which the words undoubtedly seem to authorize, I never concurred; but on the contrary objected to them as erroneous in principle, and as contradictory (in appearance at least) both to other parts of the same preface, and to the author's own practice in the greater number of the poems themselves. Mr. Wordsworth in his recent collection has, I find, degraded this prefatory disquisition to the end of his second volume, to be read or not at the reader's choice. But he has not, as far as I can discover, announced any change in his poetic creed. At all events, considering it as the source of a controversy, in which I have been honored more than I deserve by the frequent conjunction of my name with his, I think it expedient to declare once for all, in what points I coincide with his opinions, and in what points I altogether differ. But in order to render myself intelligible I must previously, in as few words as possible, explain my ideas, first, of a POEM; and secondly, of POETRY itself, in *kind*, and in *essence*.

The office of philosophical *disquisition* consists in just *distinction;* while it is the privilege of the philosopher to preserve himself constantly aware, that distinction is not division. In order to obtain adequate notions of any truth, we must intellectually separate its distinguishable parts; and this is the technical *process* of philosophy. But having so done, we must then restore them in our conceptions to the unity, in which they actually co-exist; and this is the *result* of philosophy. A poem contains the same elements as a prose composition; the difference therefore must consist in a different combination of them, in consequence of a different object being proposed. According to the difference of the object will be the difference of the combination. It is possible, that the object may be merely to facilitate the recollection of any given facts or observations by artificial arrangement; and the composition will be a poem, merely because it is distinguished from prose by metre, or by rhyme, or by both conjointly. In this, the lowest sense, a man might attribute the name of a poem to the well-known enumeration of the days in the several months;

> Thirty days hath September,
> April, June, and November, &c.

and others of the same class and purpose. And as a particular pleasure is found in anticipating the recurrence of sounds and quantities, all compositions that have this charm superadded, whatever be their contents, *may* be entitled poems.

So much for the superficial *form*. A difference of object and contents supplies an additional ground of distinction. The immediate purpose may be the communication of truths; either of truth absolute and demonstrable, as in works of science; or of facts experienced and recorded, as in history. Pleasure, and that of the highest and most permanent kind, may *result* from the *attainment* of the end; but it is not itself the immediate end. In other works the communication of pleasure may be the immediate purpose; and though truth, either moral or intellectual, ought to be the *ultimate* end, yet this will distinguish the character of the author, not the class to which the work belongs. Blest indeed is that state of society, in which the immediate purpose would be baffled by the perversion of the proper ultimate end; in which no charm of diction or imagery could exempt the Bathyllus even of an Anacreon, or the Alexis of Virgil, from disgust and aversion!

But the communication of pleasure may be the immediate object of a work not metrically composed; and that object may have been in a high degree attained, as in novels and romances. Would then the mere superaddition of metre, with or without rhyme, entitle *these* to the name of poems? The answer is, that nothing can permanently please, which does not contain in itself the reason why it is so, and not otherwise. If metre be superadded, all other parts must be made consonant with it. They must be such, as to justify the perpetual and distinct attention to each part, which an exact correspondent recurrence of accent and sound are calculated to excite. The final definition then, so deduced, may be thus worded. A poem is that species of composition, which is opposed to works of science, by proposing for its *immediate* object pleasure, not truth; and from all other species (having *this* object in common with it) it is discriminated by proposing to itself such delight from the *whole,* as is compatible with a distinct gratification from each component *part.*

Controversy is not seldom excited in consequence of the disputants attaching each a different meaning to the same word; and in few instances has this been more striking, than in disputes concerning the present subject. If a man chooses to call every composition a poem, which is rhyme, or measure, or both, I must leave his opinion uncontroverted. The distinction is at least competent to characterize the writer's intention. If it were subjoined, that the whole is likewise entertaining or affecting, as a tale, or as a series of interesting reflections, I of course admit this as another fit ingredient of a poem, and an additional merit. But if the definition sought for be that of a *legitimate* person, I answer, it must be one, the parts of which mutually support and explain each other; all in their proportion harmonizing with, and supporting the purpose and known influences of metrical arrangement. The philosophic critics of all ages coincide with the ultimate judgement of all countries, in equally denying the praises of a just poem, on the one hand, to a series of striking lines or distiches, each of which, absorbing the whole attention of the reader to itself, disjoins it from its context, and makes it a separate whole, instead of an harmonizing part; and on the other hand, to an unsustained composition, from which the reader collects rapidly the general result, unattracted by the component parts. The reader should be carried forward, not merely or chiefly by the mechanical impulse of curiosity, or by a restless desire to arrive at the final solution; but by the pleasureable activity of mind excited by the attractions of the journey itself. Like the motion of a serpent, which the Egyptians made the emblem of intellectual power; or like the path of sound through the air; at every step he pauses and half recedes, and from the retrogressive movement collects the force which again carries him onward. "Præcipitandus est *liber* spiritus [The free spirit must be carried forward]," says Petronius Arbiter most happily. The epithet, *liber*, here balances the preceding verb; and it is not easy to conceive more meaning condensed in fewer words.

But if this should be admitted as a satisfactory character of a poem, we have still to seek for a definition of poetry. The writings of PLATO, and BISHOP TAYLOR [2] and the "Theoria Sacra" of BURNET,[3] furnish undeniable proofs that poetry of the highest kind may exist without metre, and even without the contra-distinguishing objects of a poem. The first chapter of Isaiah (indeed a

[2] Jeremy Taylor (1613–67), author of *Holy Living* and *Holy Dying*.
[3] Thomas Burnet (1635–1715), author of *Telluris Theoria Sacra*, a fanciful theory of the structure of the earth.

very large portion of the whole book) is poetry in the most emphatic sense; yet it would be not less irrational than strange to assert, that pleasure, and not truth, was the immediate object of the prophet. In short, whatever *specific* import we attach to the word, poetry, there will be found involved in it, as a necessary consequence, that a poem of any length neither can be, or ought to be, all poetry. Yet if an harmonious whole is to be produced, the remaining parts must be preserved *in keeping* with the poetry; and this can be no otherwise effected than by such a studied selection and artificial arrangement, as will partake of *one*, though not a *peculiar* property of poetry. And this again can be no other than the property of exciting a more continuous and equal attention than the language of prose aims at, whether colloquial or written.

My own conclusions on the nature of poetry, in the strictest use of the word, have been in part anticipated in the preceding disquisition on the fancy and imagination. What is poetry? is so nearly the same question with, what is a poet? that the answer to the one is involved in the solution of the other. For it is a distinction resulting from the poetic genius itself, which sustains and modifies the images, thoughts, and emotions of the poet's own mind.

The poet, described in *ideal* perfection, brings the whole soul of man into activity, with the subordination of its faculties to each other, according to their relative worth and dignity. He diffuses a tone and spirit of unity, that blends, and (as it were) *fuses*, each into each, by that synthetic and magical power, to which we have exclusively appropriated the name of imagination. This power, first put in action by the will and understanding, and retained under their irremissive, though gentle and unnoticed, control (*laxis effertur habenis*) reveals itself in the balance or reconciliation of opposite or discordant qualities: of sameness, with difference; of the general, with the concrete; the idea, with the image; the individual, with the representative; the sense of novelty and freshness, with old and familiar objects; a more than usual state of emotion, with more than usual order; judgement ever awake and steady self-possession, with enthusiasm and feeling profound or vehement; and while it blends and harmonizes the natural and the artificial, still subordinates art

to nature; the manner to the matter; and our admiration of the
poet to our sympathy with the poetry. "Doubtless," as Sir John
Davies observes of the soul (and his words may with slight alteration be applied, and even more appropriately, to the poetic
IMAGINATION)

> Doubtless this could not be, but that she turns
>   Bodies to spirit by sublimation strange,
> As fire converts to fire the things it burns,
>   As we our food into our nature change.
>
> From their gross matter she abstracts their forms,
>   And draws a kind of quintessence from things;
> Which to her proper nature she transforms,
>   To bear them light on her celestial wings.
>
> Thus does she, when from individual states
>   She doth abstract the universal kinds;
> Which then re-clothed in divers names and fates
>   Steal access through our senses to our minds.[4]

Finally, GOOD SENSE is the BODY of poetic genius, FANCY its
DRAPERY, MOTION its LIFE, and IMAGINATION the SOUL that is
everywhere, and in each; and forms all into one graceful and
intelligent whole.

CHAPTER XV

The specific symptoms of poetic power elucidated in a critical analysis
of Shakespeare's Venus and Adonis, *and* Lucrece.

IN THE application of these principles to purposes of practical
criticism as employed in the appraisal of works more or less imperfect, I have endeavoured to discover what the qualities in a
poem are, which may be deemed promises and specific symptoms
of poetic power, as distinguished from general talent determined
to poetic composition by accidental motives, by an act of the will,
rather than by the inspiration of a genial and productive nature.
In this investigation, I could not, I thought, do better, than keep
before me the earliest work of the greatest genius, that perhaps

---

[4] "On the Soul of Man," section IV.

human nature has yet produced, our *myriad-minded*[5] Shakespeare. I mean the "Venus and Adonis," and the "Lucrece"; works which give at once strong promises of the strength, and yet obvious proofs of the immaturity, of his genius. From these I abstracted the following marks, as characteristics of original poetic genius in general.

1. In the "Venus and Adonis," the first and most obvious excellence is the perfect sweetness of the versification; its adaptation to the subject; and the power displayed in varying the march of the words without passing into a loftier and more majestic rhythm than was demanded by the thoughts, or permitted by the propriety of preserving a sense of melody predominant. The delight in richness and sweetness of sound, even to a faulty excess, if it be evidently original, and not the result of an easily imitable mechanism, I regard as a highly favourable promise in the compositions of a young man. "The man that hath not music in his soul" can indeed never be a genuine poet. Imagery (even taken from nature, much more when transplanted from books, as travels, voyages, and works of natural history); affecting incidents; just thoughts; interesting personal or domestic feelings; and with these the art of their combination or intertexture in the form of a poem; may all by incessant effort be acquired as a trade, by a man of talents and much reading, who, as I once before observed, has mistaken an intense desire of poetic reputation for a natural poetic genius; the love of the arbitrary end for a possession of the peculiar means. But the sense of musical delight, with the power of producing it, is a gift of imagination; and this together with the power of reducing multitude into unity of effect, and modifying a series of thoughts by some one predominant thought or feeling, may be cultivated and improved, but can never be learned. It is in these that "poeta nascitur non fit."

2. A second promise of genius is the choice of subjects very remote from the private interests and circumstances of the writer himself. At least I have found, that where the subject is taken im-

---

[5] 'Ανὴρ μυριόνους, a phrase which I have borrowed from a Greek monk, who applies it to a Patriarch of Constantinople. I might have said, that I have *reclaimed*, rather than borrowed it: for it seems to belong to Shakespeare, "de jure singulari, et ex privilegio naturæ." [Coleridge's note]

mediately from the author's personal sensations and experiences, the excellence of a particular poem is but an equivocal mark, and often a fallacious pledge, of genuine poetic power. We may perhaps remember the tale of the statuary, who had acquired considerable reputation for the legs of his goddesses, though the rest of the statue accorded but indifferently with ideal beauty; till his wife, elated by her husband's praises, modestly acknowledged that she herself had been his constant model. In the "Venus and Adonis" this proof of poetic power exists even to excess. It is throughout as if a superior spirit more intuitive, more intimately conscious, even than the characters themselves, not only of every outward look and act, but of the flux and reflux of the mind in all its subtlest thoughts and feelings, were placing the whole before our view; himself meanwhile unparticipating in the passions, and actuated only by that pleasureable excitement, which had resulted from the energetic fervor of his own spirit in so vividly exhibiting, what it had so accurately and profoundly contemplated. I think, I should have conjectured from these poems, that even then the great instinct, which impelled the poet to the drama, was secretly working in him, prompting him by a series and never broken chain of imagery, always vivid and, because unbroken, often minute; by the highest effort of the picturesque in words, of which words are capable, higher perhaps than was ever realized by any other poet, even Dante not excepted; to provide a substitute for that visual language, that constant intervention and running comment by tone, look and gesture, which in his dramatic works he was entitled to expect from the players. His "Venus and Adonis" seem at once the characters themselves, and the whole representation of those characters by the most consummate actors. You seem to be told nothing, but to see and hear everything. Hence it is, that from the perpetual activity of attention required on the part of the reader; from the rapid flow, the quick change, and the playful nature of the thoughts and images; and above all from the alienation, and, if I may hazard such an expression, the utter *aloofness* of the poet's own feelings, from those of which he is at once the painter and the analyst; that though the very subject cannot but detract from the pleasure of a delicate mind, yet never was poem less dangerous on a moral account. Instead of doing as Ariosto, and as, still more offensively, Wieland has done,

instead of degrading and deforming passion into appetite, the
trials of love into the struggles of concupiscence; Shakespeare has
here represented the animal impulse itself, so as to preclude all
sympathy with it, by dissipating the reader's notice among the
thousand outward images, and now beautiful, now fanciful circumstances, which form its dresses and its scenery; or by diverting our attention from the main subject by those frequent witty
or profound reflections, which the poet's ever active mind has
deduced from, or connected with, the imagery and the incidents.
The reader is forced into too much action to sympathize with the
merely passive of our nature. As little can a mind thus roused
and awakened be brooded on by mean and indistinct emotion, as
the low, lazy mist can creep upon the surface of a lake, while a
strong gale is driving it onward in waves and billows.

3. It has been before observed that images, however beautiful,
though faithfully copied from nature, and as accurately represented in words, do not of themselves characterize the poet. They
become proofs of original genius only as far as they are modified
by a predominant passion; or by associated thoughts or images
awakened by that passion; or when they have the effect of reducing multitude to unity, or succession to an instant; or lastly,
when a human and intellectual life is transferred to them from
the poet's own spirit,

> Which shoots its being through earth, sea, and air.

In the two following lines for instance, there is nothing objectionable, nothing which would preclude them from forming, in
their proper place, part of a descriptive poem:

> Behold yon row of pines, that shorn and bow'd
> Bend from the sea-blast, seen at twilight eve.

But with a small alteration of rhythm, the same words would
be equally in their place in a book of topography, or in a descriptive tour. The same image will rise into semblance of poetry if
thus conveyed:

> Yon row of bleak and visionary pines,
> By twilight glimpse discerned, mark! how they flee
> From the fierce sea-blast, all their tresses wild
> Streaming before them.

I have given this as an illustration, by no means as an instance, of that particular excellence which I had in view, and in which Shakespeare even in his earliest, as in his latest, works surpasses all other poets. It is by this, that he still gives a dignity and a passion to the objects which he presents. Unaided by any previous excitement, they burst upon us at once in life and in power.

> Full many a glorious morning have I seen
> *Flatter* the mountain tops with sovereign eye.
>
> Shakespeare, Sonnet 33rd.

> Not mine own fears, nor the prophetic soul
> Of the wide world dreaming on things to come—
>
> ❀   ❀   ❀   ❀   ❀   ❀   ❀
> ❀   ❀   ❀   ❀   ❀   ❀   ❀
>
> The mortal moon hath her eclipse endur'd,
> And the sad augurs mock their own presage;
> Incertainties now crown themselves assur'd,
> And Peace proclaims olives of endless age.
> Now with the drops of this most balmy time
> My Love looks fresh, and DEATH to me subscribes!
> Since spite of him, I'll live in this poor rhyme,
> While he insults o'er dull and speechless tribes.
> And thou in this shalt find thy monument,
> When tyrants' crests, and tombs of brass are spent.
>
> Sonnet 107.

As of higher worth, so doubtless still more characteristic of poetic genius does the imagery become, when it moulds and colors itself to the circumstances, passion, or character, present and foremost in the mind. For unrivalled instances of this excellence, the reader's own memory will refer him to the LEAR, OTHELLO, in short to which not of the *"great, ever living, dead man's"* dramatic works? "Inopem me copia fecit." [Abundance has made me poor.] How true it is to nature, he has himself finely expressed in the instance of love in Sonnet 98.

> From you have I been absent in the spring,
> When proud pied April drest in all its trim
> Hath put a spirit of youth in every thing,
> That heavy Saturn laugh'd and leap'd with him.

Yet nor the lays of birds, nor the sweet smell
Of different flowers in odour and in hue,
Could make me any summer's story tell,
Or from their proud lap pluck them, where they grew:
Nor did I wonder at the lilies white,
Nor praise the deep vermilion in the rose;
They were, tho' sweet, but figures of delight,
Drawn after you, you pattern of all those.
Yet seem'd it winter still, and, you away,
As with your shadow I with these did play!

Scarcely less sure, or if a less valuable, not less indispensable mark

Γονίμον μὲυ ποιητοῦ————
————ὅστις ῥῆμα γενναῖον λάχοι,

[of the productive poet, whoever achieves the noble phrase] will the imagery supply, when, with more than the power of the painter, the poet gives us the liveliest image of succession with the feeling of simultaneousness!

With this, he breaketh from the sweet embrace
Of those fair arms, that held him to her heart,
And homeward through the dark lawns runs apace:
Look! how a bright star shooteth from the sky,
So glides he in the night from Venus' eye.

4. The last character I shall mention, which would prove indeed but little, except as taken conjointly with the former; yet without which the former could scarce exist in a high degree, and (even if this were possible) would give promises only of transitory flashes and a meteoric power; is DEPTH, and ENERGY of THOUGHT. No man was ever yet a great poet, without being at the same time a profound philosopher. For poetry is the blossom and the fragrancy of all human knowledge, human thoughts, human passions, emotions, language. In Shakespeare's *poems* the creative power and the intellectual energy wrestle as in a war embrace. Each in its excess of strength seems to threaten the extinction of the other. At length in the DRAMA they were reconciled, and fought each with its shield before the breast of the other. Or like two rapid streams, that, at their first meeting

within narrow and rocky banks, mutually strive to repel each other and intermix reluctantly and in tumult; but soon finding a wider channel and more yielding shores blend, and dilate, and flow on in one current and with one voice. The "Venus and Adonis" did not perhaps allow the display of the deeper passions. But the story of Lucretia seems to favor and even demand their intensest workings. And yet we find in *Shakespeare's* management of the tale neither pathos, nor any other *dramatic* quality. There is the same minute and faithful imagery as in the former poem, in the same vivid colors, inspirited by the same impetuous vigor of thought, and diverging and contracting with the same activity of the assimilative and of the modifying faculties; and with a yet larger display, a yet wider range of knowledge and reflection; and lastly, with the same perfect dominion, often *domination,* over the whole world of language. What then shall we say? even this; that Shakespeare, no mere child of nature; no automaton of genius; no passive vehicle of inspiration possessed by the spirit, not possessing it; first studied patiently, meditated deeply, understood minutely, till knowledge, become habitual and intuitive, wedded itself to his habitual feelings, and at length gave birth to that stupendous power, by which he stands alone, with no equal or second in his own class; to that power which seated him on one of the two glory-smitten summits of the poetic mountain, with Milton as his compeer, not rival. While the former darts himself forth, and passes into all the forms of human character and passion, the one Proteus of the fire and the flood; the other attracts all forms and things to himself, into the unity of his own IDEAL. All things and modes of action shape themselves anew in the being of MILTON; while SHAKESPEARE becomes all things, yet for ever remaining himself. O what great men hast thou not produced, England! my country! truly indeed—

> Must *we* be free or die, who speak the tongue,
> Which SHAKESPEARE spake; the faith and morals hold,
> Which MILTON held. In every thing we are sprung
> Of earth's first blood, have titles manifold!
>   WORDSWORTH.

CHAPTER XVII

Examination of the tenets peculiar to Mr. Wordsworth—Rustic life (above all, low and rustic life) especially unfavorable to the formation of a human diction—The best parts of language the product of philosophers, not of clowns or shepherds—Poetry essentially ideal and generic—The language of Milton as much the language of real life, yea, incomparably more so than that of the cottager.

As FAR then as Mr. Wordsworth in his preface contended, and most ably contended, for a reformation in our poetic diction, as far as he has evinced the truth of passion, and the *dramatic* propriety of those figures and metaphors in the original poets, which, stripped of their justifying reasons, and converted into mere artifices of connection or ornament, constitute the characteristic falsity in the poetic style of the moderns; and as far as he has, with equal acuteness and clearness pointed out the process by which this change was effected, and the resemblances between that state into which the reader's mind is thrown by the pleasureable confusion of thought from an unaccustomed train of words and images; and that state which is induced by the natural language of empassioned feeling; he undertook a useful task, and deserves all praise, both for the attempt and for the execution. The provocations to this remonstrance in behalf of truth and nature were still of perpetual recurrence before and after the publication of this preface. I cannot likewise but add, that the comparison of such poems of merit, as have been given to the public within the last ten or twelve years, with the majority of those produced previously to the appearance of that preface, leave no doubt on my mind, that Mr. Wordsworth is fully justified in believing his efforts to have been by no means ineffectual. Not only in the verses of those who have professed their admiration of his genius, but even of those who have distinguished themselves by hostility to his theory, and depreciation of his writings, are the impressions of his principles plainly visible. It is possible, that with these principles others may have been blended, which are not equally evident; and some which are unsteady and subvertible from the narrowness or imperfection of their basis. But it is more than possible, that these errors of defect or exaggeration, by kindling and feeding the controversy, may have conduced not only to the wider propagation of the accompanying truths, but that, by their frequent presentation to the mind in an excited state, they may have won for them a more permanent and practical result. A man will borrow a part from his opponent the more easily, if he feels himself justified in continuing to reject a part. While there remain important points in which he can still feel himself in the right, in which he still finds firm footing for continued resistance, he will gradually adopt those opinions, which were the least remote from his own convictions, as not less congruous with his own theory than with that which he reprobates. In like manner with a kind of instinctive prudence, he will abandon by little and little his weakest posts, till at length he seems to forget that they had ever belonged to him, or affects to consider them at most as accidental and "petty annexments," the removal of which leaves the citadel unhurt and unendangered.

My own differences from certain supposed parts of Mr. Wordsworth's theory ground themselves on the assumption, that his words had been rightly interpreted, as purporting that the proper diction for poetry in general consists altogether in a language taken, with due exceptions, from the mouths of men in real life, a language which actually constitutes the natural conversation of men under the influence of natural feelings. My objection is, first, that in *any* sense this rule is applicable only to *certain* classes of poetry; secondly, that even to these classes it is not applicable, except in such a sense, as hath never by any one (as far as I know or have read) been denied or doubted; and lastly, that as far as, and in that degree in which it is *practicable,* yet as a *rule* it is useless, if not injurious, and therefore either need not, or ought not to be practised. The poet informs his reader, that he had generally chosen *low and rustic* life; but not *as* low and rustic, or in order to repeat that pleasure of doubtful moral effect, which persons of elevated rank and of superior refinement oftentimes derive from a happy *imitation* of the rude unpolished manners and discourse of their inferiors. For the pleasure so derived may be traced to three exciting causes. The first is the naturalness, in *fact,* of the things represented. The second is the apparent naturalness of the *representation,* as raised and qualified by an imperceptible infusion of the author's own knowledge and

talent, which infusion does, indeed, constitute it an *imitation* as
distinguished from a mere *copy*. The third cause may be found
in the reader's conscious feeling of his superiority awakened by
the contrast presented to him; even as for the same purpose the
kings and great barons of yore retained sometimes *actual* clowns
and fools, but more frequently shrewd and witty fellows in that
character. These, however, were not Mr. Wordsworth's objects.
He chose low and rustic life, "because in that condition the
essential passions of the heart find a better soil, in which they
can attain their maturity, are less under restraint, and speak a
plainer and more emphatic language; because in that condition
of life our elementary feelings coexist in a state of greater simplicity, and consequently may be more accurately contemplated,
and more forcibly communicated; because the manners of rural
life germinate from those elementary feelings; and from the
necessary character of rural occupations are more easily comprehended, and are more durable; and lastly, because in that
condition the passions of men are incorporated with the beautiful and permanent forms of nature."
Now it is clear to me, that in the most interesting of the poems,
in which the author is more or less dramatic, as "the Brothers,"
"Michael," "Ruth," "the Mad Mother," &c., the persons introduced are by no means taken *from low or rustic life* in the common acceptation of those words; and it is not less clear, that the
sentiments and language, as far as they can be conceived to have
been really transferred from the minds and conversation of such
persons, are attributable to causes and circumstances not necessarily connected with "their occupations and abode." The
thoughts, feelings, language, and manners of the shepherd-
farmers in the vales of Cumberland and Westmoreland, as far
as they are actually adopted in those poems, may be accounted
for from causes, which will and do produce the same results in
every state of life, whether in town or country. As the two principal I rank that INDEPENDENCE, which raises a man above ser-
vitude, or daily toil for the profit of others, yet not above the necessity of industry and a frugal simplicity of domestic life; and the
accompanying unambitious, but solid and religious, EDUCATION,
which has rendered few books familiar, but the Bible, and the
liturgy or hymn book. To this latter cause, indeed, which is so

far *accidental*, that it is the blessing of particular countries and a particular age, not the product of particular places or employments, the poet owes the show of probability, that his personages might really feel, think, and talk with any tolerable resemblance to his representation. It is an excellent remark of Dr. Henry More's, (Enthusiasmus triumphatus, Sec. XXXV.),[6] that "a man of confined education, but of good parts, by constant reading of the Bible will naturally form a more winning and commanding rhetoric than those that are learned; the intermixture of tongues and of artificial phrases debasing *their* style."

It is, moreover, to be considered that to the formation of healthy feelings, and a reflecting mind, *negations* involve impediments not less formidable than sophistication and vicious intermixture. I am convinced, that for the human soul to prosper in rustic life a certain vantage-ground is pre-requisite. It is not every man that is likely to be improved by a country life or by country labors. Education, or original sensibility, or both, must pre-exist, if the changes, forms, and incidents of nature are to prove a sufficient stimulant. And where these are not sufficient, the mind contracts and hardens by want of stimulants: and the man becomes selfish, sensual, gross, and hard-hearted. Let the management of the Poor Laws in Liverpool, Manchester, or Bristol be compared with the ordinary dispensation of the poor rates in agricultural villages, where the *farmers* are the overseers and guardians of the poor. If my own experience have not been particularly unfortunate, as well as that of the many respectable country clergymen with whom I have conversed on the subject, the result would engender more than scepticism concerning the desirable influences of low and rustic life in and for itself. Whatever may be concluded on the other side, from the stronger local attachments and enterprising spirit of the Swiss, and other mountaineers, applies to a particular mode of pastoral life, under forms of property that permit and beget manners truly republican, not to rustic life in general, or to the absence of artificial cultivation. On the contrary the mountaineers, whose manners have been so often eulogized, are in general better educated and greater readers than men of equal rank elsewhere. But where this

[6] Cambridge Platonist and mystic (1614–1687).

is not the case, as among the peasantry of North Wales, the ancient mountains, with all their terrors and all their glories, are
pictures to the blind, and music to the deaf.

I should not have entered so much into detail upon this passage, but here seems to be the point, to which all the lines of
difference converge as to their source and centre. (I mean, as far
as, and in whatever respect, my poetic creed *does* differ from the
doctrines promulged in this preface.) I adopt with full faith the
principle of Aristotle, that poetry as poetry is essentially [7] *ideal,*
that it avoids and excludes all *accident;* that its apparent individuals of rank, character, or occupation must be *representative* of a class; and that the *persons* of poetry must be
clothed with *generic* attributes, with the *common* attributes of
the class: not with such as one gifted individual might *possibly*
possess, but such as from his situation it is most probable beforehand that he *would* possess. If my premises are right and my
deductions legitimate, it follows that there can be no *poetic*

---

[7] Say not that I am recommending abstractions; for these class-character-
istics which constitute the instructiveness of a character, are so modified
and particularized in each person of the Shakespearean Drama, that life
itself does not excite more distinctly that sense of individuality which
belongs to real existence. Paradoxical as it may sound, one of the essential
properties of Geometry is not less essential to dramatic excellence; and
Aristotle has accordingly required of the poet an involution of the universal
in the individual. The chief differences are, that in Geometry it is the
universal truth, which is uppermost in the consciousness; in poetry the
individual form, in which the truth is clothed. With the ancients, and not
less with the elder dramatists of England and France, both comedy and
tragedy were considered as kinds of poetry. They neither sought in comedy
to make us laugh merely; much less to make us laugh by wry faces, accidents of jargon, *slang* phrases for the day, or the clothing of common-
place morals drawn from the shops or mechanic occupations of their
characters. Nor did they condescend in tragedy to wheedle away the
applause of the spectators, by representing before them facsimiles of
their own mean selves in all their existing meanness, or to work on the
sluggish sympathies by a pathos not a whit more respectable than the
maudlin tears of drunkenness. Their tragic scenes were meant to *affect*
us indeed; but yet within the bounds of pleasure, and in union with the
activity both of our understanding and imagination. They wished to
transport the mind to a sense of its possible greatness, and to implant the
germs of that greatness, during the temporary oblivion of the worthless
"thing we are," and of the peculiar state in which each man *happens*
to be, suspending our individual recollections and lulling them to sleep
amid the music of nobler thoughts. [Coleridge's note.]

FRIEND, Pages 251, 252.

medium between the swains of Theocritus and those of an imaginary golden age.

The characters of the vicar and the shepherd-mariner in the poem of "THE BROTHERS," that of the shepherd of Greenhead Ghyll in the "MICHAEL," have all the verisimilitude and representative quality, that the purposes of poetry can require. They are persons of a known and abiding class, and their manners and sentiments the natural product of circumstances common to the class. Take "MICHAEL" for instance:

> An old man stout of heart, and strong of limb:
> His bodily frame had been from youth to age
> Of an unusual strength: his mind was keen,
> Intense, and frugal, apt for all affairs,
> And in his shepherd's calling he was prompt
> And watchful more than ordinary men.
> Hence he had learnt the meaning of all winds,
> Of blasts of every tone; and oftentimes
> When others heeded not, he heard the South
> Make subterraneous music, like the noise
> Of bagpipers on distant Highland hills.
> The shepherd, at such warning, of his flock
> Bethought him, and he to himself would say,
> The winds are now devising work for me!
> And truly at all times the storm, that drives
> The traveller to a shelter, summon'd him
> Up to the mountains. He had been alone
> Amid the heart of many thousand mists,
> That came to him and left him on the heights.
> So liv'd he, till his eightieth year was pass'd.
> And grossly that man errs, who should suppose
> That the green vallies, and the streams and rocks,
> Were things indifferent to the shepherd's thoughts.
> Fields, where with chearful spirits he had breath'd
> The common air; the hills, which he so oft
> Had climb'd with vigorous steps; which had impress'd
> So many incidents upon his mind
> Of hardship, skill or courage, joy or fear;
> Which, like a book, preserved the memory
> Of the dumb animals, whom he had sav'd,
> Had fed or shelter'd, linking to such acts,
> So grateful in themselves, the certainty

Of honorable gain; these fields, these hills
Which were his living being, even more
Than his own blood—what could they less? had laid
Strong hold on his affections, were to him
A pleasurable feeling of blind love,
The pleasure which there is in life itself.

On the other hand, in the poems which are pitched at a lower note, as the "HARRY GILL," "IDIOT BOY," the *feelings* are those of human nature in general; though the poet has judiciously laid the *scene* in the country, in order to place *himself* in the vicinity of interesting images, without the necessity of ascribing a sentimental perception of their beauty to the persons of his drama. In the "Idiot Boy," indeed, the mother's character is not so much a real and native product of a "situation where the essential passions of the heart find a better soil, in which they can attain their maturity and speak a plainer and more emphatic language," as it is an impersonation of an instinct abandoned by judgement. Hence the two following charges seem to me not wholly groundless: at least, they are the only plausible objections, which I have heard to that fine poem. The one is, that the author has not, in the poem itself, taken sufficient care to preclude from the reader's fancy the disgusting images of *ordinary morbid idiocy*, which yet it was by no means his intention to represent. He has even by the "burr, burr, burr," uncounteracted by any preceding description of the boy's beauty, assisted in recalling them. The other is, that the idiocy of the *boy* is so evenly balanced by the folly of the *mother*, as to present to the general reader rather a laughable burlesque on the blindness of anile dotage, than an analytic display of maternal affection in its ordinary workings.

In the "Thorn" the poet himself acknowledges in a note the necessity of an introductory poem, in which he should have pourtrayed the character of the person from whom the words of the poem are supposed to proceed: a superstitious man moderately imaginative, of slow faculties and deep feelings, "a captain of a small trading vessel, for example, who, being past the middle age of life, had retired upon an annuity, or small independent income, to some village or country town of which he was not a native, or in which he had not been accustomed to

live. Such men having nothing to do become credulous and
talkative from indolence." But in a poem, still more in a lyric
poem (and the Nurse in Shakespeare's Romeo and Juliet alone
prevents me from extending the remark even to dramatic *poetry,*
if indeed the Nurse itself can be deemed altogether a case in
point) it is not possible to imitate truly a dull and garrulous dis-
courser, without repeating the effects of dullness and garrulity.
However this may be, I dare assert, that the parts (and these
form the far larger portion of the whole) which might as well or
still better have proceeded from the poet's own imagination,
and have been spoken in his own character, are those which
have given, and which will continue to give, universal delight;
and that the passages exclusively appropriate to the supposed
narrator, such as the last couplet of the third stanza;[8] the seven
last lines of the tenth; and the five following stanzas,[9] with

> [8] I've measured it from side to side;
> 'Tis three feet long, and two feet wide.
> > [Coleridge's note.]
> [9] Nay, rack your brain—'tis all in vain,
> I'll tell you everything I know;
> But to the Thorn, and to the Pond
> Which is a little step beyond,
> I wish that you would go:
> Perhaps when you are at the place,
> You something of her tale may trace.
>
> I'll give you the best help I can:
> Before you up the mountain go,
> Up to the dreary mountain-top,
> I'll tell you all I know.
> 'Tis now some two-and-twenty years
> Since she (her name is Martha Ray)
> Gave, with a maiden's true good will,
> Her company to Stephen Hill;
> And she was blithe and gay,
> And she was happy, happy still
> Whene'er she thought of Stephen Hill.
>
> And they had fix'd the wedding-day,
> The morning that must wed them both;
> But Stephen to another maid
> Had sworn another oath;
> And, with this other maid, to church
> Unthinking Stephen went—
> Poor Martha! on that woeful day
> A pang of pitiless dismay

the exception of the four admirable lines at the commencement
of the fourteenth, are felt by many unprejudiced and unsophisticated hearts, as sudden and unpleasant sinkings from the height
to which the poet had previously lifted them, and to which he
again re-elevates both himself and his reader.

If then I am compelled to doubt the theory, by which the
choice of *characters* was to be directed, not only *à priori*, from
grounds of reason, but both from the few instances in which the
poet himself *need* be supposed to have been governed by it, and

---

> Into her soul was sent;
> A fire was kindled in her breast,
> Which might not burn itself to rest.
>
> They say, full six months after this,
> While yet the summer leaves were green,
> She to the mountain-top would go,
> And there was often seen.
> 'Tis said a child was in her womb,
> As now to any eye was plain;
> She was with child, and she was mad;
> Yet often she was sober sad
> From her exceeding pain.
> Oh me! ten thousand times I'd rather
> That he had died, that cruel father!
>   ✿   ✿   ✿   ✿   ✿   ✿   ✿
>   ✿   ✿   ✿   ✿   ✿   ✿   ✿
>   ✿   ✿   ✿   ✿   ✿   ✿   ✿
>
> Last Christmas when we talked of this,
> Old farmer Simpson did maintain,
> That in her womb the infant wrought
> About its mother's heart, and brought
> Her senses back again:
> And, when at last her time drew near,
> Her looks were calm, her senses clear.
>
> No more I know, I wish I did,
> And I would tell it all to you:
> For what became of this poor child
> There's none that ever knew:
> And if a child was born or no,
> There's no one that could ever tell;
> And if 'twas born alive or dead,
> There's no one knows, as I have said:
> But some remember well,
> That Martha Ray about this time
> Would up the mountain often climb.
>
>   [Coleridge's note.]

from the comparative inferiority of those instances; still more must I hesitate in my assent to the sentence which immediately follows the former citation; and which I can neither admit as particular fact, or as general rule. "The language too of these men is adopted (purified indeed from what appear to be its real defects, from all lasting and rational causes of dislike or disgust) because such men hourly communicate with the best objects from which the best part of language is originally derived; and because, from their rank in society and the sameness and narrow circle of their intercourse, being less under the action of social vanity, they convey their feelings and notions in simple and unelaborated expressions." To this I reply; that a rustic's language, purified from all provincialism and grossness, and so far reconstructed as to be made consistent with the rules of grammar (which are in essence no other than the laws of universal logic, applied to psychological materials) will not differ from the language of any other man of common-sense, however learned or refined he may be, except as far as the notions, which the rustic has to convey, are fewer and more indiscriminate. This will become still clearer, if we add the consideration (equally important though less obvious) that the rustic, from the more imperfect development of his faculties, and from the lower state of their cultivation, aims almost solely to convey *insulated facts,* either those of his scanty experience or his traditional belief; while the educated man chiefly seeks to discover and express those *connections* of things, or those relative *bearings* of fact to fact, from which some more or less general law is deducible. For *facts* are valuable to a wise man, chiefly as they lead to the discovery of the indwelling *law,* which is the true *being* of things, the sole solution of their modes of existence, and in the knowledge of which consists our dignity and our power.

As little can I agree with the assertion, that from the objects with which the rustic hourly communicates the best part of language is formed. For first, if to communicate with an object implies such an acquaintance with it, as renders it capable of being discriminately reflected on; the distinct knowledge of an uneducated rustic would furnish a very scanty vocabulary. The few things, and modes of action, requisite for his bodily con-

veniences, would alone be individualized; while all the rest of
nature would be expressed by a small number of confused general terms. Secondly, I deny that the words and combinations
of words derived from the objects, with which the rustic is
familiar, whether with distinct or confused knowledge, can be
justly said to form the *best* part of language. It is more than
probable, that many classes of the brute creation possess discriminating sounds, by which they can convey to each other
notices of such objects as concern their food, shelter, or safety.
Yet we hesitate to call the aggregate of such sounds a language,
otherwise than metaphorically. The best part of human language, properly so called, is derived from reflection on the acts
of the mind itself. It is formed by a voluntary appropriation of
fixed symbols to internal acts, to processes and results of imagination, the greater part of which have no place in the consciousness of uneducated man; though in civilized society, by imitation and passive remembrance of what they hear from their
religious instructors and other superiors, the most uneducated
share in the harvest which they neither sowed or reaped. If the
history of the phrases in hourly currency among our peasants
were traced, a person not previously aware of the fact would
be surprised at finding so large a number, which three or four
centuries ago were the exclusive property of the universities and
the schools; and, at the commencement of the Reformation, had
been transferred from the school to the pulpit, and thus gradually passed into common life. The extreme difficulty, and often
the impossibility, of finding words for the simplest moral and
intellectual processes of the languages of uncivilized tribes has
proved perhaps the weightiest obstacle to the progress of our
most zealous and adroit missionaries. Yet these tribes are surrounded by the same nature as our peasants are; but in still
more impressive forms; and they are, moreover, obliged to
particularize many more of them. When, therefore, Mr. Wordsworth adds, "accordingly, such a language" (meaning, as before, the language of rustic life purified from provincialism)
"arising out of repeated experience and regular feelings, is a
more permanent, and a far more philosophical language, than
that which is frequently substituted for it by poets, who think
they are conferring honor upon themselves and their art in

proportion as they indulge in arbitrary and capricious habits of expression:" it may be answered, that the language, which he has in view, can be attributed to rustics with no greater right, than the style of Hooker or Bacon to Tom Brown or Sir Roger L'Estrange.[10] Doubtless, if what is peculiar to each were omitted in each, the result must needs be the same. Further, that the poet, who uses an illogical diction, or a style fitted to excite only the low and changeable pleasure of wonder by means of groundless novelty, substitutes a language of *folly* and *vanity*, not for that of the *rustic*, but for that of *good sense* and *natural feeling*.

Here let me be permitted to remind the reader, that the positions, which I controvert, are contained in the sentences— *"a selection of the* REAL *language of men;"*—*"the language of these men"* (i.e. men in low and rustic life) *"I propose to myself to imitate, and, as far as is possible, to adopt the very language of men." "Between the language of prose and that of metrical composition, there neither is, nor can be any essential difference."* It is against these exclusively that my opposition is directed.

I object, in the very first instance, to an equivocation in the use of the word "real." Every man's language varies, according to the extent of his knowledge, the activity of his faculties, and the depth or quickness of his feelings. Every man's language has, first, its *individualities;* secondly, the common properties of the *class* to which he belongs; and thirdly, words and phrases of *universal* use. The language of Hooker, Bacon, Bishop Taylor, and Burke differs from the common language of the learned class only by the superior number and novelty of the thoughts and relations which they had to convey. The language of Algernon Sidney differs not at all from that, which every well-educated gentleman would wish to write, and (with due allowances for the undeliberateness, and less connected train, of thinking natural and proper to conversation) such as he would wish to talk. Neither one nor the other differ half so much from the general language of cultivated society, as the language

[10] Richard Hooker (1554–1600), author of *Ecclesiastical Polity*, and Francis Bacon (1561–1626) were great prose writers. Thomas Brown (1663–1704) was a dull imitator of the classics, Sir Roger L'Estrange (1616–1704) a writer of scurrilous pamphlets.

of Mr. Wordsworth's homeliest composition differs from that of a common peasant. For "real" therefore, we must substitute *ordinary*, or *lingua communis*. And this, we have proved, is no more to be found in the phraseology of low and rustic life than in that of any other class. Omit the peculiarities of each, and the result of course must be common to all. And assuredly the omissions and changes to be made in the language of rustics, before it could be transferred to any species of poem, except the drama or other professed imitation, are at least as numerous and weighty, as would be required in adapting to the same purpose the ordinary language of tradesmen and manufacturers. Not to mention, that the language so highly extolled by Mr. Wordsworth varies in every county, nay in every village, according to the accidental character of the clergyman, the existence or non-existence of schools; or even, perhaps, as the exciseman, publican, or barber, happen to be, or not to be, zealous politicians, and readers of the weekly newspaper *pro bono publico*. Anterior to cultivation, the lingua communis of every country, as Dante has well observed, exists every where in parts, and no where as a whole.

Neither is the case rendered at all more tenable by the addition of the words, *in a state of excitement*. For the nature of a man's words, where he is strongly affected by joy, grief, or anger, must necessarily depend on the number and quality of the general truths, conceptions and images, and of the words expressing them, with which his mind had been previously stored. For the property of passion is not to *create*; but to set in increased activity. At least, whatever new connections of thoughts or images, or (which is equally, if not more than equally, the appropriate effect of strong excitement) whatever generalizations of truth or experience, the heat of passion may produce; yet the terms of their conveyance must have pre-existed in his former conversations, and are only collected and crowded together by the unusual stimulation. It is indeed very possible to adopt in a poem the unmeaning repetitions, habitual phrases, and other blank counters, which an unfurnished or confused understanding interposes at short intervals, in order to keep hold of his subject, which is still slipping from him, and to give him time for recollection; or in mere aid of vacancy, as in the

scanty companies of a country stage the same player pops back-
wards and forwards, in order to prevent the appearance of
empty spaces, in the procession of Macbeth, or Henry VIIIth.
But what assistance to the poet, or ornament to the poem, these
can supply, I am at a loss to conjecture. Nothing assuredly can
differ either in origin or in mode more widely from the *apparent*
tautologies of intense and turbulent feeling, in which the passion
is greater and of longer endurance than to be exhausted or
satisfied by a single representation of the image or incident
exciting it. Such repetitions I admit to be a beauty of the
highest kind; as illustrated by Mr. Wordsworth himself from the
song of Deborah. *"At her feet he bowed, he fell, he lay down;*
at her feet he bowed, he fell; where he bowed, there he fell
down dead."

CHAPTER XVIII

*Language of metrical composition, why and wherein essentially differ-
ent from that of prose—Origin and elements of metre—Its necessary consequences, and the conditions thereby imposed on the
metrical writer in the choice of his diction.*

I CONCLUDE, therefore, that the attempt is impracticable; and
that, were it not impracticable, it would still be useless. For the
very power of making the selection implies the previous possession of the language selected. Or where can the poet have
lived? And by what rules could he direct his choice, which
would not have enabled him to select and arrange his words by
the light of his own judgement? We do not adopt the language
of a class by the mere adoption of such words exclusively, as that
class would use, or at least understand; but likewise by following the *order*, in which the words of such men are wont to
succeed each other. Now this order, in the intercourse of uneducated men, is distinguished from the diction of their superiors in
knowledge and power, by the greater *disjunction* and *separation*
in the component parts of that, whatever it be, which they wish
to communicate. There is a want of that prospectiveness of mind,
that *surview*, which enables a man to foresee the whole of what
he is to convey, appertaining to any one point; and by this means
so to subordinate and arrange the different parts according to

their relative importance, as to convey it at once, and as an organized whole.

Now I will take the first stanza, on which I have chanced to open, in the Lyrical Ballads. It is one the most simple and the least peculiar in its language.

> In distant countries have I been,
> And yet I have not often seen
> A healthy man, a man full grown,
> Weep in the public roads alone.
> But such a one, on English ground,
> And in the broad highway, I met;
> Along the broad highway he came,
> His cheeks with tears were wet:
> Sturdy he seem'd, though he was sad;
> And in his arms a lamb he had.[11]

The words here are doubtless such as are current in all ranks of life; and of course not less so in the hamlet and cottage than in the shop, manufactory, college, or palace. But is this the *order,* in which the rustic would have placed the words? I am grievously deceived, if the following less *compact* mode of commencing the same tale be not a far more faithful copy. "I have been in a many parts, far and near, and I don't know that I ever saw before a man crying by himself in the public road; a grown man I mean, that was neither sick nor hurt," &c., &c. But when I turn to the following stanza in "The Thorn":

> At all times of the day and night
> This wretched woman thither goes,
> And she is known to every star,
> And every wind that blows:
> And there, beside the thorn, she sits,
> When the blue day-light's in the skies;
> And when the whirlwind's on the hill,
> Or frosty air is keen and still;
> And to herself she cries,
> Oh misery! Oh misery!
> Oh woe is me! Oh misery!

[11] Wordsworth's "The Last of the Flock."

and compare this with the language of ordinary men; or with that which I can conceive at all likely to proceed, in *real* life, from *such* a narrator, as is supposed in the note to the poem; compare it either in the succession of the images or of the sentences; I am reminded of the sublime prayer and hymn of praise, which MILTON, in opposition to an established liturgy, presents as a fair *specimen* of common extemporary devotion, and such as we might expect to hear from every self-inspired minister of a conventicle! And I reflect with delight, how little a mere theory, though of his own workmanship, interferes with the processes of genuine imagination in a man of true poetic genius, who possesses, as Mr. Wordsworth, if ever man did, most assuredly does possess, "THE VISION AND THE FACULTY DIVINE."

One point then alone remains, but that the most important; its examination having been, indeed, my chief inducement for the preceding inquisition. "*There neither is or can be any essential difference between the language of prose and metrical composition.*" Such is Mr. Wordsworth's assertion. Now prose itself, at least in all argumentative and consecutive works, differs, and ought to differ, from the language of conversation; even as [12]

---

[12] It is no less an error in teachers, than a torment to the poor children, to inforce the necessity of reading as they would talk. In order to cure them of *singing* as it is called, that is, of too great a difference, the child is made to repeat the words with his eyes from off the book; and then, indeed, his tones resemble talking, as far as his fears, tears and trembling will permit. But as soon as his eye is again directed to the printed page, the spell begins anew; for an instinctive sense tells the child's feelings, that to utter its own momentary thoughts, and to recite the written thoughts of another, as of another, and a far wiser than himself, are two widely different things; and as the two acts are accompanied with widely different feelings, so must they justify different modes of enunciation. Joseph Lancaster, among his other sophistications of the excellent Dr. Bell's invaluable system, cures this fault of *singing*, by hanging fetters and chains on the child, to the music of which one of his school-fellows, who walks before, dolefully chaunts out the child's last speech and confession, birth, parentage, and education. And this soul-benumbing ignomiy, this unholy and heart-hardening burlesque on the last fearful infliction of outraged law, in pronouncing the sentence to which the stern and familiarized judge not seldom bursts into tears, has been extolled as a happy and ingenious method of remedying—what? and how?—why, one extreme in order to introduce another, scarce less distant from good sense, and certainly likely to have worse moral effects, by enforcing a semblance of petulant ease nad self-sufficiency, in repression, and possible after-perversion of the natural feelings. I have to beg Dr. Bell's pardon for this connection of the two names, but he knows that contrast is no less powerful a cause of association than likeness.

reading ought to differ from talking. Unless therefore the difference denied be that of the mere *words*, as materials common to all styles of writing, and not of the *style* itself in the universally admitted sense of the term, it might be naturally presumed that there must exist a still greater between the ordonnance of poetic composition and that of prose, than is expected to distinguish prose from ordinary conversation.

There are not, indeed, examples wanting in the history of literature, of apparent paradoxes that have summoned the public wonder as new and startling truths, but which on examination have shrunk into tame and harmless *truisms;* as the eyes of a cat, seen in the dark, have been mistaken for flames of fire. But Mr. Wordsworth is among the last men, to whom a delusion of this kind would be attributed by anyone, who had enjoyed the slightest opportunity of understanding his mind and character. Where an objection has been anticipated by such an author as natural, his answer to it must needs be interpreted in some sense which either is, or has been, or is capable of being controverted. My object then must be to discover some other meaning for the term *"essential difference"* in this place, exclusive of the indistinction and community of the words themselves. For whether there ought to exist a class of words in the English, in any degree resembling the poetic dialect of the Greek and Italian, is a question of very subordinate importance. The number of such words would be small indeed, in our language; and even in the Italian and Greek, they consist not so much of different words, as of slight differences in the *forms* of declining and conjugating the same words; forms, doubtless, which having been, at some period more or less remote, the common grammatic flexions of some tribe or province, had been accidentally appropriated to poetry by the general admiration of certain master intellects, the first established lights of inspiration, to whom that dialect happened to be native.

Essence, in its primary signification, means the principle of *individuation*, the inmost principle of the possibility of any thing, as that particular thing. It is equivalent to the *idea* of a thing, when ever we use the word, idea, with philosophic precision. Existence, on the other hand, is distinguished from essence, by the superintroduction of *reality*. Thus we speak of the essence, and essential properties of a circle; but we do not therefore assert, that any thing, which really exists, is mathematically circular. Thus too, without any tautology we contend for the *existence* of the Supreme Being; that is, for a reality correspondent to the idea. There is, next, a *secondary* use of the word essence, in which it signifies the point or ground of contra-distinction between two modifications of the same substance or subject. Thus we should be allowed to say, that the style of architecture of Westminster Abbey is *essentially* different from that of St. Paul's, even though both had been built with blocks cut into the same form, and from the same quarry. Only in this latter sense of the term must it have been *denied* by Mr. Wordsworth (for in this sense alone is it *affirmed* by the general opinion) that the language of poetry (i.e. the formal construction, or architecture, of the words and phrases) is *essentially* different from that of prose. Now the burthen of the proof lies with the oppugner, not with the supporters of the common belief. Mr. Wordsworth, in consequence, assigns as the proof of his position, "that not only the language of a large portion of every good poem, even of the most elevated character, must necessarily, except with reference to the metre, in no respect differ from that of good prose, but likewise that some of the most interesting parts of the best poems will be found to be strictly the language of prose, when prose is well written. The truth of this assertion might be demonstrated by innumerable passages from almost all the poetical writings even of Milton himself." He then quotes Gray's sonnet—

> In vain to me the smiling mornings shine,
> And reddening Phœbus lifts his golden fire;
> The birds in vain their amorous descant join,
> Or chearful fields resume their green attire.
> These ears, alas! for other notes repine;
> *A different object do these eyes require;*
> *My lonely anguish melts no heart but mine;*
> *And in my breast the imperfect joys expire.*
> Yet morning smiles the busy race to cheer,
> And newborn pleasure brings to happier men:
> The fields to all their wonted tribute bear,
> To warm their little loves the birds complain.
> *I fruitless mourn to him that cannot hear,*
> *And weep the more because I weep in vain,*[13]

[13] Thomas Gray (1716–1771), "Sonnet on the Death of Richard West."

and adds the following remark:—"It will easily be perceived, that the only part of this Sonnet, which is of any value, is the lines printed in italics. It is equally obvious, that, except in the rhyme, and in the use of the single word 'fruitless' for 'fruitlessly,' which is so far a defect, the language of these lines does in no respect differ from that of prose."

An idealist defending his system by the fact, that when asleep we often believe ourselves awake, was well answered by his plain neighbour, "Ah, but when awake do we ever believe ourselves asleep?"—Things identical must be convertible. The preceding passage seems to rest on a similar sophism. For the question is not, whether there may not occur in prose an order of words, which would be equally proper in a poem; nor whether there are not beautiful lines and sentences of frequent occurrence in good poems, which would be equally becoming as well as beautiful in good prose; for neither the one nor the other has even been either denied or doubted by any one. The true question must be, whether there are not modes of expression, a *construction*, and an *order* of sentences, which are in their fit and natural place in a serious prose composition, but would be disproportionate and heterogeneous in metrical poetry; and, vice versa, whether in the language of a serious poem there may not be an arrangement both of words and sentences, and a use and selection of (what are called) *figures of speech*, both as to their kind, their frequency, and their occasions, which on a subject of equal weight would be vicious and alien in correct and manly prose. I contend that in both cases this unfitness of each for the place of the other frequently will and ought to exist.

And first from the *origin* of metre. This I would trace to the balance in the mind effected by that spontaneous effort which strives to hold in check the workings of passion. It might be easily explained likewise in what manner this salutary antagonism is assisted by the very state, which it counteracts; and how this balance of antagonists became organized into *metre* (in the usual acceptation of that term) by a supervening act of the will and judgement, consciously and for the foreseen purpose of pleasure. Assuming these principles, as the data of our argument, we deduce from them two legitimate conditions, which the critic is entitled to expect in every metrical work. First, that, as the *elements* of metre owe their existence to a state of increased ex-

citement, so the metre itself should be accompanied by the
natural language of excitement. Secondly, that as these elements
are formed into metre *artificially,* by a *voluntary* act, with the
design and for the purpose of blending *delight* with emotion, so
the traces of present *volition* should throughout the metrical language be proportionately discernible. Now these two conditions
must be reconciled and co-present. There must be not only a
partnership, but a union; an interpenetration of passion and of
will, of *spontaneous* impulse and of *voluntary* purpose. Again,
this union can be manifested only in a frequency of forms and
figures of speech (originally the offspring of passion, but now the
adopted children of power) greater than would be desired or
endured, where the emotion is not voluntarily encouraged and
kept up for the sake of that pleasure, which such emotion, so
tempered and mastered by the will, is found capable of communicating. It not only dictates, but of itself tends to produce, a
more frequent employment of picturesque and vivifying language, than would be natural in any other case, in which there
did not exist, as there does in the present, a previous and well
understood, though tacit, *compact* between the poet and his
reader, that the latter is entitled to expect, and the former bound
to supply, this species and degree of pleasureable excitement.
We may in some measure apply to this union the answer of
Polixenes, in the Winter's Tale, to Perdita's neglect of the
streaked gilly-flowers, because she had heard it said,

> There is an art which, in their piedness, shares
> With great creating nature.
> > *Pol:* Say there be;
> Yet nature is made better by no mean,
> But nature makes that mean; so, ev'n that art,
> Which, you say, adds to nature, is an art,
> That nature makes. You see, sweet maid, we marry
> *A gentler scyon to the wildest stock;*
> And make conceive a bark of ruder kind
> By bud of nobler race. This is an art,
> Which does mend nature—change it rather; but
> The art itself is nature.[14]

[14] Shakespeare, *The Winter's Tale,* Act IV, scene iii, ll. 86–97.

Secondly, I argue from the EFFECTS of metre. As far as metre acts in and for itself, it tends to increase the vivacity and susceptibility both of the general feelings and of the attention. This effect it produces by the continued excitement of surprize, and by the quick reciprocations of curiosity still gratified and still re-excited, which are too slight indeed to be at any one moment objects of distinct consciousness, yet become considerable in their aggregate influence. As a medicated atmosphere, or as wine during animated conversation; they act powerfully, though themselves unnoticed. Where, therefore, correspondent food and appropriate matter are not provided for the attention and feelings thus roused, there must needs be a disappointment felt; like that of leaping in the dark from the last step of a stair-case, when we had prepared our muscles for a leap of three or four.

The discussion on the powers of metre in the preface is highly ingenious and touches at all points on truth. But I cannot find any statement of its powers considered abstractly and separately. On the contrary Mr. Wordsworth seems always to estimate metre by the powers, which it exerts during (and, as I think, in *consequence of*) its combination with other elements of poetry. Thus the previous difficulty is left unanswered, *what* the elements are, with which it must be combined in order to produce its own effects to any pleasureable purpose. Double and tri-syllable rhymes, indeed, form a lower species of wit, and, attended to exclusively for their own sake, may become a source of momentary amusement; as in poor Smart's distich to the Welsh 'Squire who had promised him a hare:

> Tell me, thou son of great Cadwallader!
> Hast sent the hare? or hast thou swallow'd her?

But for any *poetic* purposes, metre resembles (if the aptness of the simile may excuse its meanness) yeast, worthless or disagreeable by itself, but giving vivacity and spirit to the liquor with which it is proportionally combined.

The reference to the "Children in the Wood," by no means satisfies my judgement. We all willingly throw ourselves back for awhile into the feelings of our childhood. This ballad, therefore, we read under such recollections of our own childish feelings, as would equally endear to us poems, which Mr. Words-

worth himself would regard as faulty in the opposite extreme
of gaudy and technical ornament. Before the invention of printing, and in a still greater degree, before the introduction of writing, metre, especially *alliterative* metre (whether alliterative at
the beginning of the words, as in "Pierce Plouman," or at the
end as in rhymes) possessed an independent value as assisting
the recollection, and consequently the preservation, of *any* series
of truths or incidents. But I am not convinced by the collation
of facts, that the "Children in the Wood" owes either its preservation, or its popularity, to its metrical form. Mr. Marshal's reposi-
tory affords a number of tales in prose inferior in pathos and
general merit, some of as old a date, and many as widely popular.
"TOM HICKATHRIFT," "JACK THE GIANT-KILLER," "GOODY TWO-
SHOES," and "LITTLE RED RIDING-HOOD" are formidable rivals.
And that they have continued in prose, cannot be fairly explained
by the assumption, that the comparative meanness of their
thoughts and images precluded even the humblest forms of
metre. The scene of GOODY TWO-SHOES in the church is perfectly
susceptible of metrical narration; and, among the Θαύματα
θαυμαστότατα [most wondrous wonders] even of the present age,
I do not recollect a more astonishing image than that of the
"whole rookery, that flew out of the giant's beard," scared by the
tremendous voice, with which this monster answered the chal-
lenge of the heroic TOM HICKATHRIFT!

If from these we turn to compositions universally, and independently of all early associations, beloved and admired; would
"THE MARIA," "THE MONK," or "THE POOR MAN'S ASS" of Sterne,
be read with more delight, or have a better chance of immortality,
had they without any change in the diction been composed in
rhyme, than in their present state? If I am not grossly mistaken,
the general reply would be in the negative. Nay, I will confess,
that, in Mr. Wordsworth's own volumes, the "ANECDOTE FOR
FATHERS," "SIMON LEE," "ALICE FELL," "THE BEGGARS," and
"THE SAILOR'S MOTHER," notwithstanding the beauties which are
to be found in each of them where the poet interposes the music
of his own thoughts, would have been more delightful to me in
prose, told and managed, as by Mr. Wordsworth they would have
been, in a moral essay, or pedestrian tour.

Metre in itself is simply a stimulant of the attention, and therefore excites the question: Why is the attention to be thus stimulated? Now the question cannot be answered by the pleasure of the metre itself: for this we have shown to be *conditional,* and dependent on the appropriateness of the thoughts and expressions, to which the metrical form is superadded. Neither can I conceive any other answer that can be rationally given, short of this: I write in metre, because I am about to use a language different from that of prose. Besides, where the language is not such, how interesting soever the reflections are, that are capable of being drawn by a philosophic mind from the thoughts or incidents of the poem, the metre itself must often become feeble. Take the last three stanzas of "THE SAILOR'S MOTHER," for instance. If I could for a moment abstract from the effect produced on the author's feelings, as a man, by the incident at the time of its real occurrence, I would dare appeal to his own judgement, whether in the *metre* itself he found a sufficient reason for *their* being written *metrically?*

> And, thus continuing, she said,
> I had a son, who many a day
> Sailed on the seas; but he is dead;
> In Denmark he was cast away:
> And I have travelled far as Hull, to see
> What clothes he might have left, or other property.
>
> The bird and cage they both were his:
> 'Twas my son's bird; and neat and trim
> He kept it: many voyages
> This singing-bird hath gone with him;
> When last he sailed he left the bird behind;
> As it might be, perhaps, from bodings of his mind.
>
> He to a fellow-lodger's care
> Had left it, to be watched and fed,
> Till he came back again; and there
> I found it when my son was dead;
> And now, God help me for my little wit!
> I trail it with me, Sir! he took so much delight in it.

If disproportioning the emphasis we read these stanzas so as to make the rhymes perceptible, even *tri-syllable* rhymes could scarcely produce an equal sense of oddity and strangeness, as we feel here in finding *rhymes at all* in sentences so exclusively colloquial. I would further ask whether, but for that visionary state, into which the figure of the woman and the susceptibility of his own genius had placed the poet's imagination, (a state which spreads its influence and coloring over all, that co-exists with the exciting cause, and in which

> The simplest, and the most familiar things
> Gain a strange power of spreading awe around [15] them,)

I would ask the poet whether he would not have felt an abrupt downfall in these verses from the preceding stanza?

> The ancient spirit is not dead;
> Old times, thought I, are breathing there;
> Proud was I that my country bred
> Such strength, a dignity so fair:
> She begged an alms, like one in poor estate;
> I looked at her again, nor did my pride abate.

It must not be omitted, and is besides worthy of notice, that those stanzas furnish the only fair instance that I have been able to discover in all Mr. Wordsworth's writings, of an *actual* adoption, or true imitation, of the *real* and *very* language of *low and rustic life,* freed from provincialisms.

Thirdly, I deduce the position from all the causes elsewhere assigned, which render metre the proper form of poetry, and poetry imperfect and defective without metre. Metre therefore having been connected with *poetry* most often and by a peculiar

---

[15] Altered from the description of Night-Mair in the "Remorse."

> Oh Heaven! 'twas frightful! Now run down and stared at
> By hideous shapes that cannot be remembered;
> Now seeing nothing and imagining nothing;
> But only being afraid—stifled with fear!
> While every goodly or familiar form
> Had a strange power of spreading terror round me!

N.B. Though Shakespeare has, for his own *all-justifying* purposes, introduced the Night-*Mare* with her own foals, yet Mair means a Sister, or perhaps a Hag. [Coleridge's note. The quotation is from Coleridge's verse-drama, *Remorse,* Act IV, scene i, ll. 68–73.]

fitness, whatever else is combined with *metre* must, though it be not itself *essentially* poetic, have nevertheless some property in common with poetry, as an intermedium of affinity, a sort (if I may dare borrow a well-known phrase from technical chemistry) of *mordaunt* between it and the superadded metre. Now poetry, Mr. Wordsworth truly affirms, does always imply PASSION: which word must be here understood in its general sense, as an excited state of the feelings and faculties. And as every passion has its proper pulse, so will it likewise have its characteristic modes of expression. But where there exists that degree of genius and talent which entitles a writer to aim at the honors of a poet, the very *act* of poetic composition *itself* is, and is *allowed* to imply and to produce, an unusual state of excitement, which of course justifies and demands a correspondent difference of language, as truly, though not perhaps in as marked a degree, as the excitement of love, fear, rage, or jealousy. The vividness of the descriptions or declamations in DONNE or DRYDEN is as much and as often derived from the force and fervor of the describer, as from the reflections, forms or incidents, which constitute their subject and materials. The wheels take fire from the mere rapidity of their motion. To what extent, and under what modifications, this may be admitted to act, I shall attempt to define in an after remark on Mr. Wordsworth's reply to this objection, or rather on his objection to this reply, as already anticipated in his preface.

Fourthly, and as intimately connected with this, if not the same argument in a more general form, I adduce the high spiritual instinct of the human being impelling us to seek unity by harmonious adjustment, and thus establishing the principle, that *all* the parts of an organized whole must be assimilated to the more *important* and *essential* parts. This and the preceding arguments may be strengthened by the reflection, that the composition of a poem is among the *imitative* arts; and that imitation, as opposed to copying, consists either in the interfusion of the SAME throughout the radically DIFFERENT, or of the different throughout a base radically the same.

Lastly, I appeal to the practice of the best poets, of all countries and in all ages, as *authorizing* the opinion (*deduced* from all the foregoing) that in every import of the word ESSENTIAL, which would not here involve a mere truism, there may be, is, and ought to be an *essential* difference between the language of prose and of metrical composition.

In Mr. Wordsworth's criticism of Gray's Sonnet, the readers' sympathy with his praise or blame of the different parts is taken for granted rather perhaps too easily. He has not, at least, attempted to win or compel it by argumentative analysis. In *my* conception at least, the lines rejected as of no value do, with the exception of the two first, differ as much and as little from the language of common life, as those which he has printed in italics as possessing genuine excellence. Of the five lines thus honourably distinguished, two of them differ from prose, even more widely than the lines which either precede or follow, in the *position* of the words.

> *A different object do these eyes require;*
> My lonely anguish melts no heart but mine;
> *And in my breast the imperfect joys expire.*

But were it otherwise, what would this prove, but a truth, of which no man ever doubted? Videlicet, that there are sentences which would be equally in their place both in verse and prose. Assuredly it does not prove the point, which alone requires proof; namely, that there are not passages, which would suit the one and not suit the other. The first line of this sonnet is distinguished from the ordinary language of men by the epithet to morning. (For we will set aside, at present, the consideration, that the particular word *"smiling"* is hackneyed and (as it involves a sort of personification) not quite congruous with the common and material attribute of *shining.*) And, doubtless, this adjunction of epithets for the purpose of additional description, where no particular attention is demanded for the quality of the thing, would be noticed as giving a poetic cast to a man's conversation. Should the sportsman exclaim, *"Come boys! the rosy morning calls you up,"* he will be supposed to have some song in his head. But no one suspects this, when he says, "A wet morning shall not confine us to our beds." This then is either a defect in poetry, or it is not. Whoever should decide in the *affirmative*, I would request him to re-peruse any one poem of any confessedly great poet from Homer to Milton, or from Æschylus to Shakespeare; and to strike out (in thought I mean) every instance of this kind. If the number of these fancied erasures did not startle him; or if he continued to deem the work improved by their total omission; he must advance reasons of no ordinary strength and evidence, reasons grounded in the essence of human nature. Otherwise, I should not hesitate to consider him as a man not so much *proof against* all authority, as *dead to* it.

The second line,

> And reddening Phœbus lifts his golden fire;

has indeed almost as many faults as words. But then it is a bad line, not because the language is distinct from that of prose; but because it conveys incongruous images, because it confounds the cause and the effect, the real *thing* with the personified *representative* of the thing; in short, because it differs from the language of GOOD SENSE! That the "Phœbus" is hackneyed, and a school-boy image, is an *accidental* fault, dependent on the age in which the author wrote, and not deduced from the nature of the thing. That it is part of an exploded mythology, is an objection more deeply grounded. Yet when the torch of ancient learning was re-kindled, so cheering were its beams, that our eldest poets, cut off by Christianity from all *accredited* machinery, and deprived of all *acknowledged* guardians and symbols of the great objects of nature, were naturally induced to adopt, as a *poetic* language, those fabulous personages, those forms of the [16] supernatural in nature, which had given them such dear delight in the poems of their great masters. Nay, even at this day what scholar of genial taste will not so far sympathize with them, as to read with pleasure in PETRARCH, CHAUCER, or SPENSER, what he would perhaps condemn as puerile in a modern poet?

I remember no poet, whose writings would safelier stand the test of Mr. Wordsworth's theory, than SPENSER. Yet will Mr. Wordsworth say, that the style of the following stanza is either undistinguished from prose, and the language of ordinary life?

[16] But still more by the mechanical system of philosophy which has needlessly infected our theological opinions, and teaching us to consider the world in its relation to God, as of building to its mason, leaves the idea of omnipresence a mere abstract notion in the stateroom of our reason. [Coleridge's note]

Or that it is vicious, and that the stanzas are *blots* in the "Faery Queen"?

> By this the northern waggoner had set
> His sevenfold teme behind the steadfast starre,
> That was in ocean waves yet never wet,
> But firme is fixt, and sendeth light from farre
> To all that in the wild deep wandering are:
> And chearful chanticleer with his note shrill
> Had warned once that Phœbus' fiery carre
> In haste was climbing up the easterne hill,
> Full envious that night so long his roome did fill.
>
> *Book I. Can. 2. St. 2.*

> At last the golden orientall gate
> Of greatest heaven gan to open fayre,
> And Phœbus fresh, as brydegrome to his mate,
> Came dauncing forth, shaking his deawie hayre,
> And hurl'd his glist'ring beams through gloomy ayre:
> Which when the wakeful elfe perceived, streightway
> He started up, and did him selfe prepayre
> In sun-bright armes and battailous array;
> For with that pagan proud he combat will that day.
>
> *B. I. Can. 5. St. 2.*

On the contrary to how many passages, both in hymn books and in blank verse poems, could I, (were it not invidious), direct the reader's attention, the style of which is most *unpoetic, because,* and only because, it is the style of *prose?* He will not suppose me capable of having in my mind such verses, as

> I put my hat upon my head
> And walk'd into the Strand;
> And there I met another man,
> Whose hat was in his hand.

To such specimens it would indeed be a fair and full reply, that these lines are not bad, because they are *unpoetic;* but because they are empty of all sense and feeling; and that it were an idle attempt to prove that an ape is not a Newton, when it is evident that he is not a man. But the sense shall be good and weighty, the language correct and dignified, the subject interesting and treated with feeling; and yet the style shall, notwithstanding all these merits, be justly blamable as *prosaic*, and solely because the words and the order of the words would find their appropriate place in prose, but are not suitable to *metrical* composition. The "Civil Wars" of Daniel is an instructive, and even interesting work; but take the following stanzas (and from the hundred instances which abound I might probably have selected others far more striking):

> And to the end we may with better ease
> Discern the true discourse, vouchsafe to shew
> What were the times foregoing near to these,
> That these we may with better profit know.
> Tell how the world fell into this disease;
> And how so great distemperature did grow;
> So shall we see with what degrees it came;
> How things at full do soon wax out of frame.
>
> Ten kings had from the Norman conqu'ror reign'd
> With intermixt and variable fate,
> When England to her greatest height attain'd
> Of power, dominion, glory, wealth, and state;
> After it had with much ado sustain'd
> The violence of princes, with debate
> For titles and the often mutinies
> Of nobles for their ancient liberties.
>
> For first, the Norman, conqu'ring all by might,
> By might was forc'd to keep what he had got;
> Mixing our customs and the form of right
> With foreign constitutions he had brought;
> Mast'ring the mighty, humbling the poorer wight,
> By all severest means that could be wrought;
> And, making the succession doubtful, rent
> His new-got state, and left it turbulent.
>
> *B. I. St. VII. VIII. & IX.*

Will it be contended on the one side, that these lines are mean and senseless? Or on the other, that they are not prosaic, and for *that* reason unpoetic? This poet's well-merited epithet is that of the *"well-languaged Daniel;"* but likewise, and by the consent of his contemporaries no less than of all succeeding critics, the "prosaic Daniel." Yet those, who thus designate this wise and amiable writer, from the frequent incorrespondency of his diction to his metre in the majority of his compositions, not only deem them valuable and interesting on other accounts; but willingly admit, that there are to be found throughout his poems, and especially in his *Epistles* and in his *Hymen's Triumph,* many and exquisite specimens of that style which, as the *neutral ground* of prose and verse, is common to both. A fine and almost faultless extract, eminent, as for other beauties, so for its perfection in this species of diction, may be seen in LAMB's Dramatic Specimens, &c., a work of various interest from the nature of the selections themselves, (all from the plays of Shakespeare's contemporaries), and deriving a high additional value from the notes, which are full of just and original criticism, expressed with all the freshness of originality.

Among the possible effects of practical adherence to a theory, that aims to *identify* the style of prose and verse, (if it does not indeed claim for the latter a yet nearer resemblance to the average style of men in the vivâ voce intercourse of real life) we might anticipate the following as not the least likely to occur. It will happen, as I have indeed before observed, that the metre itself, the sole acknowledged difference, will occasionally become metre to the eye only. The existence of *prosaisms,* and that they detract from the merit of a poem, *must* at length be conceded, when a number of successive lines can be rendered, even to the most delicate ear, unrecognizable as verse, or as having even been intended for verse, by simply transcribing them as prose; when, if the poem be in blank verse, this can be effected without any alteration, or at most by merely restoring one or two words to their proper places, from which they have been [17] transplanted

----

[17] As the ingenious gentleman under the influence of the Tragic Muse contrived to dislocate, "I wish you a good morning, Sir! Thank you, Sir, and I wish you the same," into two blank-verse heroics:—

> To you a morning good, good Sir! I wish.
> You, Sir! I thank: to you the same wish I.

In those parts of Mr. Wordsworth's works which I have thoroughly studied, I find fewer instances in which this would be practicable than I have met in many poems, where an approximation of prose has been sedulously and on system guarded against. Indeed excepting the stanzas already quoted

for no assignable cause or reason but that of the author's convenience; but, if it be in rhyme, by the mere exchange of the final word of each line for some other of the same meaning, equally appropriate, dignified, and euphonic.

The answer or objection in the preface to the anticipated remark "that metre paves the way to other distinctions," is contained in the following words. "The distinction of rhyme and metre is voluntary and uniform, and not, like that produced by (what is called) poetic diction, arbitrary, and subject to infinite caprices, upon which no calculation whatever can be made. In the one case the reader is utterly at the mercy of the poet respecting what imagery or diction he may choose to connect with the passion." But is this a *poet*, of whom a poet is speaking? No surely! rather of a fool or madman: or at best of a vain or ignorant phantast! And might not brains so wild and so deficient make just the same havock with rhymes and metres, as they are supposed to effect with modes and figures of speech? How is the reader at the *mercy* of such men? If he continue to read their nonsense, is it not his own fault? The ultimate end of criticism is much more to establish the principles of writing, than to furnish *rules* how to pass judgement on what has been written by others; if indeed it were possible that the two could be separated. But if it be asked, by what principles the poet is to regulate his own style, if he do not adhere closely to the sort and

from "THE SAILOR'S MOTHER," I can recollect but one instance: viz. a short passage of four or five lines in "THE BROTHERS," that model of English pastoral, which I have never yet read with unclouded eye.—"James, pointing to its summit, over which they had all purposed to return together, informed them that he would wait for them there. They parted, and his comrades passed that way some two hours after, but they did not find him at the appointed place, *a circumstance of which they took no heed:* but one of them, going by chance into the house, which at this time was James's house, learnt *there,* that nobody had seen him all that day." The only change which has been made is in the position of the little word *there* in two instances, the position in the original being clearly such as is not adopted in ordinary conversation. The other words printed in *italics* were so marked because, though good and genuine English, they are not the phraseology of common conversation either in the word put in apposition, or in the connection by the genitive pronoun. Men in general would have said, "but that was a circumstance they paid no attention to, or took no notice of," and the language is, on the theory of the preface, justified only by the narrator's being the *Vicar.* Yet if any ear *could* suspect, that these sentences were ever printed as metre, on these very words alone could the suspicion have been grounded.

[Coleridge's note.]

order of words which he hears in the market, wake, high-road, or plough-field? I reply; by principles, the ignorance or neglect of which would convict him of being no *poet,* but a silly or presumptuous usurper of the name! By the principles of grammar, logic, psychology! In one word by such a knowledge of the facts, material and spiritual, that most appertain to his art, as, if it have been governed and applied by *good sense,* and rendered instinctive by habit, becomes the representative and reward of our past conscious reasonings, insights, and conclusions, and acquires the name of TASTE. By what *rule* that does not leave the reader at the poet's mercy, and the poet at his own, is the latter to distinguish between the language suitable to *suppressed,* and the language, which is characteristic of *indulged,* anger? Or between that of rage and that of jealousy? Is it obtained by wandering about in search of angry or jealous people in uncultivated society, in order to copy their words? Or not far rather by the power of imagination proceeding upon the *all in each* of human nature? By *meditation,* rather than by *observation?* And by the latter in consequence only of the former? As eyes, for which the former has pre-determined their field of vision, and to which, as to *its* organ, it communicates a microscopic power? There is not, I firmly believe, a man now living, who has, from his own inward experience, a clearer intuition, than Mr. Wordsworth himself, that the last mentioned are the true sources of *genial* discrimination. Through the same process and by the same creative agency will the poet distinguish the degree and kind of the excitement produced by the very act of poetic composition. As intuitively will he know, what differences of style it at once inspires and justifies; what intermixture of conscious volition is natural to that state; and in what instances such figures and colors of speech degenerate into mere creatures of an arbitrary purpose, cold technical artifices of ornament or connection. For, even as truth is its own light and evidence, discovering at once itself and falsehood, so is it the prerogative of poetic genius to distinguish by parental instinct its proper offspring from the changelings, which the gnomes of vanity or the fairies of fashion may have laid in its cradle or called by its names. Could a rule be given from *without,* poetry would cease to be poetry, and sink into a mechanical art. It would be μόρφωσις, not ποίησις [a shaping, not a creating]. The *rules* of the IMAGINATION are themselves the very powers of growth and production. The *words*, to which they are reducible, present only the outlines and external appearance of the fruit. A deceptive counterfeit of the superficial form and colors may be elaborated; but the marble peach feels cold and heavy, and *children* only put it to their mouths. We find no difficulty in admitting as excellent, and the legitimate language of poetic fervor self-impassioned, DONNE's apostrophe to the Sun in the second stanza of his "Progress of the Soul:"

> Thee, eye of heaven! this great soul envies not:
> By thy male force is all, we have, begot.
> In the first East thou now beginn'st to shine,
> Suck'st early balm and island spices there,
> And wilt anon in thy loose-rein'd career
> At Tagus, Po, Seine, Thames, and Danow dine,
> And see at night this western world of mine:
> Yet hast thou not more nations seen than she,
> Who before thee one day began to be,
> And, thy frail light being quench'd, shall long, long outlive thee!

Or the next stanza but one:

> Great destiny, the commissary of God,
> That hast mark'd out a path and period
> For ev'ry thing! Who, where we offspring took,
> Our ways and ends see'st at one instant: thou
> Knot of all causes! Thou, whose changeless brow
> Ne'er smiles or frowns! O! vouchsafe thou to look,
> And shew my story in thy eternal book, &c.

As little difficulty do we find in excluding from the honors of unaffected warmth and elevation the madness prepense of pseudo-poesy, or the startling *hysteric* of weakness over-exerting itself, which bursts on the unprepared reader in sundry odes and apostrophes to abstract terms. Such are the Odes to Jealousy, to Hope, to Oblivion, and the like, in Dodsley's collection [18] and

[18] Robert Dodsley (1703–64), publisher of *Poems by Several Hands* (1748–58), a popular anthology of the time.

the magazines of that day, which seldom fail to remind me of
an Oxford copy of verses on the two Suttons, commencing with

INOCULATION, heavenly maid! descend!

It is not to be denied that men of undoubted talents, and even
poets of true, though not of first-rate, genius, have from a mistaken theory deluded both themselves and others in the opposite
extreme. I once read to a company of sensible and well-educated
women the introductory period of Cowley's preface to his *"Pin-
daric Odes, written in imitation of the style and manner of the
odes of Pindar."* "If, (says Cowley), a man should undertake to
translate Pindar, word for word, it would be thought that one
madman had translated another; as may appear, when he, that
understands not the original, reads the verbal traduction of him
into Latin prose, than which nothing seems more raving." I then
proceeded with his own free version of the second Olympic,
composed for the charitable purpose of *rationalizing* the Theban
Eagle.

> Queen of all harmonious things,
> Dancing words and speaking strings,
> What God, what hero, wilt thou sing?
> What happy man to equal glories bring?
> Begin, begin thy noble choice,
> And let the hills around reflect the image of thy voice.
> Pisa does to Jove belong,
> Jove and Pisa claim thy song.
> The fair first-fruits of war, th' Olympic games,
> Alcides offer'd up to Jove;
> Alcides too thy strings may move!
> But, oh! what man to join with these can worthy prove?
> Join Theron boldly to their sacred names;
> Theron the next honor claims;
> Theron to no man gives place,
> Is first in Pisa's and in Virtue's race;
> Theron there, and he alone,
> Ev'n his own swift forefathers has outgone.

One of the company exclaimed, with the full assent of the rest,
that if the original were madder than this, it must be incurably

mad. I then translated the ode from the Greek, and as nearly as possible, word for word; and the impression was, that in the general movement of the periods, in the form of the connections and transitions, and in the sober majesty of lofty sense, it appeared to them to approach more nearly, than any other poetry they had heard, to the style of our Bible in the prophetic books. The first strophe will suffice as a specimen:

> Ye harp-controuling hymns! (or) ye hymns the sovereigns of harps!
> What God? what Hero?
> What Man shall we celebrate?
> Truly Pisa indeed is of Jove,
> But the Olympiad (or the Olympic games) did Hercules establish,
> The first-fruits of the spoils of war.
> But Theron for the four-horsed car,
> That bore victory to him,
> It behoves us now to voice aloud:
> The Just, the Hospitable,
> The Bulwark of Agrigentum,
> Of renowned fathers
> The Flower, even him
> Who preserves his native city erect and safe.

But are such rhetorical caprices condemnable only for their deviation from the language of real life? and are they by no other means to be precluded, but by the rejection of all distinctions between prose and verse, save that of metre? Surely good sense, and a moderate insight into the constitution of the human mind, would be amply sufficient to prove, that such language and such combinations are the native produce neither of the fancy nor of the imagination; that their operation consists in the excitement of surprise by the juxta-position and *apparent* reconciliation of widely different or incompatible things. As when, for instance, the hills are made to reflect the image of a *voice*. Surely, no unusual taste is requisite to see clearly, that this compulsory juxta-position is not produced by the presentation of impressive or delightful forms to the inward vision, nor by any sympathy with the modifying powers with which the genius of the poet had united and inspired all the objects of his thought; that it is therefore a species of *wit*, a pure work of the *will*, and implies a leisure and self-possession both of thought and of feeling, incompatible with the steady fervor of a mind possessed and filled with the grandeur of its subject. To sum up the whole in one sentence. When a poem, or a part of a poem, shall be adduced, which is evidently vicious in the figures and contexture of its style, yet for the condemnation of which no reason can be assigned, except that it differs from the style in which men actually converse, then, and not till then, can I hold this theory to be either plausible, or practicable, or capable of furnishing either rule, guidance, or precaution, that might not, more easily and more safely, as well as more naturally, have been deduced in the author's own mind from considerations of grammar, logic, and the truth and nature of things, confirmed by the authority of works, whose fame is not of ONE country nor of ONE age.

George Noel Gordon, Lord Byron

[1788-1824]

BYRON'S LIFE IS THE best example we have of a Romantic literary cliché—the Romantic Rebel, or Byronic Hero. He was educated at Harrow and Cambridge, and published his first volume of poems while still an undergraduate. After leaving Cambridge he traveled for two years through Portugal, Spain, Greece, and the Near East; this tour provided the materials for the first two cantos of *Childe Harold's Pilgrimage* (1812), the poem which defined the Byronic stance and made him famous. Byron was for a time active in English society and in the House of Lords, but the failure of his marriage and his subsequent notoriety forced him to leave England, and he spent the last years of his life on the Continent. He joined the movement for Greek independence in 1823, and died of fever at Missolonghi the following year.

Byron's literary criticism, like his poetry, reveals a divided mind. He thought of himself as in the tradition of Pope, and in his attacks on the Lake Poets he assumed a neo-classical position, both in critical principles and in satiric method. But he was also a Romantic, and this side of his character has its critical theory too. For this Romantic Byron, the creative act is an uninvited frenzy ("it comes over me in a kind of rage every now and then," he wrote to Thomas Moore, "and then, if I don't write to empty my mind, I go mad"), which brings emotional release; or it is a way of living "a being more intense," a conscious heightening of experience. In either case, the action of the work of art is upon the emotional life of the artist, an idea entirely alien to neo-classicism.

Byron's literary criticism is occasional and unsystematic. *English Bards and Scotch Reviewers* was published as a retaliation of the severe criticism of Byron's first book of poems in the *Edinburgh Review*. The Bowles-Byron quarrel was one skirmish in a longer battle over the reputation of Pope which lasted through most of the nine-

teenth century. Bowles began it with his edition of Pope's *Works*
(1806), in which he criticized Pope's poetical and moral character.
Some years later Thomas Campbell defended Pope in an essay prefixed to his *Specimens of the British Poets.* Bowles replied the same
year in a pamphlet, and the controversy soon spread to the quarterly
reviews. There Byron's name was mentioned, and he took the opportunity to enter the fray with two letters (of which, however, only the
first was printed at the time). The quarrel continued in pamphlets
and quarterlies, but Byron took no further part.

The principal question between Byron and Bowles was, as Bowles
put it in his reply to Byron, "whether POETRY be more immediately
indebted to what is SUBLIME or BEAUTIFUL in the Works of
NATURE, or the Works of ART." Bowles argued that works of nature
are more poetical than works of art, and that the passions of the
human heart are more poetical than artificial manners. Judged by these
principles, Pope—and neo-classical art in general—fared badly. Byron,
in his neo-classical stance, replied with arguments for Art, for Ethical
Poetry, and for Pope.

BIBLIOGRAPHY. *Works: Poetry,* ed. E. H. Coleridge, 7 vols.; *Letters
and Journals,* ed. R. E. Prothero, 6 vols. (London, 1898–1904); *Lord
Byron's Correspondence,* ed. John Murray, 2 vols. (London, 1922).
    Ernest J. Lovell, Jr., *Byron: The Record of a Quest* (Austin, Texas,
1949); William J. Calvert, *Byron: Romantic Paradox* (Chapel Hill,
N. C., 1935).

TEXT. *Works: Poetry,* ed. Coleridge, vol. I; *Letters and Journals,* ed.
Prothero, vols. X, XII.

from

ENGLISH BARDS AND SCOTCH REVIEWERS

[1809]

Time was, ere yet in these degenerate days
Ignoble themes obtained mistaken praise,
When Sense and Wit with Poesy allied,
No fabled Graces, flourished side by side;

From the same fount their inspiration drew,
And, reared by Taste, bloomed fairer as they grew.
Then, in this happy Isle, a Pope's pure strain
Sought the rapt soul to charm, nor sought in vain;
A polished nation's praise aspired to claim,
And raised the people's, as the poet's fame.
Like him great Dryden poured the tide of song,
In stream less smooth, indeed, yet doubly strong.
Then Congreve's scenes could cheer, or Otway's melt; [1]
For Nature then an English audience felt—
But why these names, or greater still, retrace,
When all to feebler Bards resign their place?
Yet to such times our lingering looks are cast,
When taste and reason with those times are past.
Now look around, and turn each trifling page,
Survey the precious works that please the age;
This truth at least let Satire's self allow,
No dearth of Bards can be complained of now.
The loaded Press beneath her labour groans,
And Printers' devils shake their weary bones;
While Southey's Epics cram the creaking shelves,[2]
And Little's Lyrics shine in hot-pressed twelves.[3]
Thus saith the *Preacher:* "Nought beneath the sun
Is new," [4] yet still from change to change we run.
What varied wonders tempt us as they pass!
The Cow-pox, Tractors, Galvanism, and Gas,
In turns appear, to make the vulgar stare,
Till the swoln bubble bursts—and all is air!
Nor less new schools of Poetry arise,
Where dull pretenders grapple for the prize:
O'er Taste awhile these pseudo-bards prevail;
Each country Book-club bows the knee to Baal,

[1] William Congreve (1670–1729), best of the Restoration comic dramatists; Thomas Otway (1652–1685), known for his tragedies.
[2] Robert Southey (1774–1843), Lake poet and friend of Coleridge; poet laureate 1813–1843. Byron satirized Southey's poetry and politics in "The Vision of Judgment" and "Don Juan."
[3] Little: a pseudonym used by Thomas Moore (1779–1852) for his early poems.
[4] *Ecclesiastes* 1:9.

And, hurling lawful Genius from the throne,
Erects a shrine and idol of its own;
Some leaden calf—but whom it matters not,
From soaring SOUTHEY, down to groveling STOTT.[5]

Behold! in various throngs the scribbling crew,
For notice eager, pass in long review:
Each spurs his jaded Pegasus apace,
And Rhyme and Blank maintain an equal race;
Sonnets on sonnets crowd, and ode on ode;
And Tales of Terror jostle on the road;
Immeasurable measures move along;
For simpering Folly loves a varied song,
To strange, mysterious Dulness still the friend,
Admires the strain she cannot comprehend.
Thus Lays of Minstrels—may they be the last!—
On half-strung harps whine mournful to the blast,
While mountain spirits prate to river sprites,
That dames may listen to the sound at nights;
And goblin brats, of Gilpin Horner's brood [6]
Decoy young Border-nobles through the wood,
And skip at every step, Lord knows how high,
And frighten foolish babes, the Lord knows why;
While high-born ladies in their magic cell,
Forbidding Knights to read who cannot spell,
Despatch a courier to a wizard's grave,
And fight with honest men to shield a knave.

Next view in state, proud prancing on his roan,
The golden-crested haughty Marmion,[7]
Now forging scrolls, now foremost in the fight,
Not quite a Felon, yet but half a Knight,
The gibbet or the field prepared to grace—

5 Stott, a newspaper poet whom Byron called "the most impudent and execrable of literary poachers for the Daily Prints."
6 Sir Walter Scott's *Lay of the Last Minstrel* originated in a suggestion of the Countess of Dalkeith that he write a ballad on the border legend of Gilpin Horner.
7 Scott's romantic epic, *Marmion*, was published in 1808.

A mighty mixture of the great and base.
And think'st thou, SCOTT! by vain conceit perchance,
On public taste to foist thy stale romance,
Though MURRAY with his MILLER may combine [8]
To yield thy muse just half-a-crown per line?
No! when the sons of song descend to trade,
Their bays are sear, their former laurels fade,
Let such forego the poet's sacred name,
Who rack their brains for lucre, not for fame:
Still for stern Mammon may they toil in vain!
And sadly gaze on gold they cannot gain!
Such be their meed, such still the just reward
Of prostituted Muse and hireling bard!
For this we spurn Apollo's venal son,
And bid a long "good night to Marmion."

    These are the themes that claim our plaudits now;
These are the Bards to whom the Muse must bow;
While MILTON, DRYDEN, POPE, alike forgot,
Resign their hallowed Bays to WALTER SCOTT.

    The time has been, when yet the Muse was young,
When HOMER swept the lyre, and MARO sung,
An Epic scarce ten centuries could claim,
While awe-struck nations hailed the magic name:
The work of each immortal Bard appears
The single wonder of a thousand years.
Empires have mouldered from the face of earth,
Tongues have expired with those who gave them birth,
Without the glory such a strain can give,
As even in ruin bids the language live.
Not so with us, though minor Bards content,
On one great work a life of labour spent:
With eagle pinion soaring to the skies,
Behold the Ballad-monger SOUTHEY rise!
To him let CAMOËNS, MILTON, TASSO yield,

[8] Murray and Miller were London publishers who owned part of the copy-right of *Marmion*.

Whose annual strains, like armies, take the field.[9]
First in the ranks see Joan of Arc advance,
The scourge of England and the boast of France!
Though burnt by wicked BEDFORD for a witch,
Behold her statue placed in Glory's niche;
Her fetters burst, and just released from prison,
A virgin Phœnix from her ashes risen.
Next see tremendous Thalaba come on,
Arabia's monstrous, wild, and wond'rous son;
Domdaniel's dread destroyer, who o'erthrew
More mad magicians than the world e'er knew.
Immortal Hero! all thy foes o'ercome,
For ever reign—the rival of Tom Thumb!
Since startled Metre fled before thy face,
Well wert thou doomed the last of all thy race!
Well might triumphant Genii bear thee hence,
Illustrious conqueror of common sense!
Now, last and greatest, Madoc spreads his sails,
Cacique in Mexico, and Prince in Wales;
Tells us strange tales, as other travellers do,
More old than Mandeville's, and not so true.
Oh, SOUTHEY! SOUTHEY! cease thy varied song!
A bard may chaunt too often and too long:
As thou art strong in verse, in mercy spare!
A fourth, alas! were more than we could bear.
But if, in spite of all the world can say,
Thou still wilt verseward plod thy weary way;
If still in Berkeley-Ballads most uncivil,
Thou wilt devote old women to the devil,
The babe unborn thy dread intent may rue:
"God help thee," SOUTHEY, and thy readers too.

Next comes the dull disciple of thy school,
That mild apostate from poetic rule,
The simple WORDSWORTH, framer of a lay
As soft as evening in his favourite May,
Who warns his friend "to shake off toil and trouble,

---

[9] In the lines that follow, Byron ridicules Southey's long poems, *Joan of Arc* (1796), *Thalaba the Destroyer* (1801), and *Madoc* (1805).

And quit his books, for fear of growing double";
Who, both by precept and example, shows
That prose is verse, and verse is merely prose; [10]
Convincing all, by demonstration plain,
Poetic souls delight in prose insane;
And Christmas stories tortured into rhyme
Contain the essence of the true sublime.
Thus, when he tells the tale of Betty Foy,
The idiot mother of "an idiot Boy";
A moon-struck, silly lad, who lost his way,
And, like his bard, confounded night with day;
So close on each pathetic part he dwells,
And each adventure so sublimely tells,
That all who view the "idiot in his glory"
Conceive the Bard the hero of the story.

Shall gentle COLERIDGE pass unnoticed here,
To turgid ode and tumid stanza dear?
Though themes of innocence amuse him best,
Yet still Obscurity's a welcome guest.
If Inspiration should her aid refuse
To him who takes a Pixy for a muse,
Yet none in lofty numbers can surpass
The bard who soars to elegize an ass:
So well the subject suits his noble mind,
He brays, the Laureate of the long-eared kind. . . .

from

LETTER TO MISS MILBANKE

[Nov. 10, 1813]

. . . I BY NO MEANS rank poetry or poets high in the scale of intellect. This may look like affectation, but it is my real opinion. It is
the lava of the imagination whose eruption prevents an earth-

[10] See Preface to *Lyrical Ballads*, above, p. 13.

quake. They say poets never or rarely go *mad*. Cowper and Collins are instances to the contrary (but Cowper was no poet). It is, however, to be remarked that they rarely do, but are generally so near it that I cannot help thinking rhyme is so far useful in anticipating and preventing the disorder. I prefer the talents of action —of war, or the senate, or even of science,—to all the speculations of those mere dreamers of another existence (I don't mean religiously but fancifully) and spectators of this apathy. Disgust and perhaps incapacity have rendered me now a mere spectator; but I have occasionally mixed in the active and tumultuous departments of existence, and in these alone my recollection rests with any satisfaction, though not the best parts of it.

from

LETTER TO JOHN MURRAY, ESQ.*

[1821]

. . . MR. B[OWLES] ASSERTS THAT Campbell's "Ship of the Line" derives all its poetry, not from "*art*," but from "*Nature*." "Take away the waves, the winds, the sun, etc., etc., etc., *one* will become a stripe of blue bunting; and the other a piece of coarse canvas on three tall poles." Very true; take away the "waves," "the winds," and there will be no ship at all, not only for poetical, but for any other purpose; and take away "the sun," and we must read Mr. B.'s pamphlet by candlelight. But the "poetry" of the "Ship" does *not* depend on the "waves," etc.; on the contrary, the "Ship of the line" confers its own poetry upon the waters, and heightens *theirs*. I do not deny, that the "waves and winds," and above all "the sun," are highly poetical; we know it to our cost, by the many descriptions of them in verse: but if the waves bore only the foam upon their bosoms, if the winds wafted only the sea-weed to the shore, if the sun shone neither upon pyramids, nor fleets, nor fortresses, would its beams be equally poetical? I

* This letter is on the Rev. W. L. Bowles' *Strictures on the Life and Writings of Pope.*

think not: the poetry is at least reciprocal. Take away "the Ship of the Line" "swinging round" the "calm water," and the calm water becomes a somewhat monotonous thing to look at, particularly if not transparently *clear*; witness the thousands who pass by without looking on it at all. What was it attracted the thousands to the launch? They might have seen the poetical "calm water" at Wapping, or in the "London Dock," or in the Paddington Canal, or in a horse-pond, or in a slop-basin, or in any other vase. They might have heard the poetical winds howling through the chinks of a pig-stye, or the garret window; they might have seen the sun shining on a footman's livery, or on a brass warming pan; but could the "calm water," or the "wind," or the "sun," make all, or any of these "poetical?" I think not. Mr. B. admits "the Ship" to be poetical, but only from those accessories: now if they *confer* poetry so as to make one thing poetical, they would make other things poetical; the more so, as Mr. B. calls a "ship of the line" without them,—that is to say, its "masts and sails and streamers,"—"blue bunting," and "coarse canvas," and "tall poles." So they are; and porcelain is clay, and man is dust, and flesh is grass, and yet the two latter at least are the subjects of much poesy. . . .

Mr. B. contends again that the Pyramids of Ægypt are poetical, because of "the association with boundless deserts," and that a "pyramid of the same dimensions" would not be sublime in "Lincoln's Inn Fields:" not *so* poetical certainly; but take away the "pyramids," and what is the *desert?* Take away Stone-henge from Salisbury Plain, and it is nothing more than Hounslow Heath, or any other uninclosed down. It appears to me that St. Peter's, the Coliseum, the Pantheon, the Palatine, the Apollo, the Laocoon, the Venus di medicis, the Hercules, the dying Gladiator, the Moses of Michel Agnolo, and all the higher work of Canova, (I have already spoken of those of antient Greece, still extant in that country, or transported to England,) are as *poetical* as Mont Blanc or Mount Ætna, perhaps still more so, as they are direct manifestations of mind, and *presuppose* poetry in their very conception; and have, moreover, as being such, a something of actual life, which cannot belong to any part of inanimate nature, unless we adopt the System of Spinosa, that the World is the deity. There can be nothing more poetical in its aspect than the

city of Venice; does this depend upon the sea, or the canals?—
     "The dirt and sea-weed when proud Venice rose?" [11]

Is it the canal which runs between the palace and the prison, or
the "Bridge of Sighs," which connects them, that render it poetical? Is it the "Canal Grande," or Rialto which arches it, the
churches which tower over it, the palaces which line, and the gondolas which glide over the waters, that render this city more poetical than Rome itself? Mr. B. will say, perhaps, that the Rialto is
but marble, the palaces and churches only stone, and the gondolas
a "coarse" black cloth, thrown over some planks of carved wood,
with a shining bit of fantastically formed iron at the prow,
"*without*" the water. And I tell him that without these, the water
would be nothing but a clay-coloured ditch; and whoever says
the contrary, deserves to be at the bottom of that, where Pope's
heroes are embraced by the mud nymphs. There would be nothing to make the Canal of Venice more poetical than that of Paddington, were it not for the artificial adjuncts above mentioned,
although it is a perfectly natural canal, formed by the sea, and
the innumerable islands which constitute the site of this extraordinary city.

The very Cloacæ of Tarquin at Rome are as poetical as Rich-
mond Hill; many will think more so: take away Rome, and leave
the Tybur and the seven Hills, in the Nature of Evander's time.
Let Mr. Bowles or Mr. Wordsworth, or Mr. Southey, or any of the
other "Naturals," make a poem upon them, and then see which
is most poetical,—their production, or the commonest guide-
book, which tells you the road from St. Peter's to the Coliseum,
and informs you what you will see by the way. The Ground
interests in Virgil, because it *will* be *Rome,* and not because it is
Evander's rural domain.

Mr. B. then proceeds to press Homer into his service, in
answer to a remark of Mr. Campbell's that "Homer was a great
describer of works of art." Mr. B. contends that all his great
power, even in this, depends upon their connection with nature.
The "shield of Achilles derives its poetical interest from the
subjects described on it." And from what does the *spear* of
Achilles derive its interest? and the helmet and the mail worn

[11] Pope, *Essay on Man,* Epistle IV, 292.

by Patroclus, and the celestial armour, and the very brazen greaves of the well-booted Greeks? Is it solely from the legs, and the back, and the breast, and the human body, which they enclose? In that case, it would have been more poetical to have made them fight naked; and Gulley and Gregson, as being nearer to a state of nature, are more poetical boxing in a pair of drawers than Hector and Achilles in radiant armour, and with heroic weapons.

Instead of the clash of helmets, and the rushing of chariots, and the whizzing of spears, and the glancing of swords, and the cleaving of shields, and the piercing of breast-plates, why not represent the Greeks and Trojans like two savage tribes, tugging and tearing, and kicking and biting, and gnashing, foaming, grinning, and gouging, in all the poetry of martial nature, unincumbered with gross, prosaic, artificial arms; an equal superfluity to the natural warrior and his natural poet? Is there any thing unpoetical in Ulysses striking the horses of Rhesus with *his bow* (having forgotten his thong), or would Mr. B. have had him kick them with his foot, or smack them with his hand, as being more unsophisticated?

In Gray's Elegy, is there an image more striking than his "shapeless sculpture?" Of sculpture in general, it may be observed, that it is more poetical than nature itself, inasmuch as it represents and bodies forth that ideal beauty and sublimity which is never to be found in actual Nature. This at least is the general opinion. But, always excepting the Venus di Medicis, I differ from this opinion, at least as far as regards female beauty; for the head of Lady Charlemont (when I first saw her nine years ago) seemed to possess all that sculpture could require for its ideal. I recollect seeing something of the same kind in the head of an Albanian girl, who was actually employed in mending a road in the mountains, and in some Greek, and one or two Italian, faces. But of *sublimity*, I have never seen anything in human nature at all to approach the expression of sculpture, either in the Apollo, the Moses, or other of the sterner works of ancient or modern art. . . .

Had Gray written nothing but his Elegy, high as he stands, I am not sure that he would not stand higher; it is the cornerstone of his glory: without it, his odes would be insufficient for

his fame. The depreciation of Pope is partly founded upon a false
idea of the dignity of his order of poetry, to which he has partly
contributed by the ingenious boast,

> "That not in fancy's maze he wandered long,
> But *stooped* to Truth, and moralised his song." 12

He should have written "rose to truth." In my mind, the highest
of all poetry is ethical poetry, as the highest of all earthly objects
must be moral truth. Religion does not make a part of my
subject; it is something beyond human powers, and has failed
in all human hands except Milton's and Dante's, and even Dante's
powers are involved in his delineation of human passions, though
in supernatural circumstances. What made Socrates the greatest
of men? His moral truth—his ethics. What proved Jesus Christ
the Son of God hardly less than his miracles? His moral precepts.
And if ethics have made a philosopher the first of men, and have
not been disdained as an adjunct to his Gospel by the Deity
himself, are we to be told that ethical poetry, or didactic poetry,
or by whatever name you term it, whose object is to make men
better and wiser, is not the *very first order* of poetry; and are
we to be told this too by one of the priesthood? It requires more
mind, more wisdom, more power, than all the "forests" that ever
were "walked for their description," and all the epics that ever
were founded upon fields of battle. The Georgics are indisputably,
and I believe, *undisputedly,* even a finer poem than the Æneid.
Virgil knew this; he did not order *them* to be burnt.

> "The proper study of mankind is man." 13

It is the fashion of the day to lay great stress upon what they
call "imagination" and "invention," the two commonest of qualities: an Irish peasant with a little whisky in his head will
imagine and invent more than would furnish forth a modern
poem. If Lucretius had not been spoiled by the Epicurean sys-

---

12 Pope, "Epistle to Dr. Arbuthnot," ll. 340–41. Byron seems unaware of
the gloss on this figure by William Warburton, Pope's first editor (1751):
"The term is from falconry; and the allusion to one of those untamed birds
of spirit, which sometimes wantons at large in airy circles before it regards,
or *stoops to,* its prey."
13 *Essay on Man,* II, 2.

tem, we should have had a far superior poem to any now in
Existence. As mere poetry, it is the first of Latin poems. What
then has ruined it? His ethics. Pope has not this defect; his moral
is as pure as his poetry is glorious. . . .

The attempt of the poetical populace of the present day to
obtain an ostracism against Pope is as easily accounted for as the
Athenian's shell against Aristides; they are tired of hearing him
always called "the Just." They are also fighting for life; for, if
he maintains his station, they will reach their own—by falling.
They have raised a mosque by the side of a Grecian temple of the
purest architecture; and, more barbarous than the barbarians
from whose practice I have borrowed the figure, they are not
contented with their own grotesque edifice, unless they destroy
the prior, and purely beautiful fabric which preceded, and which
shames them and theirs for ever and ever. I shall be told that
amongst those I *have* been (or it may be still *am*) conspicuous—
true, and I am ashamed of it. I *have* been amongst the builders
of this Babel, attended by a confusion of tongues, but *never*
amongst the envious destroyers of the classic temple of our
predecessor. I have loved and honoured the fame and name of
that illustrious and unrivalled man, far more than my own paltry
renown, and the trashy jingle of the crowd of "Schools" and up-
starts, who pretend to rival, or even surpass him. Sooner than a
single leaf should be torn from his laurel, it were better that all
which these men, and that I, as one of their set, have ever written, should

> "Line trunks, clothe spice, or, fluttering in a row,
> Befringe the rails of Bedlam, or Soho!" [14]

There are those who will believe this, and those who will not.
You, sir, know how far I am sincere, and whether my opinion,
not only in the short work intended for publication, and in private
letters which can never be published, has or has not been the
same. I look upon this as the declining age of English poetry; no
regard for others, no selfish feeling, can prevent me from seeing
this, and expressing the truth. There can be no worse sign for
the taste of the times than the depreciation of Pope. It would

[14] Pope, "First Epistle of the Second Book of Horace," ll. 418–19.

be better to receive for proof Mr. Cobbett's rough but strong
attack upon Shakespeare and Milton, than to allow this smooth
and "candid" undermining of the reputation of the most *perfect*
of our poets, and the purest of our moralists. Of his power in the
passions, in description, in the mock heroic, I leave others to
descant. I take him on his strong ground as an *ethical* poet: in the
former, none excel; in the mock heroic and the ethical, none equal
him; and, in my mind, the latter is the highest of all poetry, because it does that in *verse,* which the greatest of men have
wished to accomplish in prose. If the essence of poetry must be a
lie, throw it to the dogs, or banish it from your republic, as
Plato would have done. He who can reconcile poetry with truth
and wisdom, is the only true "*poet*" in its real sense, "the *maker,*"
"the *creator,*"—why must this mean the "liar," the "feigner," the
"tale-teller?" A man may make and create better things than these.

I shall not presume to say that Pope is as high a poet as
Shakespeare and Milton, though his enemy, Warton, places him
immediately under them. I would no more say this than I would
assert in the mosque (once Saint Sophia's), that Socrates was
a greater man than Mahomet. But if I say that he is very near
them, it is no more than has been asserted of Burns, who is
supposed:

> "To rival all but Shakespeare's name below."

I say nothing against this opinion. But of what "*order,*" according
to the poetical aristocracy, are Burns's poems? There are his *opus
magnum,* "Tam O'Shanter," a *tale*; the Cotter's Saturday Night,
a descriptive sketch; some others in the same style: the rest are
songs. So much for the *rank* of his productions; the *rank* of *Burns*
is the very first of his art. Of Pope I have expressed my opinion
elsewhere, as also of the effects which the present attempts at
poetry have had upon our literature. If any great national or
natural convulsion could or should overwhelm your country in
such sort as to sweep Great Britain from the kingdoms of the
earth, and leave only that, after all, the most living of human
things, a *dead language,* to be studied and read, and imitated by
the wise of future and far generations, upon foreign shores; if
your literature should become the learning of mankind, divested
of party cabals, temporary fashions, and national pride and

prejudice;—an Englishman, anxious that the posterity of strangers should know that there had been such a thing as a British Epic and Tragedy, might wish for the preservation of Shakespeare and Milton; but the surviving World would snatch Pope from the wreck, and let the rest sink with the people. He is the moral poet of all civilisation; and as such, let us hope that he will one day be the national poet of mankind. He is the only poet that never shocks; the only poet whose *faultlessness* has been made his reproach. Cast your eye over his productions; consider their extent, and contemplate their variety:—pastoral, passion, mock heroic, translation, satire, ethics.—all excellent, and often perfect. If his great charm be his *melody*, how comes it that foreigners adore him even in their diluted translations? But I have made this letter too long. Give my compliments to Mr. Bowles.

Yours ever very truly,
BYRON

John Keats

[1795–1821]

కఠిశ

KEATS WAS BORN IN LONDON, the son of a livery-stable keeper. He studied medicine for a time, but soon abandoned it, as he told his guardian, "to rely upon my abilities as a poet." He became a member of Leigh Hunt's literary circle, and began to publish verse; his first volume appeared in 1817. Keats reached the pinnacle of his brief career in 1819, when he wrote his great odes; a year later he was seriously ill with tuberculosis. In a last effort to regain his health he traveled to Rome, where he died.

Keats is unique among English critics in that he holds his place there entirely on the basis of his familiar letters. It is well to keep in mind (and Keats' spelling and punctuation should be reminders enough) that these are personal letters, not intended for publication; in them Keats tosses off remarks on his own and other poets' work which are full of his own intelligence and wit, but he does not propose a system.

Keats' critical position may be inferred from a single remark, "O for a Life of Sensation rather than of Thoughts!" This idea that Poetry and Reason are antithetical is common among Romantic poets, but Keats went farther than most, both in his verse and in his scattered critical statements. He was hostile to didactic poetry ("We hate poetry that has a palpable design upon us," he wrote) and to poets whose sensibilities were dictated to by their opinions or personalities. His own idea of the poet was of a sensibility unviolated by either personality or opinion, a sensitive Nothing, "capable of being in uncertainties, mysteries, doubts, without any irritable reaching after fact and reason." This latter condition, which Keats called *Negative Capability*, was a quality which he thought went to form a "Man of Achievement" in Literature.

From this idea of the poet a theory of poetry follows. True poetry will come naturally, leaving no trace of thought or effort, and will celebrate "the holiness of the Heart's affections and the truth of Imagination." Keats' repeated assertion that what is beautiful is true has

108

troubled his commentators, but it seems clear enough in the light of his other theories. In a life of Sensation and Negative Capability, there is no standard of truth left except the sensitive man's imaginative, sympathetic response to experience. This is the message of the Grecian Urn.

BIBLIOGRAPHY. *Complete Works,* ed. H. Buxton Forman, 5 vols. (Edinburgh, 1900–01); *Letters,* ed. Hyder Edward Rollins, 2 vols. (Cambridge, Mass., 1958).

W. J. Bate, *Negative Capability* (Cambridge, Mass., 1939); J. R. Caldwell, *John Keats' Fancy* (Ithaca, 1945); Neville Ford, *The Prefigurative Imagination of John Keats* (Stanford, 1951); C. D. Thorpe, *The Mind of John Keats* (New York, 1926); Lionel Trilling, "The Poet as Hero: Keats in his Letters," in *The Opposing Self* (New York, 1955).

TEXT. *Letters,* ed. Hyder Edward Rollins.

LETTERS *

[1817–1818]

TO BENJAMIN BAILEY.

Saturday 22 Nov. 1817.

MY DEAR BAILEY,

I will get over the first part of this (*unsaid*) Letter as soon as possible for it relates to the affair of poor Crips—To a Man of your nature, such a Letter as Haydon's [1] must have been extremely cutting—What occasions the greater part of the World's Quarrels? simply this, two Minds meet and do not understand each other time enough to p[r]ævent any shock or surprise at the conduct of either party—As soon as I had known Haydon three days I had got enough of his character not to have been surp[r]ised at such a

* *The Letters of John Keats 1814–1821,* ed. Hyder Edward Rollins (Copyright 1958), reprinted by permission of The President and Fellows of Harvard College.

[1] Benjamin Robert Haydon (1786–1846), English painter. His posthumous *Autobiography* (1853) is an entertaining record of the period.

Letter as he has hurt you with. Nor when I knew it was it a
principle with me to drop his acquaintance although with you it
would have been an imperious feeling. I wish you knew all that
I think about Genius and the Heart—and yet I think you are
thoroughly acquainted with my innermost breast in that respect,
or you could not have known me even thus long and still hold me
worthy to be your dear friend. In passing however I must say of
one thing that has pressed upon me lately and encreased my
Humility and capability of submission and that is this truth—Men
of Genius are great as certain ethereal Chemicals operating on
the Mass of neutral intellect—by [*for* but] they have not any
individuality, any determined Character—I would call the top
and head of those who have a proper self Men of Power—

But I am running my head into a Subject which I am certain I
could not do justice to under five years s[t]udy and 3 vols octavo
—and moreover long to be talking about the Imagination—so my
dear Bailey do not think of this unpleasant affair if possible—do
not—I defy any ha[r]m to come of it—I defy—I'll shall write to
Crips this Week and reque[s]t him to tell me all his goings on from
time to time by Letter wherever I may be—it will all go on well—
so dont because you have suddenly discover'd a Coldness in Haydon suffer yourself to be teased. Do not my dear fellow. O I wish
I was as certain of the end of all your troubles as that of your momentary start about the authenticity of the Imagination. I am certain of nothing but of the holiness of the Heart's affections and
the truth of Imagination—What the imagination seizes as Beauty
must be truth—whether it existed before or not—for I have the
same Idea of all our Passions as of Love they are all in their sublime, creative of essential Beauty—In a Word, you may know
my favorite Speculation by my first Book and the little song I
sent in my last—which is a representation from the fancy of the
probable mode of operating in these Matters—The Imagination
may be compared to Adam's dream [2]—he awoke and found it
truth. I am the more zealous in this affair, because I have never
yet been able to perceive how any thing can be known for truth
by consequitive reasoning—and yet it must be—Can it be that
even the greatest Philosopher ever arrived at his goal without

---

[2] *Paradise Lost,* Book VIII, ll. 460–490.

putting aside numerous objections—However it may be, O for a
Life of Sensations rather than of Thoughts! It is 'a Vision in the
form of Youth' a Shadow of reality to come—and this consideration has further conv[i]nced me for it has come as auxiliary to
another favorite Speculation of mine, that we shall enjoy ourselves here after by having what we called happiness on Earth
repeated in a finer tone and so repeated—And yet such a fate can
only befall those who delight in sensation rather than hunger as
you do after Truth—Adam's dream will do here and seems to be a
conviction that Imagination and its empyreal reflection is the same
as human Life and its Spiritual repetition. But as I was saying—
the simple imaginative Mind may have its rewards in the repeti-
[ti]on of its own silent Working coming continually on the
Spirit with a fine Suddenness—to compare great things with small
—have you never by being Surprised with an old Melody—in a
delicious place—by a delicious voice, fe[l]t over again your very
Speculations and Surmises at the time it first operated on your
Soul—do you not remember forming to yourself the singer's face
more beautiful that [*for* than] it was possible and yet with the
elevation of the Moment you did not think so—even then you
were mounted on the Wings of Imagination so high—that the
Prototype must be here after—that delicious face you will see—
What a time! I am continually running away from the subject
—sure this cannot be exactly the case with a complex Mind—
one that is imaginative and at the same time careful of its fruits
—who would exist partly on sensation partly on thought—to
whom it is necessary that years should bring the philosophic
Mind—such an one I consider your's and therefore it is necessary to your eternal Happiness that you not only drink this
old Wine of Heaven which I shall call the redigestion of our
most ethereal Musings on Earth; but also increase in knowledge and know all things. I am glad to hear you are in a fair
Way for Easter—you will soon get through your unpleasant reading and then!—but the world is full of troubles
and I have not much reason to think myself pesterd with many
—I think Jane or Marianne [3] has a better opinion of me than I
deserve—for really and truly I do not think my Brothers illness

[3] The sisters of Keats' friend John Hamilton Reynolds.

connected with mine—you know more of the real Cause than
they do—nor have I any chance of being rack'd as you have been
—you perhaps at one time thought there was such a thing as
Worldly Happiness to be arrived at, at certain periods of time
marked out—you have of necessity from your disposition been
thus led away—I scarcely remember counting upon any Happiness—I look not for it if it be not in the present hour—nothing
startles me beyond the Moment. The setting sun will always set
me to rights—or if a Sparrow come before my Window I take
part in its existence and pick about the Gravel. The first thing
that strikes me on hearing a Misfortune having befalled another
is this. 'Well it cannot be helped.—he will have the pleasure of
trying the resources of his spirit,'—and I beg now my dear Bailey
that hereafter should you observe any thing cold in me not to but
[*for* put] it to the account of heartlessness but abstraction—for I
assure you I sometimes feel not the influence of a Passion or Affection during a whole week—and so long this sometimes continues
I begin to suspect myself and the genuiness of my feelings at
other times—thinking them a few barren Tragedy-tears—My
brother Tom is much improved—he is going to Devonshire—
whither I shall follow him—at present I am just arrived at Dorking to change the Scene—change the Air and give me a spur to
wind up my Poem, of which there are wanting 500 Lines. I should
have been here a day sooner but the Reynoldses persuaded me to
spop [stop] in Town to meet your friend Christie—There were
Rice and Martin—we talked about Ghosts—I will have some
talk with Taylor and let you know—when please God I come
down a[t] Christmas—I will find that Examiner if possible. My
best regards to Gleig. My Brothers to you and Mrs Bentley['s]

Your affectionate friend
John Keats—

I want to say much more to you—a few hints will set me going.
Direct Burford Bridge near dorking

TO GEORGE AND THOMAS KEATS

Hampstead Sunday
22 December 1818
[*for* 21, 27 (?) December 1817]

MY DEAR BROTHERS

I must crave your pardon for not having written ere this & &
I saw Kean return to the public in Richard III, and finely he did
it, & at the request of Reynolds I went to criticise his Luke in
Riches—the critique is in today's champion, which I send you,
with the Examiner in which you will find very proper lamentation
on the obsoletion of christmas Gambols and pastimes [4]: but it was
mixed up with so much egotism of that drivelling nature that
pleasure is entirely lost. Hone, the publisher's trial, you must find
very amusing; & as Englishmen, very encouraging—his *Not Guilty*
is a thing, which not to have been, would have dulled still more
Liberty's Emblazoning—Lord Ellenborough has been paid in his
own coin—Wooler & Hone [5] have done us an essential service—
I have had two very pleasant evenings with Dilke,[6] yesterday &
to-day; & am at this moment just come from him & feel in the
humour to go on with this, began in the morning, & from which
he came to fetch me. I spent Friday evening with Wells & went
next morning to see *Death on the Pale horse*. It is a wonderful
picture, when West's [7] age is considered; But there is nothing
to be intense upon; no women one feels mad to kiss, no face
swelling into reality. The excellence of every art is its intensity,
capable of making all disagreeables evaporate, from their being
in close relationship with Beauty & Truth—Examine King Lear
& you will find this exemplified throughout; but in this picture
we have unpleasantness without any momentous depth of speculation excited, in which to bury its repulsiveness—The picture is

[4] "Christmas and other old National Merry-makings considered, with reference to the Nature of the Age, and to the Desirableness of their Revival,"
an essay by Leigh Hunt.
[5] Publishers tried for libel, December, 1817.
[6] Charles Wentworth Dilke (1789–1864), friend of Keats, minor author
and editor.
[7] Benjamin West (1738–1820), American-born painter, president of the
Royal Academy in London, was 79 at the time.

larger than Christ rejected—I dined with Haydon the Sunday after you left, and had a very pleasant day, I dined too (for I have been out too much lately) with Horace Smith & met his two Brothers with Hill & Kingston & one Du Bois, they only served to convince me, how superior humour is to wit in respect to enjoyment—These men say things which make one start, without making one feel, they are all alike; their manners are alike; they all know fashionables; they have a mannerism in their eating & drinking, in their mere handling a Decanter—They talked of Kean and his low company—Would I were with that company instead of yours said I to myself! I know such like acquaintance will never do for me & yet I am going to Reynolds, on wednesday —Brown & Dilke walked with me & back from the Christmas pantomime. I had not a dispute but a disquisition with Dilke, on various subjects; several things dovetailed in my mind, & at once it struck me what quality went to form a Man of Achievement especially in Literature & which Shakespeare possessed so enormously—I mean *Negative Capability,* that is when a man is capable of being in uncertainties, Mysteries, doubts, without any irritable reaching after fact & reason—Coleridge, for instance, would let go by a fine isolated verisimilitude caught from the Penetralium of mystery, from being incapable of remaining content with half knowledge. This pursued through Volumes would perhaps take us no further than this, that with a great poet the sense of Beauty overcomes every other consideration, or rather obliterates all consideration.

Shelley's poem is out & there are words about its being objected too, as much as Queen Mab was. Poor Shelley I think he has his Quota of good qualities, in sooth la!! Write soon to your most sincere friend & affectionate Brother

John

Messrs Keats
Teignmouth Devonshire

TO JOHN HAMILTON REYNOLDS

Thursday 19 Feb. 1818

MY DEAR REYNOLDS,

I have an idea that a Man might pass a very pleasant life in this manner—let him on a certain day read a certain Page of full Poesy or distilled Prose and let him wander with it, and muse upon it, and reflect upon it, and bring home to it, and prophesy upon it, and dream upon it—untill it becomes stale—but when will it do so? Never—When Man has arrived at a certain ripeness in intellect any one grand and spiritual passage serves him as a starting post towards all "the two-and-thirty Pallaces"[.] How happy is such a "voyage of conception," what delicious diligent Indolence! A doze upon a Sofa does not hinder it, and a nap upon Clover engenders ethereal finger-pointings—the prattle of a child gives it wings, and the converse of middle-age a strength to beat them—a strain of musick conducts to "an odd angle of the Isle",[8] and when the leaves whisper it puts a "girdle round the earth.["] [9] Nor will this sparing touch of noble Books be any irreverence to their Writers—for perhaps the honors paid by Man to Man are trifles in comparison to the Benefit done by great Works to the "Spirit and pulse of good" [10] by their mere passive existence. Memory should not be called knowledge—Many have original minds who do not think it—they are led away by Custom—Now it appears to me that almost any Man may like the Spider spin from his own inwards his own airy Citadel—the points of leaves and twigs on which the Spider begins her work are few and she fills the air with a beautiful circuiting: man should be content with as few points to tip with the fine Webb of his Soul, and weave a tapestry empyrean full of Symbols for his spiritual eye, of softness for his spiritual touch, of space for his wandering of distinctness for his Luxury—But the Minds of Mortals are so different and bent on such diverse Journeys that it may at first appear impossible for any common taste and fellowship to exist between two or three under these suppositions—It is however quite the contrary—Minds would leave each other in contrary directions, traverse each other in Numberless points, and all [for at] last greet each other at the Journeys end—A old Man and a child would talk together and the old Man be led on his Path and the child left thinking—Man should not dispute or assert but whisper results to his neighbour, and thus by every germ of Spirit sucking the Sap from mould ethereal every human might become great, and Humanity instead of being a wide heath of

8 Shakespeare, *The Tempest*, Act I, scene ii, l. 223.
9 *Midsummer-Night's Dream*, Act II, scene i, l. 175.
10 Wordsworth, "The Old Cumberland Beggar," l. 77.

Furze and Briars with here and there a remote Oak or Pine, would
become a grand democracy of Forest Trees. It has been an old
Comparison for our urging on—the Bee hive—however it seems
to me that we should rather be the flower than the Bee—for it is
a false notion that more is gained by receiving than giving—no
the receiver and the giver are equal in their benefits—The flower I
doubt not receives a fair guerdon from the Bee—its leaves blush
deeper in the next spring—and who shall say between Man and
Woman which is the most delighted? Now it is more noble to sit
like Jove that [*for* than] to fly like Mercury—let us not therefore
go hurrying about and collecting honey-bee like, buzzing here
and there impatiently from a knowledge of what is to be
arrived at; but let us open our leaves like a flower and be passive
and receptive—budding patiently under the eye of Apollo and
taking hints from every noble insect that favours us with a visit—
sap will be given us for meat and dew for drink. I was led into
these thoughts, my dear Reynolds, by the beauty of the morning
operating on a sense of Idleness—I have not read any Books—
the Morning said I was right—I had no Idea but of the Morning,
and the Thrush said I was right—seeming to say—

> 'O thou whose face hath felt the Winter's wind,
> Whose eye has seen the Snow clouds hung in Mist
> And the black-elm tops 'mong the freezing Stars
> To thee the Spring will be a harvest-time—
> O thou whose only book has been the light
> Of supreme darkness which thou feddest on
> Night after night, when Phœbus was away
> To thee the Spring shall be a triple morn—
> O fret not after knowledge—I have none
> And yet my song comes native with the warmth.
> O fret not after knowledge—I have none
> And yet the Evening listens—He who saddens
> At thought of Idleness cannot be idle,
> And he's awake who thinks himself asleep.'

Now I am sensible all this is a mere sophistication, however it
may neighbour to any truths, to excuse my own indolence—so I
will not deceive myself that Man should be equal with jove—but

think himself very well off as a sort of scullion-Mercury or even a humble Bee—It is not [*for* no] matter whether I am right or wrong either one way or another, if there is sufficient to lift a little time from your Shoulders.

Your affectionate friend
John Keats—

TO JOHN TAYLOR

Friday 27 Feb. [1818].
Hampstead 27 Feby—

MY DEAR TAYLOR

Your alteration strikes me as being a great improvement—the page looks much better. And now I will attend to the Punctuations you speak of—the comma should be at *soberly,* and in the other passage the comma should follow *quiet,*.[11] I am extremely indebted to you for this attention and also for your after admonitions—It is a sorry thing for me that any one should have to overcome Prejudices in reading my Verses—that affects me more than any hyper-criticism on any particular Passage. In *Endymion* I have most likely but moved into the Go-cart from the leading strings. In Poetry I have a few Axioms, and you will see how far I am from their Centre. 1st. I think Poetry should surprise by a fine excess and not by Singularity—it should strike the Reader as a wording of his own highest thoughts and appear almost a Remembrance—2nd. Its touches of Beauty should never be half way ther[e]by making the reader breathless instead of content: the rise, the progress, the setting of imagery should like the Sun come natural too him—shine over him and set soberly although in magnificence leaving him in the Luxury of twilight —but it is easier to think what Poetry should be than to write it —and this leads me on to another axiom. That if Poetry comes not as naturally as the Leaves to a tree it had better not come at all. However it may be with me I cannot help looking into new countries with 'O for a Muse of fire to ascend!'[12] If Endymion serves me as a Pioneer perhaps I ought to be content. I have great reason to be content, for thank God I can read and perhaps

[11] Revisions to Keats' *Endymion,* I, lines 149 and 247.
[12] *Henry V,* Prologue i.

understand Shakespeare to his depths, and I have I am sure
many friends, who, if I fail, will attribute any change in my Life
and Temper to Humbleness rather than to Pride—to a cowering
under the Wings of great Poets rather than to a Bitterness that
I am not appreciated. I am anxious to get Endymion printed that
I may forget it and proceed. I have coppied the 3rd Book and
have begun the 4th. On running my Eye over the Proofs—I saw
one Mistake I will notice it presently and also any others if there
be any—There should be no comma in 'the raft branch down
sweeping from a tall Ash top'—I have besides made one or two
alteration[s] and also altered the 13 Line Page 32 to make sense
of it as you will see. I will take care the Printer shall not trip up
my Heels—There should be no dash after Dryope in this Line
'Dryope's lone lulling of her Child. Remember me to Percy
Street.

Your sincere and oblig^d friend
John Keats—

P. S. You shall have a sho[r]t *Preface* in good time—

William Hazlitt

[1778–1830]

❧❧

HAZLITT TRIED IN TURN theology, philosophical writing, and painting, before he turned to a career in journalism. He was a parliamentary reporter, a prolific contributor to periodicals, and a popular lecturer on literary subjects. His independent, impatient mind made him a difficult, controversial figure, and at one time or another he managed to alienate most of his friends, including Wordsworth, Coleridge, and Lamb. He died in poverty at the age of 52.

As a critic, Hazlitt was in many central ways characteristic of his time. In his concern with the psychology of art, and in his treatment of the nature and operations of the imagination, he was close to the position of his friend Coleridge. Like many Romantic critics (but perhaps more than most), Hazlitt was an impressionist, offering as criticism his own responses to authors and their inventions; his collection of essays on Shakespeare he called *Characters of Shakespeare's Plays,* and his lectures on the English comic writers might well have been titled *Characters of English Comedy.* The dangers of this sort of criticism are twofold: it may blur the distinction between art and reality, treating fictional characters as though they had actual existence; and it may become undiscriminatingly and subjectively enthusiastic. Hazlitt is occasionally guilty of both lapses.

Hazlitt's criticism is essentially applied criticism—the personal judgment of authors and works—rather than theory. Even when, as in the essay that follows, he was laying theoretical groundwork for such judgments, he did so by example, filling his pages with literary illustrations, with anecdotes, and with homely paradigm cases from nature and from ordinary human experience. This particularity makes him one of the most readable of critics.

Hazlitt's "On Wit and Humor" has its place in the great tradition of English comic theory which began with Ben Jonson, but it is distinctly a *Romantic* place. Like his neo-classical predecessors, Hazlitt recognizes the role of incongruity and of ridicule in comedy; but he differs from them in two significant ways: he treats the problem of comedy as essentially a psychological, rather than a moral one, and he concludes that wit is inferior to "poetry or imagination." On both these points he is a representative Romantic.

BIBLIOGRAPHY. *Complete Works*, ed. P. P. Howe, 21 vols. (New York, 1930–34).

Elisabeth Schneider, *The Aesthetics of William Hazlitt* (Philadelphia, 1933); René Wellek, *A History of Modern Criticism, 1750–1950*, vol. II (New Haven, 1955); Jacob Zeitlin, "Introduction" to *Hazlitt on English Literature* (New York, 1913).

TEXT. *Lectures on the English Comic Writers* (London, 1819).

from

ON WIT AND HUMOUR *

[1819]

MAN IS THE ONLY animal that laughs and weeps; for he is the only animal that is struck with the difference between what things are, and what they ought to be. We weep at what thwarts or exceeds our desires in serious matters: we laugh at what only disappoints our expectations in trifles. We shed tears from sympathy with real and necessary distress; as we burst into laughter from want of sympathy with that which is unreasonable and unnecessary, the absurdity of which provokes our spleen or mirth, rather than any serious reflections on it.

To explain the nature of laughter and tears, is to account for the condition of human life; for it is in a manner compounded of these two! It is a tragedy or a comedy—sad or merry, as it happens. The crimes and misfortunes that are inseparable from it, shock and wound the mind when they once seize upon it, and when the pressure can no longer be borne, seek relief in tears: the follies and absurdities that men commit, or the odd accidents that befal them, afford us amusement from the very rejection of

* "On Wit and Humor" is found in *Lectures on the English Comic Writers*, 1819.

these false claims upon our sympathy, and end in laughter. If everything that went wrong, if every vanity or weakness in another gave us a sensible pang, it would be hard indeed: but as long as the disagreeableness of the consequences of a sudden disaster is kept out of sight by the immediate oddity of the circumstances, and the absurdity or unaccountableness of a foolish action is the most striking thing in it, the ludicrous prevails over the pathetic, and we receive pleasure instead of pain from the farce of life which is played before us, and which discomposes our gravity as often as it fails to move our anger or our pity!

Tears may be considered as the natural and involuntary resource of the mind overcome by some sudden and violent emotion, before it has had time to reconcile its feelings to the change of circumstances: while laughter may be defined to be the same sort of convulsive and involuntary movement, occasioned by mere surprise or contrast (in the absence of any more serious emotion), before it has time to reconcile its belief to contradictory appearances. If we hold a mask before our face, and approach a child with this disguise on, it will at first, from the oddity and incongruity of the appearance, be inclined to laugh; if we go nearer to it, steadily, and without saying a word, it will begin to be alarmed, and be half inclined to cry: if we suddenly take off the mask, it will recover from its fears, and burst out a-laughing; but if, instead of presenting the old well-known countenance, we have concealed a satyr's head or some frightful caricature behind the first mask, the suddenness of the change will not in this case be a source of merriment to it, but will convert its surprise into an agony of consternation, and will make it scream out for help, even though it may be convinced that the whole is a trick at bottom.

The alternation of tears and laughter, in this little episode in common life, depends almost entirely on the greater or less degree of interest attached to the different changes of appearance. The mere suddenness of the transition, the mere baulking our expectations, and turning them abruptly into another channel, seems to give additional liveliness and gaiety to the animal spirits; but the instant the change is not only sudden, but threatens serious consequences, or calls up the shape of danger, terror supersedes our disposition to mirth, and laughter gives place to tears.

It is usual to play with infants, and make them laugh by clapping your hands suddenly before them; but if you clap your hands too loud, or too near their sight, their countenances immediately change, and they hide them in the nurse's arms. Or suppose the same child, grown up a little older, comes to a place, expecting to meet a person it is particularly fond of, and does not find that person there, its countenance suddenly falls, its lips begin to quiver, its cheek turns pale, its eye glistens, and it vents its little sorrow (grown too big to be concealed) in a flood of tears. Again, if the child meets the same person unexpectedly after long absence, the same effect will be produced by an excess of joy, with different accompaniments; that is, the surprise and the emotion excited will make the blood come into his face, his eyes sparkle, his tongue falter or be mute, but in either case the tears will gush to his relief, and lighten the pressure about his heart. On the other hand, if a child is playing at hide-and-seek, or blindman's-bluff, with persons it is ever so fond of, and either misses them where it had made sure of finding them, or suddenly runs up against them where it had least expected it, the shock or additional impetus given to the imagination by the disappointment or the discovery, in a matter of this indifference, will only vent itself in a fit of laughter.[1] The transition here is not from one thing of importance to another, or from a state of indifference to a state of strong excitement; but merely from one impression to another that we did not at all expect, and when we had expected just the contrary. The mind having been led to form a certain conclusion, and the result producing an immediate solution of continuity in the chain of our ideas, this alternate excitement and relaxation of the imagination, the object also striking upon the mind more vividly in its loose unsettled state, and before it has had time to recover and collect itself, causes that alternate excitement and relaxation, or irregular convulsive movement of the muscular and nervous system, which constitutes physical laughter. The *discontinuous* in our sensations produces a correspondent jar and discord in the frame. The steadiness of our

---

[1] A child that has hid itself out of the way in sport, is under a great temptation to laugh at the unconsciousness of others as to its situation. A person concealed from assassins, is in no danger of betraying his situation by laughing. [Hazlitt's note.]

faith and of our features begins to give way at the same time. We turn with an incredulous smile from a story that staggers our belief: and we are ready to split our sides with laughing at an extravagance that sets all common sense and serious concern at defiance.

To understand or define the ludicrous, we must first know what the serious is. Now the serious is the habitual stress which the mind lays upon the expectation of a given order of events, following one another with a certain regularity and weight of interest attached to them. When this stress is increased beyond its usual pitch of intensity, so as to overstrain the feelings by the violent opposition of good to bad, or of objects to our desires, it becomes the pathetic or tragical. The ludicrous, or comic, is the unexpected loosening or relaxing this stress below its usual pitch of intensity, by such an abrupt transposition of the order of our ideas, as taking the mind unawares, throws it off its guard, startles it into a lively sense of pleasure, and leaves no time nor inclination for painful reflections.

The essence of the laughable then is the incongruous, the disconnecting one idea from another, or the jostling of one feeling against another. The first and most obvious cause of laughter is to be found in the simple succession of events, as in the sudden shifting of a disguise, or some unlooked-for accident, without any absurdity of character or situation. The accidental contradiction between our expectations and the event can hardly be said, however, to amount to the ludicrous: it is merely laughable. The ludicrous is where there is the same contradiction between the object and our expectations, heightened by some deformity or inconvenience, that is, by its being contrary to what is customary or desirable; as the ridiculous, which is the highest degree of the laughable, is that which is contrary not only to custom but to sense and reason, or is a voluntary departure from what we have a right to expect from those who are conscious of absurdity and propriety in words, looks, and actions.

Of these different kinds of degrees of the laughable, the first is the most shallow and short-lived; for the instant the immediate surprise of a thing's merely happening one way or another is over, there is nothing to throw us back upon our former expectation, and renew our wonder at the event a second time. The second

sort, that is, the ludicrous arising out of the improbable or dis-
tressing, is more deep and lasting, either because the painful
catastrophe excites a greater curiosity, or because the old impression, from its habitual hold on the imagination, still recurs
mechanically, so that it is longer before we can seriously make
up our minds to the unaccountable deviation from it. The third
sort, or the ridiculous arising out of absurdity as well as improbability, that is, where the defect or weakness is of a man's own
seeking, is the most refined of all, but not always so pleasant as
the last, because the same contempt and disapprobation which
sharpens and subtilises our sense of the impropriety, adds a severity to it inconsistent with perfect ease and enjoyment. This last
species is properly the province of satire. The principle of contrast is, however, the same in all the stages, in the simply laughable, the ludicrous, the ridiculous; and the effect is only the more
complete, the more durably and pointedly this principle operates.

To give some examples in these different kinds. We laugh,
when children, at the sudden removing of a pasteboard mask:
we laugh, when grown up, more gravely at the tearing off the
mask of deceit. We laugh at absurdity; we laugh at deformity.
We laugh at a bottle-nose in a caricature; at a stuffed figure
of an alderman in a pantomime, and at the tale of Slauken-
bergius.[2] A giant standing by a dwarf makes a contemptible
figure enough. Rosinante and Dapple [3] are laughable from contrast, as their masters from the same principle make two for a
pair. We laugh at the dress of foreigners, and they at ours.
Three chimney-sweepers meeting three Chinese in Lincoln's-
inn Fields, they laughed at one other till they were ready to drop
down. Country people laugh at a person because they never saw
him before. Any one dressed in the height of the fashion, or
quite out of it, is equally an object of ridicule. One rich source
of the ludicrous is distress with which we cannot sympathise
from its absurdity or insignificance. Women laugh at their lovers.
We laugh at a damned author, in spite of our teeth, and though
he may be our friend. "There is something in the misfortunes
of our best friends that pleases us." [4] We laugh at people on the

2 In Sterne's *Tristram Shandy*, Book IV.
3 Don Quixote's horse; Sancho Panza's donkey.
4 La Rochefoucauld.

top of a stage-coach, or in it, if they seem in great extremity. It is hard to hinder children from laughing at a stammerer, at a negro, at a drunken man, or even at a madman. We laugh at mischief. We laugh at what we do not believe. We say that an argument or an assertion that is very absurd, is quite ludicrous. We laugh to shew our satisfaction with ourselves, or our contempt for those about us, or to conceal our envy or our ignorance. We laugh at fools, and at those who pretend to be wise—at extreme simplicity, awkwardness, hypocrisy, and affectation. "They were talking of me," says Scrub, "for they laughed *consumedly.*" Lord Foppington's insensibility to ridicule, and airs of ineffable self-conceit, are no less admirable; and Joseph Surface's [5] cant maxims of morality, when once disarmed of their power to do hurt, become sufficiently ludicrous.—We laugh at that in others which is a serious matter to ourselves; because our self-love is stronger than our sympathy, sooner takes the alarm, and instantly turns our heedless mirth into gravity, which only enhances the jest to others. Some one is generally sure to be the sufferer by a joke. What is sport to one, is death to another. It is only very sensible or very honest people, who laugh as freely at their own absurdities as at those of their neighbours. In general the contrary rule holds, and we only laugh at those misfortunes in which we are spectators, not sharers. The injury, the disappointment, shame, and vexation that we feel, put a stop to our mirth; while the disasters that come home to us, and excite our repugnance and dismay, are an amusing spectacle to others. The greater resistance we make, and the greater the perplexity into which we are thrown, the more lively and *piquant* is the intellectual display of cross-purposes to the by-standers. Our humiliation is their triumph. We are occupied with the disagreeableness of the result instead of its oddity or unexpectedness. Others see only the conflict of motives, and the sudden alternation of events; we feel the pain as well, which more than counterbalances the speculative entertainment we might receive from the contemplation of our abstract situation.

You cannot force people to laugh: you cannot give a reason why they should laugh: they must laugh of themselves, or not

[5] Scrub from Farquhar's *Beaux' Strategem;* Lord Foppington from Vanbrugh's *Relapse;* Surface from Sheridan's *School for Scandal.*

at all. As we laugh from a spontaneous impulse, we laugh the more at any restraint upon this impulse. We laugh at a thing merely because we ought not. If we think we must not laugh, this perverse impediment makes our temptation to laugh the greater; for by endeavouring to keep the obnoxious image out of sight, it comes upon us more irresistibly and repeatedly; and the inclination to indulge our mirth, the longer it is held back, collects its force, and breaks out the more violently in peals of laughter. In like manner, any thing we must not think of makes us laugh, by its coming upon us by stealth and unawares, and from the very efforts we make to exclude it. A secret, a loose word, a wanton jest, make people laugh. Aretine laughed himself to death at hearing a lascivious story. Wickedness is often made a substitute for wit; and in most of our good old comedies, the intrigue of the plot and the double meaning of the dialogue go hand-in-hand, and keep up the ball with wonderful spirit between them. The consciousness, however it may arise, that there is something that we ought to look grave at, is almost always a signal for laughing outright: we can hardly keep our countenance at a sermon, a funeral, or a wedding. What an excellent old custom was that of throwing the stocking! What a deal of innocent mirth has been spoiled by the disuse of it!—It is not an easy matter to preserve decorum in courts of justice. The smallest circumstance that interferes with the solemnity of the proceedings, throws the whole place into an uproar of laughter. People at the point of death often say smart things. Sir Thomas More jested with his executioner. Rabelais and Wycherley both died with a *bon-mot* in their mouths.

Misunderstandings, (*malentendus*) where one person means one thing, and another is aiming at something else, are another great source of comic humour, on the same principle of ambiguity and contrast. There is a high-wrought instance of this in the dialogue between Aimwell and Gibbet, in the Beaux' Stratagem, where Aimwell mistakes his companion for an officer in a marching regiment, and Gibbet takes it for granted that the gentleman is a highwayman. The alarm and consternation occasioned by some one saying to him, in the course of common conversation, "I apprehend you," is the most ludicrous thing in that admirably natural and powerful performance, Mr. Emery's Robert

Tyke.[6] Again, unconsciousness in the person himself of what he is about, or of what others think of him, is also a great heightener of the sense of absurdity. It makes it come the fuller home upon us from his insensibility to it. His simplicity sets off the satire, and gives it a finer edge. It is a more extreme case still where the person is aware of being the object of ridicule, and yet seems perfectly reconciled to it as a matter of course. So wit is often the more forcible and pointed for being dry and serious, for it then seems as if the speaker himself had no intention in it, and we were the first to find it out. Irony, as a species of wit, owes its force to the same principle. In such cases it is the contrast between the appearance and the reality, the suspense of belief, and the seeming incongruity, that gives point to the ridicule, and makes it enter the deeper when the first impression is overcome. Excessive impudence, as in the Liar; or excessive modesty, as in the hero of She Stoops to Conquer; or a mixture of the two, as in the Busy Body,[7] are equally amusing. Lying is a species of wit and humour. To lay any thing to a person's charge from which he is perfectly free, shews spirit and invention; and the more incredible the effrontery, the greater is the joke.

There is nothing more powerfully humorous than what is called *keeping* in comic character, as we see it very finely exemplified in Sancho Panza and Don Quixote. The proverbial phlegm and the romantic gravity of these two celebrated persons may be regarded as the height of this kind of excellence. The deep feeling of character strengthens the sense of the ludicrous. Keeping in comic character is consistency in absurdity; a determined and laudable attachment to the incongruous and singular. The regularity completes the contradiction; for the number of instances of deviation from the right line, branching out in all directions, shews the inveteracy of the original bias to any extravagance or folly, the natural improbability, as it were, increasing every time with the multiplication of chances for a return to common sense, and in the end mounting up to an incredible and unaccountably ridiculous height, when we find our expectations as invariably baffled. The most curious problem of all, is this truth of absurdity

[6] In Thomas Morton's *School of Reform* (1805).
[7] Samuel Foote, *The Liar* (1762); Oliver Goldsmith, *She Stoops to Conquer* (1773); Susannah Centlivre, *The Busybody* (1709).

to itself. That reason and good sense should be consistent, is not wonderful: but that caprice, and whim, and fantastical prejudice, should be uniform and infallible in their results, is the surprising thing. But while this characteristic clue to absurdity helps on the ridicule, it also softens and harmonises its excesses; and the ludicrous is here blended with a certain beauty and decorum, from this very truth of habit and sentiment, or from the principle of similitude in dissimilitude. The devotion to nonsense, and enthusiasm about trifles, is highly affecting as a moral lesson: it is one of the striking weaknesses and greatest happinesses of our nature. That which excites so lively and lasting an interest in itself, even though it should not be wisdom, is not despicable in the sight of reason and humanity. We cannot suppress the smile on the lip; but the tear should also stand ready to start from the eye. The history of hobby-horses is equally instructive and delightful; and after the pair I have just alluded to, My Uncle Toby's [8] is one of the best and gentlest that "ever lifted leg!" The inconveniences, odd accidents, falls, and bruises, to which they expose their riders, contribute their share to the amusement of the spectators; and the blows and wounds that the Knight of the Sorrowful Countenance received in his many perilous adventures, have applied their healing influence to many a hurt mind.—In what relates to the laughable, as it arises from unforeseen accidents or self-willed scrapes, the pain, the shame, the mortification, and the utter helplessness of situation, add to the joke, provided they are momentary, or overwhelming only to the imagination of the sufferer. Malvolio's punishment and apprehensions are as comic, from our knowing that they are not real, as Christopher Sly's drunken transformation and short-lived dream of happiness are for the like reason. Parson Adams's fall into the tub at the 'Squire's, or his being discovered in bed with Mrs. Slipslop, though pitiable, are laughable accidents: nor do we read with much gravity of the loss of his Æschylus, serious as it was to him at the time.—[9] . . .

There is another source of comic humour which has been but little touched on or attended to by the critics—not the infliction of casual pain, but the pursuit of uncertain pleasure and idle

---

[8] *Tristram Shandy*, Book I, Chapters 24 and 25.
[9] Incidents from Fielding's *Joseph Andrews*.

gallantry. Half the business and gaiety of comedy turns upon this. Most of the adventures, difficulties, demurs, hair-breadth 'scapes, disguises, deceptions, blunders, disappointments, successes, excuses, all the dextrous manœuvres, artful inuendos, assignations, billets-doux, *double entendres,* sly allusions, and elegant flattery, have an eye to this— to the obtaining of those "favours secret, sweet, and precious," in which love and pleasure consist, and which when attained, and the *equivoque* is at an end, the curtain drops, and the play is over. All the attractions of a subject that can only be glanced at indirectly, that is a sort of forbidden ground to the imagination, except under severe restrictions, which are constantly broken through; all the resources it supplies for intrigue and invention; the bashfulness of the clownish lover, his looks of alarm and petrified astonishment; the foppish affectation and easy confidence of the happy man; the dress, the airs, the languor, the scorn, and indifference of the fine lady; the bustle, pertness, loquaciousness, and tricks of the chambermaid; the impudence, lies, and roguery of the valet; the match-making and unmaking; the wisdom of the wise; the sayings of the witty, the folly of the fool; "the soldier's, scholar's, courtier's eye, tongue, sword, the glass of fashion and the mould of form," have all a view to this. It is the closet in Blue Beard. It is the life and soul of Wycherley, Congreve, Vanbrugh, and Farquhar's plays. It is the salt of comedy, without which it would be worthless and insipid. It makes Horner decent, and Millamant divine. It is the jest between Tattle and Miss Prue. It is the bait with which Olivia, in the Plain Dealer, plays with honest Manly. It lurks at the bottom of the catechism which Archer teaches Cherry, and which she learns by heart. It gives the finishing grace to Mrs. Amlet's confession—"Though I'm old, I'm chaste." Valentine and his Angelica would be nothing without it; Miss Peggy would not be worth a gallant; and Slender's "sweet Anne Page" would be no more! "The age of comedy would be gone, and the glory of our play-houses extinguished for ever." Our old comedies would be invaluable, were it only for this, that they keep alive this sentiment, which still survives in all its fluttering grace and breathless palpitations on the stage.

Humour is the describing the ludicrous as it is in itself; wit is the exposing it, by comparing or contrasting it with something else. Humour is, as it were, the growth of nature and accident; wit is the product of art and fancy. Humour, as it is shewn in books, is an imitation of the natural or acquired absurdities of mankind, or of the ludicrous in accident, situation, and character: wit is the illustrating and heightening the sense of that absurdity by some sudden and unexpected likeness or opposition of one thing to another, which sets off the quality we laugh at or despise in a still more contemptible or striking point of view. Wit, as distinguished from poetry, is the imagination or fancy inverted, and so applied to given objects, as to make the little look less, the mean more light and worthless; or to divert our admiration or wean our affections from that which is lofty and impressive, instead of producing a more intense admiration and exalted passion, as poetry does. Wit may sometimes, indeed, be shewn in compliments as well as satire; as in the common epigram—

> Accept a miracle, instead of wit:
> See two dull lines with Stanhope's pencil writ.[10]

But then the mode of paying it is playful and ironical, and contradicts itself in the very act of making its own performance an humble foil to another's. Wit hovers round the borders of the light and trifling, whether in matters of pleasure or pain; for as soon as it describes the serious seriously, it ceases to be wit, and passes into a different form. Wit is, in fact, the eloquence of indifference, or an ingenious and striking exposition of those evanescent and glancing impressions of objects which affect us more from surprise or contrast to the train of our ordinary and literal preconceptions, than from any thing in the objects themselves exciting our necessary sympathy or lasting hatred. The favourite employment of wit is to add littleness to littleness, and heap contempt on insignificance by all the arts of petty and incessant warfare; or if it ever affects to aggrandise, and use the language of hyperbole, it is only to betray into derision by a fatal comparison, as in the mock-heroic; or if it treats of serious passion, it must do it so as to lower the tone of intense and high-wrought sentiment, by the introduction of burlesque and familiar circumstances. To

[10] By Edward Young (1683–1765); quoted in Joseph Spence, *Anecdotes* (London, 1820), p. 378.

give an instance or two. Butler, in his Hudibras, compares the
change of night into day, to the change of colour in a boiled lob-
ster.

> The sun had long since, in the lap
> Of Thetis, taken out his nap;
> And, like a lobster boil'd, the morn
> From black to red, began to turn:
> When Hudibras, whom thoughts and aching
> 'Twixt sleeping kept all night, and waking,
> Began to rub his drowsy eyes,
> And from his couch prepared to rise,
> Resolving to dispatch the deed
> He vow'd to do with trusty speed.

Compare this with the following stanzas in Spenser, treating of
the same subject:—

> By this the Northern Waggoner had set
> His seven-fold team behind the stedfast star,
> That was in Ocean waves yet never wet,
> But firm is fix'd and sendeth light from far
> To all that in the wide deep wand'ring are:
> And cheerful chanticleer with his note shrill,
> Had warned once that Phœbus' fiery car
> In haste was climbing up the eastern hill,
> Full envious that night so long his room did fill.

> At last the golden oriental gate
> Of greatest heaven 'gan to open fair,
> And Phœbus, fresh as bridgegroom to his mate,
> Came dancing forth, shaking his dewy hair,
> And hurl'd his glist'ring beams through gloomy air:
> Which when the wakeful elf perceiv'd, straitway
> He started up and did himself prepare
> In sun-bright arms and battailous array,
> For with that pagan proud he combat will that day.[11]

In this last passage, every image is brought forward that can
give effect to our natural impression of the beauty, the splen-

[11] *Faerie Queene*, I, ii, 1 and I, v, 2.

dour, and solemn grandeur of the rising sun; pleasure and power wait on every line and word: whereas, in the other, the only memorable thing is a grotesque and ludicrous illustration of the alteration which takes place from darkness to gorgeous light, and that brought from the lowest instance, and with associations that can only disturb and perplex the imagination in its conception of the real object it describes. There cannot be a more witty, and at the same time degrading comparison, than that in the same author, of the Bear turning round the pole-star to a bear tied to a stake:—

> But now a sport more formidable
> Had raked together village rabble;
> 'Twas an old way of recreating
> Which learned butchers call bear-baiting,
> A bold adventrous exercise
> With ancient heroes in high prize,
> For authors do affirm it came
> From Isthmian or Nemæan game;
> Others derive it from the Bear
> That's fixed in Northern hemisphere,
> And round about his pole does make
> A circle like a bear at stake,
> That at the chain's end wheels about
> And overturns the rabble rout.[12]

I need not multiply examples of this sort.—Wit or ludicrous invention produces its effect oftenest by comparison, but not always. It frequently effects its purposes by unexpected and subtle distinctions. For instance, in the first kind, Mr. Sheridan's description of Mr. Addington's administration as the fag-end of Mr. Pitt's, who had remained so long on the treasury bench that, like Nicias in the fable, "he left the sitting part of the man behind him," is as fine an example of metaphorical wit as any on record. The same idea seems, however, to have been included in the old well-known nickname of the *Rump* Parliament. Almost as happy an instance of the other kind of wit, which consists in sudden retorts, in turns upon an idea, and diverting the train of your adversary's argument abruptly and adroitly into another channel,

[12] *Hudibras*, Part I, Canto i, ll. 215–216.

may be seen in the sarcastic reply of Porson, who hearing some one observe, that "certain modern poets would be read and admired when Homer and Virgil were forgotten," made answer—"And not till then!" Sir Robert Walpole's definition of the gratitude of place-expectants, "That it is a lively sense of *future* favours," is no doubt wit, but it does not consist in the finding out any coincidence or likeness, but in suddenly transposing the order of time in the common account of this feeling, so as to make the professions of those who pretend to it correspond more with their practice. It is filling up a blank in the human heart with a word that explains its hollowness at once. Voltaire's saying, in answer to a stranger who was observing how tall his trees grew—"That they had nothing else to do"—was a quaint mixture of wit and humour, making it out as if they really led a lazy, laborious life; but there was here neither allusion or metaphor. Again, that master-stroke in Hudibras is sterling wit and profound satire, where speaking of certain religious hypocrites he says, that they

> Compound for sins they are inclin'd to,
> By damning those they have no mind to;

but the wit consists in the truth of the character, and in the happy exposure of the ludicrous contradiction between the pretext and the practice; between their lenity towards their own vices, and their severity to those of others. The same principle of nice distinction must be allowed to prevail in those lines of the same author, where he is professing to expound the dreams of judicial astrology.

> There's but the twinkling of a star
> Betwixt a man of peace and war,
> A thief and justice, fool and knave,
> A huffing officer and a slave;
> A crafty lawyer and pickpocket;
> A great philosopher and a blockhead;
> A formal preacher and a player;
> A learn'd physician and man slayer.

The finest piece of wit I know of, is in the lines of Pope on the Lord Mayor's show—

> Now night descending, the proud scene is o'er,
> But lives in Settle's numbers one day more.[13]

This is certainly as mortifying an inversion of the idea of poetical
immortality as could be thought of; it fixes the *maximum* of
littleness and insignificance: but it is not by likeness to any thing
else that it does this, but by literally taking the lowest possible
duration of ephemeral reputation, marking it (as with a slider)
on the scale of endless renown, and giving a rival credit for it as
his loftiest praise. In a word, the shrewd separation or disentan-
gling of ideas that seem the same, or where the secret contradiction is not sufficiently suspected, and is of a ludicrous and whimsi-
cal nature, is wit just as much as the bringing together those that
appear at first sight totally different. There is then no sufficient
ground for admitting Mr. Locke's celebrated definition of wit,
which he makes to consist in the finding out striking and unexpected resemblances in things so as to make pleasant pictures
in the fancy, while judgment and reason, according to him, lie
the clean contrary way, in separating and nicely distinguishing
those wherein the smallest difference is to be found.[14]

[13] *Dunciad,* I, 89–90.

[14] His words are—"If in having our ideas in the memory ready at hand
consists quickness of parts, in this of having them unconfused, and being
able nicely to distinguish one thing from another, where there is but the
least difference, consists in a great measure the exactness of judgment and
clearness of reason, which is to be observed in one man above another. And
hence, perhaps, may be given some reason of that common observation, that
men who have a great deal of wit and prompt memories, have not always
the clearest judgment or deepest reason. For wit lying mostly in the assemblage of ideas, and putting them together with quickness and variety, wherein
can be found any resemblance or congruity, thereby to make up pleasant
pictures and agreeable visions in the fancy; judgment, on the contrary, lies
quite on the other side, in separating carefully one from another, ideas
wherein can be found the least difference, thereby to avoid being misled by
similitude, and by affinity to take one thing for another." (*Essay,* vol. i, p.
143.) This definition, such as it is, Mr.Locke took without acknowledgment
from Hobbes, who says in his Leviathan, "This difference of quickness in
imagining is caused by the difference of men's passions, that love and dislike
some one thing, some another, and therefore some men's thoughts run one
way, some another, and are held to and observed differently the things that
pass through their imagination. And whereas in this succession of thoughts
there is nothing to observe in the things they think on, but either in what
they be like one another, or in what they be unlike, those that observe their
similitudes, in case they be such as are but rarely observed by others, are
said to have a good wit, by which is meant on this occasion a good fancy.

On this definition Harris, the author of Hermes, has very well observed that the demonstrating the equality of the three angles of a right-angled triangle to two right ones, would, upon the principle here stated, be a piece of wit instead of an act of the judgment or understanding, and Euclid's Elements a collection of epigrams. On the contrary it has appeared, that the detection and exposure of difference, particularly where this implies nice and subtle observation, as in discriminating between pretence and practice, between appearance and reality, is common to wit and satire with judgment and reasoning, and certainly the comparing and connecting our ideas together is an essential part of reason and judgment, as well as of wit and fancy.—Mere wit, as opposed to reason or argument, consists in striking out some casual and partial coincidence which has nothing to do, or at least implies no necessary connection with the nature of the things, which are forced into a seeming analogy by a play upon words, or some irrelevant conceit, as in puns, riddles, alliteration, &c. The jest, in all such cases, lies in the sort of mock-identity, or nominal resemblance, established by the intervention of the same words expressing different ideas, and countenancing as it were, by a fatality of language, the mischievous insinuation which the person who has the wit to take advantage of it wishes to convey. So when the disaffected French wits applied to the new order of the *Fleur du lys* the *double entendre* of *Compagnons d'Ulysse*, or companions of Ulysses, meaning the animal into which the fellow-travellers of the hero of the Odyssey were transformed, this was a shrewd and biting intimation of a galling truth (if truth it were) by a fortuitous concourse of letters of the alphabet, jumping in "a foregone conclusion," but there was no proof of the thing, unless it was self-evident. And, indeed, this may be considered as the best defence of the contested maxim—That *ridicule is the test of truth;* viz. that it does not contain or attempt a formal proof of

---

But they that observe their differences and dissimilitudes, which is called distinguishing and discerning and judging between thing and thing; in case such discerning be not easy, are said to have a good judgment; and particularly in matter of conversation and business, wherein times, places, and persons are to be discerned, this virtue is called discretion. The former, that is, fancy, without the help of judgment, is not commended for a virtue; but the latter, which is judgment or discretion, is commended for itself, without the help of fancy." *Leviathan,* p. 32. [Hazlitt.]

it, but owes its power of conviction to the bare suggestion of it, so that if the thing when once hinted is not clear in itself, the satire fails of its effect and falls to the ground. The sarcasm here glanced at the character of the new or old French noblesse may not be well founded; but it is so like truth, and "comes in such a questionable shape," backed with the appearance of an identical proposition, that it would require a long train of facts and laboured arguments to do away the impression, even if we were sure of the honesty and wisdom of the person who undertook to refute it. A flippant jest is as good a test of truth as a solid bribe; and there are serious sophistries,

Soul-killing lies, and truths that work small good,[15]

as well as idle pleasantries. Of this we may be sure, that ridicule fastens on the vulnerable points of a cause, and finds out the weak sides of an argument; if those who resort to it sometimes rely too much on its success, those who are chiefly annoyed by it almost always are so with reason, and cannot be too much on their guard against deserving it. Before we can laugh at a thing, its absurdity must at least be open and palpable to common apprehension. Ridicule is necessarily built on certain supposed facts, whether true or false, and on their inconsistency with certain acknowledged maxims, whether right or wrong. It is, therefore, a fair test, if not of philosophical or abstract truth, at least of what is truth according to public opinion and common sense; for it can only expose to instantaneous contempt that which is condemned by public opinion, and is hostile to the common sense of mankind. Or to put it differently, it is the test of the quantity of truth that there is in our favourite prejudices.—To shew how nearly allied wit is thought to be to truth, it is not unusual to say of any person—"Such a one is a man of sense, for though he said nothing, he laughed in the right place."—Alliteration comes in here under the head of a certain sort of verbal wit; or, by pointing the expression, sometimes points the sense. Mr. Grattan's wit or eloquence (I don't know by what name to call it) would be nothing without this accompaniment. Speaking of some ministers whom he did not like, he said, "Their only means of government are the

[15] Charles Lamb, *John Woodvil*, Act II.

guinea and the gallows." There can scarcely, it must be confessed, be a more effectual mode of political conversion than one of these applied to a man's friends, and the other to himself. The fine sarcasm of Junius on the effect of the supposed ingratitude of the Duke of Grafton at court—"The instance might be painful, but the principle would please"—notwithstanding the profound insight into human nature it implies, would hardly pass for wit without the alliteration, as some poetry would hardly be acknowledged as such without the rhyme to clench it. A quotation or a hackneyed phrase dextrously turned or wrested to another purpose, has often the effect of the liveliest wit. An idle fellow who had only fourpence left in the world, which had been put by to pay for the baking some meat for his dinner, went and laid it out to buy a new string for a guitar. An old acquaintance on hearing this story, repeated those lines out of the Allegro—

> And ever against *eating* cares
> Lap me in soft Lydian airs.

The reply of the author of the periodical paper called the World to a lady at church, who seeing him look thoughtful, asked what he was thinking of—"The next World,"—is a perversion of an established formula of language, something of the same kind.— Rhymes are sometimes a species of wit, where there is an alternate combination and resolution or decomposition of the elements of sound, contrary to our usual division and classification of them in ordinary speech, not unlike the sudden separation and re-union of the component parts of the machinery in a pantomime. The author who excels infinitely the most in this way is the writer of Hudibras. He also excels in the invention of single words and names which have the effect of wit by sounding big, and meaning nothing:—"full of sound and fury, signifying nothing." But of the artifices of this author's burlesque style I shall have occasion to speak hereafter.—It is not always easy to distinguish between the wit of words and that of things. "For thin partitions do their bounds divide." Some of the late Mr. Curran's *bon mots* or *jeux d'esprit*, might be said to owe their birth to this sort of equivocal generation; or were a happy mixture of verbal wit and a lively and picturesque fancy, of legal acuteness in detecting the variable applications of words, and of a mind apt at perceiving the ludicrous in external objects. "Do you see any thing ridiculous in this wig?" said one of his brother judges to him. "Nothing but the head," was the answer. Now here instantaneous advantage was taken of the slight technical ambiguity in the construction of language, and the matter-of-fact is flung into the scale as a thumping makeweight. After all, verbal and accidental strokes of wit, though the most surprising and laughable, are not the best and most lasting. That wit is the most refined and effectual, which is founded on the detection of unexpected likeness or distinction in things, rather than in words. It is more severe and galling, that is, it is more unpardonable though less surprising, in proportion as the thought suggested is more complete and satisfactory, from its being inherent in the nature of the things themselves. *Hæret lateri lethalis arundo.* Truth makes the greatest libel; and it is that which barbs the darts of wit. The Duke of Buckingham's saying, "Laws are not, like women, the worse for being old," is an instance of a harmless truism and the utmost malice of wit united. That is, perhaps, what has been meant by the distinction between true and false wit. Mr. Addison, indeed, goes so far as to make it the exclusive test of true wit that it will bear translation into another language, that is to say, that it does not depend at all on the form of expression. But this is by no means the case. Swift would hardly have allowed of such a strait-laced theory, to make havoc with his darling conundrums; though there is no one whose serious wit is more that of things, as opposed to a mere play either of words or fancy. I ought, I believe, to have noticed before, in speaking of the difference between wit and humour, that wit is often pretended absurdity, where the person overacts or exaggerates a certain part with a conscious design to expose it as if it were another person, as when Mandrake in the Twin Rivals says, "This glass is too big, carry it away, I'll drink out of the bottle." On the contrary, when Sir Hugh Evans says very innocently, "'Od's plessed will, I will not be absence at the grace," though there is here a great deal of humour, there is no wit. This kind of wit of the humorist, where the person makes a butt of himself, and exhibits his own absurdities or foibles purposely in the most pointed and glaring lights, runs through the whole of the character of Falstaff, and is, in truth, the principle on which it is founded. It is an irony directed against one's-self. Wit is, in fact, a voluntary act of the mind, or exercise of the invention, shewing the absurd and ludicrous consciously, whether in ourselves or another. Cross-readings, where the blunders are designed, are wit: but if any one were to light upon them through ignorance or accident, they would be merely ludicrous.

It might be made an argument of the intrinsic superiority of poetry or imagination to wit, that the former does not admit of mere verbal combinations. Whenever they do occur, they are uniformly blemishes. It requires something more solid and substantial to raise admiration or passion. The general forms and aggregate masses of our ideas must be brought more into play, to give weight and magnitude. Imagination may be said to be the finding out something similar in things generally alike, or with like feelings attached to them; while wit principally aims at finding out something that seems the same, or amounts to a momentary deception where you least expected it, viz. in things totally opposite. The reason why more slight and partial, or merely accidental and nominal resemblances serve the purposes of wit, and indeed characterise its essence as a distinct operation and faculty of the mind, is, that the object of ludicrous poetry is naturally to let down and lessen; and it is easier to let down than to raise up, to weaken than to strengthen, to disconnect our sympathy from passion and power, than to attach and rivet it to any object of grandeur or interest, to startle and shock our preconceptions by incongruous and equivocal combinations, than to confirm, enforce, and expand them by powerful and lasting associations of ideas, or striking and true analogies. A slight cause is sufficient to produce a slight effect. To be indifferent or sceptical, requires no effort; to be enthusiastic and in earnest, requires a strong impulse, and collective power. Wit and humour (comparatively speaking, or taking the extremes to judge of the gradations by) appeal to our indolence, our vanity, our weakness, and insensibility; serious and impassioned poetry appeals to our strength, our magnanimity, our virtue, and humanity. Any thing is sufficient to heap contempt upon an object; even the bare suggestion of a mischievous allusion to what is improper, dissolves the whole charm, and puts an end to our admiration of the sublime or beautiful. Reading the finest passage in Milton's Paradise Lost in a false tone, will make it seem insipid and absurd. The cavilling at, or invidiously pointing out, a few slips of the pen, will embitter the pleasure, or alter our opinion of a whole work, and make us throw it down in disgust. The critics are aware of this vice and infirmity in our nature, and play upon it with periodical success. The meanest weapons are strong enough for this kind of warfare, and the meanest hands can wield them. Spleen can subsist on any kind of food. The shadow of a doubt, the hint of an inconsistency, a word, a look, a syllable, will destroy our best-formed convictions. What puts this argument in as striking a point of view as any thing, is the nature of parody or burlesque, the secret of which lies merely in transposing or applying at a venture to any thing, or to the lowest objects, that which is applicable only to certain given things, or to the highest matters. "From the sublime to the ridiculous, there is but one step." The slightest want of unity of impression destroys the sublime; the detection of the smallest incongruity is an infallible ground to rest the ludicrous upon. But in serious poetry, which aims at rivetting our affections, every blow must tell home. The missing a single time is fatal, and undoes the spell. We see how difficult it is to sustain a continued flight of impressive sentiment: how easy it must be then to travestie or burlesque it, to flounder into nonsense, and be witty by playing the fool. It is a common mistake, however, to suppose that parodies degrade, or imply a stigma on the subject: on the contrary, they in general imply something serious or sacred in the originals. Without this, they would be good for nothing; for the immediate contrast would be wanting, and with this they are sure to tell. The best parodies are, accordingly, the best and most striking things reversed. Witness the common travesties of Homer and Virgil. Mr. Canning's court parodies on Mr. Southey's popular odes, are also an instance in point (I do not know which were the cleverest); and the best of the Rejected Addresses is the parody on Crabbe, though I do not certainly think that Crabbe is the most ridiculous poet now living.

Lear and the Fool are the sublimest instance I know of passion and wit united, or of imagination unfolding the most tremendous sufferings, and of burlesque on passion playing with it, aiding and relieving its intensity by the most pointed, but familiar and indifferent illustrations of the same thing in different objects, and on a meaner scale. The Fool's reproaching Lear with "making

his daughters his mothers," his snatches of proverbs and old ballads, "The hedge-sparrow fed the cuckoo so long, that it had its
head bit off by its young," and "Whoop jug, I know when the
horse follows the cart," are a running commentary of trite truisms, pointing out the extreme folly of the infatuated old mon-
arch, and in a manner reconciling us to its inevitable consequences.

Lastly, there is a wit of sense and observation, which consists
in the acute illustration of good sense and practical wisdom, by
means of some far-fetched conceit or quaint imagery. The matter
is sense, but the form is wit. Thus the lines in Pope—

> 'Tis with our judgments as our watches, none
> Go just alike; yet each believes his own— [16]

are witty, rather than poetical; because the truth they convey is
a mere dry observation on human life, without elevation or enthusiasm, and the illustration of it is of that quaint and familiar
kind that is merely curious and fanciful. Cowley is an instance of
the same kind in almost all his writings. Many of the jests and
witticisms in the best comedies are moral aphorisms and rules for
the conduct of life, sparkling with wit and fancy in the mode of
expression. The ancient philosophers also abounded in the same
kind of wit, in telling home truths in the most unexpected manner.—In this sense Æsop was the greatest wit and moralist that
ever lived. Ape and slave, he looked askance at human nature,
and beheld its weaknesses and errors transferred to another
species. Vice and virtue were to him as plain as any objects of
sense. He saw in man a talking, absurd, obstinate, proud, angry
animal; and clothed these abstractions with wings, or a beak, or
tail, or claws, or long ears, as they appeared embodied in these
hieroglyphics in the brute creation. His moral philosophy is
natural history. He makes an ass bray wisdom, and a frog croak
humanity. The store of moral truth, and the fund of invention
in exhibiting it in eternal forms, palpable and intelligible, and
delightful to children and grown persons, and to all ages and
nations, are almost miraculous. The invention of a fable is to me
the most enviable exertion of human genius: it is the discovering

[16] *Essay on Criticism*, 9–10.

a truth to which there is no clue, and which, when once found
out, can never be forgotten. I would rather have been the author
of Æsop's Fables, than of Euclid's Elements!—That popular entertainment, Punch and the Puppet-show, owes part of its irresistible and universal attraction to nearly the same principle of
inspiring inanimate and mechanical agents with sense and consciousness. The drollery and wit of a piece of wood is doubly droll
and farcical. Punch is not merry in himself, but "he is the cause
of heartfelt mirth in other men." The wires and pulleys that
govern his motions are conductors to carry off the spleen, and all
"that perilous stuff that weighs upon the heart." If we see a
number of people turning the corner of a street, ready to burst
with secret satisfaction, and with their faces bathed in laughter,
we know what is the matter—that they are just come from a
puppet-show. Who can see three little painted, patched-up figures, no bigger than one's thumb, strut, squeak and gibber, sing,
dance, chatter, scold, knock one another about the head, give
themselves airs of importance, and "imitate humanity most
abominably," without laughing immoderately? We overlook the
farce and mummery of human life in little, and for nothing; and
what is still better, it costs them who have to play in it nothing.
We place the mirth, and glee, and triumph, to our own account;
and we know that the bangs and blows they have received go for
nothing, as soon as the showman puts them up in his box and
marches off quietly with them, as jugglers of a less amusing
description sometimes march off with the wrongs and rights of
mankind in their pockets!—I have heard no bad judge of such
matters say, "he liked a comedy better than a tragedy, a farce
better than a comedy, a pantomime better than a farce, but a
puppet-show best of all." I look upon it, that he who invented
puppet-shows was a greater benefactor to his species, than he
who invented Operas! . . .

Thomas Love Peacock

[1785–1866]

THE WORKS AND OPINIONS of Peacock are a useful reminder that the neo-classical temper did not disappear when Wordsworth published the *Lyrical Ballads*. Though Peacock lived through the Romantic Period and well into the reign of Queen Victoria, his closest intellectual kin are the poets and novelists of the eighteenth century. Perhaps because he was a literary amateur (he earned his living with the East India Company), Peacock preserved an independence of mind and an eccentricity of method which make him a refreshing and attractive minor figure. His seven novels have no parallels in English fiction; they are virtually plotless, composed largely of witty dialogues among characters who are often satiric portraits of his contemporaries (both Coleridge and Shelley appear in *Nightmare Abbey*). Through his dialogues Peacock satirizes the ideas of his time, and particularly those which he associated with excessive Romanticism—sentimentality, emotionalism, and obscure metaphysics.

"The Four Ages of Poetry" is typical Peacock, both in its ironic, epigrammatic style, and in its neo-classical ideas. The idea that society (and with it literature) had declined from a classical Golden Age is, of course, a stock eighteenth-century notion (it underlies Pope's "Essay on Criticism"); Peacock's opinions of the Middle Ages and of Romantic primitivism, based as they are on Reason as the primary human value, are equally neo-classical.

Peacock sent a copy of his essay to his friend Shelley, and Shelley responded with his *Defence of Poetry*, which is essentially a defense against Peacock. No better contrast of the neo-classical and romantic tempers could be found than these two essays, read side by side.

BIBLIOGRAPHY. *Works*, ed. H. F. B. Brett-Smith and C. E. Jones, 10 vols. (London, 1934).

A. H. Able, *Meredith and Peacock. A Study in Literary Influence*

(Philadelphia, 1933); J. B. Priestley, *Thomas Love Peacock* (London, 1927).

TEXT. *Olliers Literary Miscellany*, No. 1 (London, 1820).

THE FOUR AGES OF POETRY

[1820]

Qui inter haec nutriuntur non magis sapere possunt, quam bene olere qui in culinâ habitant.   PETRONIUS
[Boys, nourished by things like these, can no more acquire real taste than those who live in a kitchen can smell sweet.]

POETRY, LIKE THE WORLD, may be said to have four ages, but in a different order; the first age of poetry being the age of iron; the second, of gold; the third, of silver; and the fourth, of brass.

The first, or iron age of poetry, is that in which rude bards celebrate in rough numbers the exploits of ruder chiefs, in days when every man is a warrior, and when the great practical maxim of every form of society, "to keep what we have and to catch what we can," is not yet disguised under names of justice and forms of law, but is the naked motto of the naked sword, which is the only judge and jury in every question of *meum* and *tuum* [mine and yours]. In these days, the only three trades flourishing (besides that of priest which flourishes always) are those of king, thief, and beggar: the beggar being for the most part a king deject, and the thief a king expectant. The first question asked of a stranger is, whether he is a beggar or a thief:[1] the stranger, in reply, usually assumes the first, and awaits a convenient opportunity to prove his claim to the second appellation.

The natural desire of every man to engross to himself as much power and property as he can acquire by any of the means which might makes right, is accompanied by the no less natural desire of making known to as many people as possible the extent to which he has been a winner in this universal game. The successful

[1] See the Odyssey, passim: and Thucydides, I. 5. [Peacock's note.]

warrior becomes a chief; the successful chief becomes a king: his next want is an organ to disseminate the fame of his achievements and the extent of his possessions; and this organ he finds in a bard, who is always ready to celebrate the strength of his arm, being first duly inspired by that of his liquor. This is the origin of poetry, which, like all other trades, takes its rise in the demand for the commodity, and flourishes in proportion to the extent of the market.

Poetry is thus in its origin panegyrical. The first rude songs of all nations appear to be a sort of brief historical notices, in a strain of tumid hyperbole, of the exploits and possessions of a few pre-eminent individuals. They tell us how many battles such an one has fought, how many helmets he has cleft, how many breastplates he has pierced, how many widows he has made, how much land he has appropriated, how many houses he has demolished for other people, what a large one he has built for himself, how much gold he has stowed away in it, and how liberally and plentifully he pays, feeds, and intoxicates the divine and immortal bards, the sons of Jupiter, but for whose everlasting songs the names of heroes would perish.

This is the first stage of poetry before the invention of written letters. The numerical modulation is at once useful as a help to memory, and pleasant to the ears of uncultured men, who are easily caught by sound: and from the exceeding flexibility of the yet unformed language, the poet does no violence to his ideas in subjecting them to the fetters of number. The savage indeed lisps in numbers, and all rude and uncivilized people express themselves in the manner which we call poetical.

The scenery by which he is surrounded, and the superstitions which are the creed of his age, form the poet's mind. Rocks, mountains, seas, unsubdued forests, unnavigable rivers, surround him with forms of power and mystery, which ignorance and fear have peopled with spirits, under multifarious names of gods, goddesses, nymphs, genii, and daemons. Of all these personages marvellous tales are in existence: the nymphs are not indifferent to handsome young men, and the gentlemen-genii are much troubled and very troublesome with a propensity to be rude to pretty maidens: the bard therefore finds no difficulty in tracing the genealogy of his chief to any of the deities in his neighborhood with whom the said chief may be most desirous of claiming relationship.

In this pursuit, as in all others, some of course will attain a very marked pre-eminence; and these will be held in high honor, like Demodocus in the Odyssey, and will be consequently inflated with boundless vanity, like Thamyris in the Iliad. Poets are as yet the only historians and chroniclers of their time, and the sole depositories of all the knowledge of their age; and though this knowledge is rather a crude congeries of traditional phantasies than a collection of useful truths, yet, such as it is, they have it to themselves. They are observing and thinking, while others are robbing and fighting: and though their object be nothing more than to secure a share of the spoil, yet they accomplish this end by intellectual, not by physical, power: their success excites emulation to the attainment of intellectual eminence: thus they sharpen their own wits and awaken those of others, at the same time that they gratify vanity and amuse curiosity. A skilful display of the little knowledge they have gains them credit for the possession of much more which they have not. Their familiarity with the secret history of gods and genii obtains for them, without much difficulty, the reputation of inspiration; thus they are not only historians but theologians, moralists, and legislators: delivering their oracles *ex cathedrâ,* and being indeed often themselves (as Orpheus and Amphion) regarded as portions and emanations of divinity: building cities with a song, and leading brutes with a symphony; which are only metaphors for the faculty of leading multitudes by the nose.

The golden age of poetry finds its materials in the age of iron. This age begins when poetry begins to be retrospective; when something like a more extended system of civil polity is established; when personal strength and courage avail less to the aggrandizing of their possessor and to the making and marring of kings and kingdoms, and are checked by organized bodies, social institutions, and hereditary successions. Men also live more in the light of truth and within the interchange of observation; and thus perceive that the agency of gods and genii is not so frequent among themselves as, to judge from the songs and legends of the past time, it was among their ancestors. From these two circumstances, really diminished personal power, and apparently diminished familiarity with gods and genii, they very easily and naturally deduce two conclusions: 1st, That men are degenerated, and 2nd, That they are less in favor with the gods. The people of the petty states and colonies, which have now acquired stability and form, which owed their origin and first prosperity to the talents and courage of a single chief, magnify their founder through the mists of distance and tradition, and perceive him achieving wonders with a god or goddess always at his elbow. They find his name and his exploits thus magnified and accompanied in their traditionary songs, which are their only memorials. All that is said of him is in this character. There is nothing to contradict it. The man and his exploits and his tutelary deities are mixed and blended in one invariable association. The marvellous too is very much like a snowball: it grows as it rolls downward, till the little nucleus of truth which began its descent from the summit is hidden in the accumulation of superinduced hyperbole.

When tradition, thus adorned and exaggerated, has surrounded the founders of families and states with so much adventitious power and magnificence, there is no praise which a living poet can, without fear of being kicked for clumsy flattery, address to a living chief, that will not still leave the impression that the latter is not so great a man as his ancestors. The man must in this case be praised through his ancestors. Their greatness must be established, and he must be shown to be their worthy descendant. All the people of a state are interested in the founder of their state. All states that have harmonized into a common form of society, are interested in their respective founders. All men are interested in their ancestors. All men love to look back into the days that are past. In these circumstances traditional national poetry is reconstructed and brought like chaos into order and form. The interest is more universal: understanding is enlarged: passion still has scope and play: character is still various and strong: nature is still unsubdued and existing in all her beauty and magnificence, and men are not yet excluded from her observation by the magnitude of cities or the daily confinement of civic life: poetry is more an art: it requires greater skill in numbers, greater command of language, more extensive and various knowledge, and greater comprehensiveness of mind. It still exists without rivals in any other department of literature; and even the arts, painting and sculpture certainly, and music probably, are comparatively rude and imperfect. The whole field of intellect is its own. It has no rivals in history, nor in philosophy, nor in science. It is cultivated by the greatest intellects of the age, and listened to by all the rest. This is the age of Homer, the golden age of poetry. Poetry has now attained its perfection: it has attained the point which it cannot pass: genius therefore seeks new forms for the treatment of the same subjects: hence the lyric poetry of Pindar and Alcaeus, and the tragic poetry of Æschylus and Sophocles. The favor of kings, the honor of the Olympic crown, the applause of present multitudes, all that can feed vanity and stimulate rivalry, await the successful cultivator of this art, till its forms become exhausted, and new rivals arise around it in new fields of literature, which gradually acquire more influence as, with the progress of reason and civilization, facts become more interesting than fiction: indeed the maturity of poetry may be considered the infancy of history. The transition from Homer to Herodotus is scarcely more remarkable than that from Herodotus to Thucydides: in the gradual dereliction of fabulous incident and ornamented language, Herodotus is as much a poet in relation to Thucydides as Homer is in relation to Herodotus. The history of Herodotus is half a poem: it was written while the whole field of literature belonged to the Muses, and the nine books of which it was composed were therefore of right, as well as of courtesy, superinscribed with their nine names.

Speculations, too, and disputes, on the nature of man and of mind; on moral duties and on good and evil; on the animate and inanimate components of the visible world; begin to share attention with the eggs of Leda and the horns of Io, and to draw off from poetry a portion of its once undivided audience.

Then comes the silver age, or the poetry of civilized life. This poetry is of two kinds, imitative and original. The imitative consists in recasting, and giving an exquisite polish to, the poetry of the age of gold: of this Virgil is the most obvious and striking example. The original is chiefly comic, didactic, or satiric: as in Menander, Aristophanes, Horace, and Juvenal. The poetry of this age is characterized by an exquisite and fastidious selection of words, and a labored and somewhat monotonous harmony of expression: but its monotony consists in this, that experience having exhausted all the varieties of modulation, the civilized poetry selects the most beautiful, and prefers the repetition of these to ranging through the variety of all. But the best expression being that into which the idea naturally falls, it requires the utmost labor and care so to reconcile the inflexibility of civilized language and the labored polish of versification with the idea intended to be expressed, that sense may not appear to be sacrificed to sound. Hence numerous efforts and rare success.

This state of poetry is however a step towards its extinction. Feeling and passion are best painted in, and roused by, ornamental and figurative language; but the reason and the understanding are best addressed in the simplest and most unvarnished phrase. Pure reason and dispassionate truth would be perfectly ridiculous in verse, as we may judge by versifying one of Euclid's demonstrations. This will be found true of all dispassionate reasoning whatever, and all reasoning that requires comprehensive views and enlarged combinations. It is only the more tangible points of morality, those which command assent at once, those which have a mirror in every mind, and in which the severity of reason is warmed and rendered palatable by being mixed up with feeling and imagination, that are applicable even to what is called moral poetry: and as the sciences of morals and of mind advance towards perfection, as they become more enlarged and comprehensive in their views, as reason gains the ascendancy in them over imagination and feeling, poetry can no longer accompany them in their progress, but drops into the back ground, and leaves them to advance alone. Thus the empire of thought is withdrawn from poetry, as the empire of facts had been before. In respect of the latter, the poet of the age of iron celebrates the achievements of his contemporaries; the poet of the age of gold celebrates the heroes of the age of iron; the poet of the age of silver re-casts the poems of the age of gold: we may here see how very slight a ray of historical truth is sufficient to dissipate all the illusions of poetry. We know no more of the men than of the gods of the Iliad; no more of Achilles than we do of Thetis; no more of Hector and Andromache than we do of Vulcan and Venus: these belong altogether to poetry; history has no share in them: but Virgil knew better than to write an epic about Caesar; he left him to Livy; and travelled out of the confines of truth and history into the old regions of poetry and fiction.

Good sense and elegant learning, conveyed in polished and somewhat monotonous verse, are the perfection of the original and imitative poetry of civilized life. Its range is limited, and when exhausted, nothing remains but the *crambe repetita* [warmed-over cabbage] of common-place, which at length becomes thoroughly wearisome, even to the most indefatigable readers of the newest new nothings.

It is now evident that poetry must either cease to be cultivated, or strike into a new path. The poets of the age of gold have been imitated and repeated till no new imitation will attract notice: the limited range of ethical and didactic poetry is exhausted: the associations of daily life in an advanced state of society are of very dry, methodical, unpoetical matters-of-fact: but there is always a multitude of listless idlers, yawning for amusement, and gaping for novelty: and the poet makes it his glory to be foremost among their purveyors.

Then comes the age of brass, which, by rejecting the polish and the learning of the age of silver, and taking a retrograde stride to the barbarisms and crude traditions of the age of iron, professes to return to nature and revive the age of gold. This is the second childhood of poetry. To the comprehensive energy of the Homeric Muse, which, by giving at once the grand outline of things, presented to the mind a vivid picture in one or two verses, inimitable alike in simplicity and magnificence, is substituted a verbose and minutely detailed description of thoughts, passions, actions, persons, and things, in that loose rambling style of verse, which any one may write, *stans pede in uno* [standing on one foot], at the rate of two hundred lines in an hour. To this age may be referred all the poets who flourished in the decline of the Roman Empire. The best specimen of it, though not the most generally known, is the Dionysiaca of Nonnus,[2] which contains many passages of exceeding beauty in the midst of masses of amplification and repetition.

[2] Greek epic poet of Egypt, late 4th or early 5th century A.D.

The iron age of classical poetry may be called the bardic; the golden, the Homeric; the silver, the Virgilian; and the brass, the Nonnic.

Modern poetry has also its four ages: but "it wears its rue with a difference."

To the age of brass in the ancient world succeeded the dark ages, in which the light of the Gospel began to spread over Europe, and in which, by a mysterious and inscrutable dispensation, the darkness thickened with the progress of the light. The tribes that overran the Roman Empire brought back the days of barbarism, but with this difference, that there were many books in the world, many places in which they were preserved, and occasionally some one by whom they were read, who indeed (if he escaped being burned *pour l'amour de Dieu* [for the love of God],) generally lived an object of mysterious fear, with the reputation of magician, alchymist, and astrologer. The emerging of the nations of Europe from this superinduced barbarism, and their settling into new forms of polity, was accompanied, as the first ages of Greece had been, with a wild spirit of adventure, which, co-operating with new manners and new superstitions, raised up a fresh crop of chimaeras, not less fruitful, though far less beautiful, than those of Greece. The semi-deification of women by the maxims of the age of chivalry, combining with these new fables, produced the romance of the middle ages. The founders of the new line of heroes took the place of the demi-gods of Grecian poetry. Charlemagne and his Paladins, Arthur and his knights of the round table, the heroes of the iron age of chivalrous poetry, were seen through the same magnifying mist of distance, and their exploits were celebrated with even more extravagant hyperbole. These legends, combined with the ex-aggerated love that pervades the songs of the troubadours, the reputation of magic that attached to learned men, the infant wonders of natural philosophy, the crazy fanaticism of the cru-sades, the power and privileges of the great feudal chiefs, and the holy mysteries of monks and nuns, formed a state of society in which no two laymen could meet without fighting, and in which the three staple ingredients of lover, prize-fighter, and fanatic, that composed the basis of the character of every true man, were mixed up and diversified, in different individuals and

classes, with so many distinctive excellencies, and under such an
infinite motley variety of costume, as gave the range of a most
extensive and picturesque field to the two great constituents of
poetry, love and battle.

From these ingredients of the iron age of modern poetry, dis-
persed in the rhymes of minstrels and the songs of the troubadours, arose the golden age, in which the scattered materials were
harmonized and blended about the time of the revival of learning; but with this peculiar difference, that Greek and Roman
literature pervaded all the poetry of the golden age of modern
poetry, and hence resulted a heterogeneous compound of all ages
and nations in one picture; an infinite licence, which gave to the
poet the free range of the whole field of imagination and memory. This was carried very far by Ariosto, but farthest of all by
Shakespeare and his contemporaries, who used time and locality
merely because they could not do without them, because every
action must have its when and where: but they made no scruple
of deposing a Roman Emperor by an Italian Count, and sending him off in the disguise of a French pilgrim to be shot with a
blunderbuss by an English archer. This makes the old English
drama very picturesque, at any rate, in the variety of costume,
and very diversified in action and character; though it is a picture of nothing that ever was seen on earth except a Venetian
carnival.

The greatest of English poets, Milton, may be said to stand
alone between the ages of gold and silver, combining the excellencies of both; for with all the energy, and power, and freshness of the first, he united all the studied and elaborate magnificence of the second.

The silver age succeeded; beginning with Dryden, coming to
perfection with Pope, and ending with Goldsmith, Collins, and
Gray.

Cowper divested verse of its exquisite polish; he thought in
meter, but paid more attention to his thoughts than his verse.
It would be difficult to draw the boundary of prose and blank
verse between his letters and his poetry.

The silver age was the reign of authority; but authority now
began to be shaken, not only in poetry but in the whole sphere
of its dominion. The contemporaries of Gray and Cowper were

deep and elaborate thinkers. The subtle scepticism of Hume, the solemn irony of Gibbon, the daring paradoxes of Rousseau, and the biting ridicule of Voltaire, directed the energies of four extraordinary minds to shake every portion of the reign of authority. Enquiry was roused, the activity of intellect was excited, and poetry came in for its share of the general result. The changes had been rung on lovely maid and sylvan shade, summer heat and green retreat, waving trees and sighing breeze, gentle swains and amorous pains, by versifiers who took them on trust, as meaning something very soft and tender, without much caring what: but with this general activity of intellect came a necessity for even poets to appear to know something of what they professed to talk of. Thomson and Cowper looked at the trees and hills which so many ingenious gentlemen had rhymed about so long without looking at them at all, and the effect of the operation on poetry was like the discovery of a new world. Painting shared the influence, and the principles of picturesque beauty were explored by adventurous essayists with indefatigable pertinacity. The success which attended these experiments, and the pleasure which resulted from them, had the usual effect of all new enthusiasms, that of turning the heads of a few unfortunate persons, the patriarchs of the age of brass, who, mistaking the prominent novelty for the all-important totality, seem to have ratiocinated much in the following manner: "Poetical genius is the finest of all things, and we feel that we have more of it than any one ever had. The way to bring it to perfection is to cultivate poetical impressions exclusively. Poetical impressions can be received only among natural scenes: for all that is artificial is anti-poetical. Society is artificial, therefore we will live out of society. The mountains are natural, therefore we will live in the mountains. There we shall be shining models of purity and virtue, passing the whole day in the innocent and amiable occupation of going up and down hill, receiving poetical impressions, and communicating them in immortal verse to admiring generations." To some such perversion of intellect we owe that egregious confraternity of rhymesters, known by the name of the Lake Poets; who certainly did receive and communicate to the world some of the most extraordinary poetical impressions that ever were heard of, and ripened into models of public virtue, too splendid to need illustration. They wrote verses on a new principle; saw rocks and rivers in a new light; and remaining studiously ignorant of history, society, and human nature, cultivated the phantasy only at the expence of the memory and the reason; and contrived, though they had retreated from the world for the express purpose of seeing nature as she was, to see her only as she was not, converting the land they lived in into a sort of fairy-land, which they peopled with mysticisms and chimaeras. This gave what is called a new tone to poetry, and conjured up a herd of desperate imitators, who have brought the age of brass prematurely to its dotage.

The descriptive poetry of the present day has been called by its cultivators a return to nature. Nothing is more impertinent than this pretension. Poetry cannot travel out of the regions of its birth, the uncultivated lands of semi-civilized men. Mr. Wordsworth, the great leader of the returners to nature, cannot describe a scene under his own eyes without putting into it the shadow of a Danish boy or the living ghost of Lucy Gray, or some similar phantastical parturition of the moods of his own mind.

In the origin and perfection of poetry, all the associations of life were composed of poetical materials. With us it is decidedly the reverse. We know too that there are no Dryads in Hyde-park nor Naiads in the Regent's-canal. But barbaric manners and supernatural interventions are essential to poetry. Either in the scene, or in the time, or in both, it must be remote from our ordinary perceptions. While the historian and the philosopher are advancing in, and accelerating, the progress of knowledge, the poet is wallowing in the rubbish of departed ignorance, and raking up the ashes of dead savages to find gewgaws and rattles for the grown babies of the age. Mr. Scott digs up the poachers and cattle-stealers of the ancient border. Lord Byron cruises for thieves and pirates on the shores of the Morea and among the Greek Islands. Mr. Southey wades through ponderous volumes of travels and old chronicles, from which he carefully selects all that is false, useless, and absurd, as being essentially poetical; and when he has a commonplace book full of monstrosities, strings them into an epic. Mr. Wordsworth picks up village legends from old women and sextons; and Mr. Coleridge, to the valuable information acquired from similar sources, superadds the dreams of crazy theologians and the mysticisms of German metaphysics, and favors the world with visions in verse, in which the quadruple elements of sexton, old woman, Jeremy Taylor, and Emanuel Kant, are harmonized into a delicious poetical compound. Mr. Moore presents us with a Persian, and Mr. Campbell with a Pennsylvanian tale, both formed on the same principle as Mr. Southey's epics, by extracting from a perfunctory and desultory perusal of a collection of voyages and travels, all that useful investigation would not seek for and that common sense would reject.

These disjointed relics of tradition and fragments of second-hand observation, being woven into a tissue of verse, constructed on what Mr. Coleridge calls a new principle (that is, no principle at all), compose a modern-antique compound of frippery and barbarism, in which the puling sentimentality of the present time is grafted on the misrepresented ruggedness of the past into a heterogeneous congeries of unamalgamating manners, sufficient to impose on the common readers of poetry, over whose understanding the poet of this class possesses that commanding advantage, which, in all circumstances and conditions of life, a man who knows something, however little, always possesses over one who knows nothing.

A poet in our times is a semi-barbarian in a civilized community. He lives in the days that are past. His ideas, thoughts, feelings, associations, are all with barbarous manners, obsolete customs, and exploded superstitions. The march of his intellect is like that of a crab, backward. The brighter the light diffused around him by the progress of reason, the thicker is the darkness of antiquated barbarism, in which he buries himself like a mole, to throw up the barren hillocks of his Cimmerian labors. The philosophic mental tranquillity which looks round with an equal eye on all external things, collects a store of ideas, discriminates their relative value, assigns to all their proper place, and from the materials of useful knowledge thus collected, appreciated, and arranged, forms new combinations that impress the stamp of their power and utility on the real business of life, is diametrically the reverse of that frame of mind which poetry inspires, or from which poetry can emanate. The highest inspirations of poetry are resolvable into three ingredients: the rant of unregu-

lated passion, the whining of exaggerated feeling, and the cant
of factitious sentiment: and can therefore serve only to ripen
a splendid lunatic like Alexander, a puling driveller like Werter,[3]
or a morbid dreamer like Wordsworth. It can never make a
philosopher, nor a statesman, nor in any class of life an useful or
rational man. It cannot claim the slightest share in any one of
the comforts and utilities of life of which we have witnessed so
many and so rapid advances. But though not useful, it may be
said it is highly ornamental, and deserves to be cultivated for
the pleasure it yields. Even if this be granted, it does not follow
that a writer of poetry in the present state of society is not a
waster of his own time, and a robber of that of others. Poetry
is not one of those arts which, like painting, require repetition
and multiplication, in order to be diffused among society. There
are more good poems already existing than are sufficient to employ that portion of life which any mere reader and recipient
of poetical impressions should devote to them, and these having
been produced in poetical times, are far superior in all the characteristics of poetry to the artificial reconstructions of a few
morbid ascetics in unpoetical times. To read the promiscuous
rubbish of the present time to the exclusion of the select treasures of the past, is to substitute the worse for the better variety
of the same mode of enjoyment.

But in whatever degree poetry is cultivated, it must necessarily be to the neglect of some branch of useful study: and it is
a lamentable spectacle to see minds, capable of better things,
running to seed in the specious indolence of these empty aim-
less mockeries of intellectual exertion. Poetry was the mental
rattle that awakened the attention of intellect in the infancy of
civil society: but for the maturity of mind to make a serious
business of the playthings of its childhood, is as absurd as for
a full-grown man to rub his gums with coral, and cry to be
charmed to sleep by the jingle of silver bells.

As to that small portion of our contemporary poetry, which is
neither descriptive, nor narrative, nor dramatic, and which, for
want of a better name, may be called ethical, the most distinguished portion of it, consisting merely of querulous, egotistical

---

[3] Werther, the morbidly sentimental hero of Goethe's *The Sorrows of
Werther* (1774).

rhapsodies, to express the writer's high dissatisfaction with the world and every thing in it, serves only to confirm what has been said of the semi-barbarous character of poets, who from singing dithyrambics and "Io Triumphe," while society was savage, grow rabid, and out of their element, as it becomes polished and enlightened.

Now when we consider that it is not to the thinking and studious, and scientific and philosophical part of the community, not to those whose minds are bent on the pursuit and promotion of permanently useful ends and aims, that poets must address their minstrelsy, but to that much larger portion of the reading public, whose minds are not awakened to the desire of valuable knowledge, and who are indifferent to any thing beyond being charmed, moved, excited, affected, and exalted: charmed by harmony, moved by sentiment, excited by passion, affected by pathos, and exalted by sublimity: harmony, which is language on the rack of Procrustes; sentiment, which is canting egotism in the mask of refined feeling; passion, which is the commotion of a weak and selfish mind; pathos, which is the whining of an unmanly spirit; and sublimity, which is the inflation of an empty head: when we consider that the great and permanent interests of human society become more and more the main spring of intellectual pursuit; that in proportion as they become so, the subordinacy of the ornamental to the useful will be more and more seen and acknowledged; and that therefore the progress of useful art and science, and of moral and political knowledge, will continue more and more to withdraw attention from frivolous and unconducive, to solid and conducive studies: that therefore the poetical audience will not only continually diminish in the proportion of its number to that of the rest of the reading public, but will also sink lower and lower in the comparison of intellectual acquirement: when we consider that the poet must still please his audience, and must therefore continue to sink to their level, while the rest of the community is rising above it: we may easily conceive that the day is not distant, when the degraded state of every species of poetry will be as generally recognized as that of dramatic poetry has long been: and this not from any decrease either of intellectual power, or intellectual acquisition, but because intellectual power and intellectual acquisition have turned themselves into other and better channels, and have abandoned the cultivation and the fate of poetry to the degenerate fry of modern rhymesters, and their olympic judges, the magazine critics, who continue to debate and promulgate oracles about poetry, as if it were still what it was in the Homeric age, the all-in-all of intellectual progression, and as if there were no such things in existence as mathematicians, astronomers, chemists, moralists, metaphysicians, historians, politicians, and political economists, who have built into the upper air of intelligence a pyramid, from the summit of which they see the modern Parnassus far beneath them, and, knowing how small a place it occupies in the comprehensiveness of their prospect, smile at the little ambition and the circumscribed perceptions with which the drivellers and mountebanks upon it are contending for the poetical palm and the critical chair.

Percy Bysshe Shelley

[1792–1822]

❦

SHELLEY, THE ELDEST SON of Sir Timothy Shelley, Bart., was educated at Eton and at Oxford, from which he was expelled for writing a pamphlet on *The Necessity of Atheism*. The radicalism of his ideas and the turmoil of his private life made it difficult for him to remain in England, and in 1818 he left his home to live the rest of his life on the Continent. He was drowned while sailing off the Italian coast.

Shelley's *Defence* was written as a rebuttal to Peacock's *Four Ages of Poetry* (see above, pp. 144 to 158), and takes its form in part from the arguments which Shelley was opposing. Thus the first part of the essay argues for an innate poetic faculty in man, and the second for the historical effects of poetry upon society, because Peacock had treated poetry as a primitive practice of declining value and social utility. In the final pages Shelley abandons argument altogether, and ends his essay with an emotional testament of his faith in his art.

Of the Romantic poets, Shelley was the most influenced by Platonism, as both his poetry and this essay demonstrate. He regarded the word *poetry* as including all forms of order and of beauty—all works of man, that is, which bring him into touch with "the eternal, the infinite, and the one." Such a definition obviously eliminates formal distinctions altogether (as Romantic theory tends to do); it also encourages an "inspirational" theory of poetic creation, since a poet cannot reason himself into contact with the infinite. But most of all it glorifies poetry, making it co-extensive with everything that is most valuable, and most real, in human experience. The poet perceives the universal laws of order and beauty, and transmits his perceptions to his fellow men; it is in this sense of law-giver that he is the "unacknowledged legislator of mankind."

Because the poet apprehends "the true and the beautiful, in a word, the good," his utterances are by definition moral. One of Shelley's most interesting arguments is his attempt to defend the morality of poetry while distinguishing its moral function from ethics. The Horatian "instruction and delight," which had been good enough for most of the

eighteenth-century, was too rational and didactic a formulation for
Shelley; he chose instead to make the moral operation of poetry psychological, a kind of process which creates new materials of knowledge,
power, and pleasure, and at the same time "engenders in the mind a
desire to reproduce and arrange them according to a certain rhythm
and order which may be called the beautiful and the good." The
formative, creative power which this argument ascribes to poetry is
greater than any critic had previously asserted: Shelley is by far the
most grandiloquent of poetry's defenders.

BIBLIOGRAPHY. *Complete Works,* ed. H. Buxton Forman, 8 vols. (London, 1880); *Literary and Philosophical Criticism,* ed. John Shawcross
(London, 1909).

    David Lee Clark, ed. *Shelley's Prose; or, The Trumpet of a Prophecy*
(Albuquerque, 1954); Carl H. Grabo, *The Magic Plant* (Chapel Hill,
1936); Melvin T. Solve, *Shelley: His Theory of Poetry* (Chicago,
1927).

TEXT. *Works,* ed. Forman, vol. 7.

A DEFENCE OF POETRY *

[1821]

ACCORDING TO ONE MODE of regarding those two classes of mental
action, which are called reason and imagination, the former may
be considered as mind contemplating the relations borne by one
thought to another, however produced; and the latter, as mind
acting upon those thoughts so as to colour them with its own
light, and composing from them, as from elements, other
thoughts, each containing within itself the principle of its own
integrity. The one is the τὸ ποιεῖν, or the principle of synthesis,
and has for its objects those forms which are common to universal
nature and existence itself; the other is the τὸ λογίζειν, or principle of analysis, and its action regards the relations of things,
simply as relations; considering thoughts, not in their integral
unity, but as the algebraical representations which conduct to

* This *Defence* was not published until 1840.

certain general results. Reason is the enumeration of quantities already known; imagination is the perception of the value of those quantities, both separately and as a whole. Reason respects the differences, and imagination the similitudes of things. Reason is to the imagination as the instrument to the agent, as the body to the spirit, as the shadow to the substance.

Poetry, in a general sense, may be defined to be 'the expression of the imagination': and poetry is connate with the origin of man. Man is an instrument over which a series of external and internal impressions are driven, like the alternations of an ever-changing wind over an Aeolian lyre, which move it by their motion to ever-changing melody. But there is a principle within the human being, and perhaps within all sentient beings, which acts otherwise than in the lyre, and produces not melody alone, but harmony, by an internal adjustment of the sounds or motions thus excited to the impressions which excite them. It is as if the lyre could accommodate its chords to the motions of that which strikes them, in a determined proportion of sound; even as the musician can accommodate his voice to the sound of the lyre. A child at play by itself will express its delight by its voice and motions; and every inflexion of tone and every gesture will bear exact relation to a corresponding antitype in the pleasurable impressions which awakened it; it will be the reflected image of that impression; and as the lyre trembles and sounds after the wind has died away, so the child seeks, by prolonging in its voice and motions the duration of the effect, to prolong also a consciousness of the cause. In relation to the objects which delight a child, these expressions are, what poetry is to higher objects. The savage (for the savage is to ages what the child is to years) expresses the emotions produced in him by surrounding objects in a similar manner; and language and gesture, together with plastic or pictorial imitation, become the image of the combined effect of those objects, and of his apprehension of them. Man in society, with all his passions and his pleasures, next becomes the object of the passions and pleasures of man; an additional class of emotions produces an augmented treasure of expressions; and language, gesture, and the imitative arts, become at once the representation and the medium, the pencil and the picture, the chisel and the statue, the chord and the harmony.

The social sympathies, or those laws from which, as from its elements, society results, begin to develop themselves from the moment that two human beings coexist; the future is contained within the present, as the plant within the seed; and equality, diversity, unity, contrast, mutual dependence, become the principles alone capable of affording the motives according to which the will of a social being is determined to action, inasmuch as he is social; and constitute pleasure in sensation, virtue in sentiment, beauty in art, truth in reasoning, and love in the intercourse of kind. Hence men, even in the infancy of society, observe a certain order in their words and actions, distinct from that of the objects and the impressions represented by them, all expression being subject to the laws of that from which it proceeds. But let us dismiss those more general considerations which might involve an inquiry into the principles of society itself, and restrict our view to the manner in which the imagination is expressed upon its forms.

In the youth of the world, men dance and sing and imitate natural objects, observing in these actions, as in all others, a certain rhythm or order. And, although all men observe a similar, they observe not the same order, in the motions of the dance, in the melody of the song, in the combinations of language, in the series of their imitations of natural objects. For there is a certain order or rhythm belonging to each of these classes of mimetic representation, from which the hearer and the spectator receive an intenser and purer pleasure than from any other: the sense of an approximation to this order has been called taste by modern writers. Every man in the infancy of art observes an order which approximates more or less closely to that from which this highest delight results: but the diversity is not sufficiently marked, as that its gradations should be sensible, except in those instances where the predominance of this faculty of approximation to the beautiful (for so we may be permitted to name the relation between this highest pleasure and its cause) is very great. Those in whom it exists in excess are poets, in the most universal sense of the word; and the pleasure resulting from the manner in which they express the influence of society or nature upon their own minds, communicates itself to others, and gathers a sort of reduplication from that community. Their language is vitally metaphorical; that is, it marks the before unapprehended relations of things and perpetuates their apprehension, until the words which represent them become, through time, signs for portions or classes of thoughts instead of pictures of integral thoughts; and then if no new poets should arise to create afresh the associations which have been thus disorganized, language will be dead to all the nobler purposes of human intercourse. These similitudes or relations are finely said by Lord Bacon to be 'the same footsteps of nature impressed upon the various subjects of the world'; [1] and he considers the faculty which perceives them as the storehouse of axioms common to all knowledge. In the infancy of society every author is necessarily a poet, because language itself is poetry; and to be a poet is to apprehend the true and the beautiful, in a word, the good which exists in the relation, subsisting, first between existence and perception, and secondly between perception and expression. Every original language near to its source is in itself the chaos of a cyclic poem: the copiousness of lexicography and the distinctions of grammar are the works of a later age, and are merely the catalogue and the form of the creations of poetry.

But poets, or those who imagine and express this indestructible order, are not only the authors of language and of music, of the dance, and architecture, and statuary, and painting; they are the institutors of laws, and the founders of civil society, and the inventors of the arts of life, and the teachers, who draw into a certain propinquity with the beautiful and the true, that partial apprehension of the agencies of the invisible world which is called religion. Hence all original religions are allegorical, or susceptible of allegory, and, like Janus, have a double face of false and true. Poets, according to the circumstances of the age and nation in which they appeared, were called, in the earlier epochs of the world, legislators, or prophets: a poet essentially comprises and unites both these characters. For he not only beholds intensely the present as it is, and discovers those laws according to which present things ought to be ordered, but he beholds the future in the present, and his thoughts are the germs of the flower and the fruit of latest time. Not that I assert poets

---

[1] *De Augment. Scient.* cap. i, lib. iii. [Shelley's note.]

to be prophets in the gross sense of the word, or that they can
foretell the form as surely as they foreknow the spirit of events:
such is the pretence of superstition, which would make poetry
an attribute of prophecy, rather than prophecy an attribute of
poetry. A poet participates in the eternal, the infinite, and the
one; as far as relates to his conceptions, time and place and
number are not. The grammatical forms which express the moods
of time, and the difference of persons, and the distinction of
place, are convertible with respect to the highest poetry without
injuring it as poetry; and the choruses of Aeschylus, and the
book of Job, and Dante's Paradise, would afford, more than
any other writings, examples of this fact, if the limits of this
essay did not forbid citation. The creations of sculpture, painting,
and music, are illustrations still more decisive.

Language, colour, form, and religious and civil habits of
action, are all the instruments and materials of poetry; they may
be called poetry by that figure of speech which considers the
effect as a synonym of the cause. But poetry in a more restricted
sense expresses those arrangements of language, and especially
metrical language, which are created by that imperial faculty,
whose throne is curtained within the invisible nature of man.
And this springs from the nature itself of language, which is a
more direct representation of the actions and passions of our
internal being, and is susceptible of more various and delicate
combinations, than colour, form, or motion, and is more plastic
and obedient to the control of that faculty of which it is the
creation. For language is arbitrarily produced by the imagination,
and has relation to thoughts alone; but all other materials, instruments, and conditions of art, have relations among each
other, which limit and interpose between conception and expression. The former is as a mirror which reflects, the latter as a
cloud which enfeebles, the light of which both are mediums of
communications. Hence the fame of sculptors, painters, and
musicians, although the intrinsic powers of the great masters of
these arts may yield in no degree to that of those who have
employed language as the hieroglyphic of their thoughts, has
never equalled that of poets in the restricted sense of the term;
as two performers of equal skill will produce unequal effects
from a guitar and a harp. The fame of legislators and founders

of religions, so long as their institutions last, alone seems to exceed that of poets in the restricted sense; but it can scarcely be a question, whether, if we deduct the celebrity which their flattery of the gross opinions of the vulgar usually conciliates, together with that which belonged to them in their higher character of poets, any excess will remain.

We have thus circumscribed the word poetry within the limits of that art which is the most familiar and the most perfect expression of the faculty itself. It is necessary, however, to make the circle still narrower, and to determine the distinction between measured and unmeasured language; for the popular division into prose and verse is inadmissible in accurate philosophy.

Sounds as well as thoughts have relation both between each other and towards that which they represent, and a perception of the order of those relations has always been found connected with a perception of the order of the relations of thoughts. Hence the language of poets has ever affected a certain uniform and harmonious recurrence of sound, without which it were not poetry, and which is scarcely less indispensable to the communication of its influence, than the words themselves, without reference to that peculiar order. Hence the vanity of translation; it were as wise to cast a violet into a crucible that you might discover the formal principle of its colour and odour, as seek to transfuse from one language into another the creations of a poet. The plant must spring again from its seed, or it will bear no flower—and this is the burthen of the curse of Babel.

An observation of the regular mode of the recurrence of harmony in the language of poetical minds, together with its relation to music, produced metre, or a certain system of traditional forms of harmony and language. Yet it is by no means essential that a poet should accommodate his language to this traditional form, so that the harmony, which is its spirit, be observed. The practice is indeed convenient and popular, and to be preferred, especially in such composition as includes much action: but every great poet must inevitably innovate upon the example of his predecessors in the exact structure of his peculiar versification. The distinction between poets and prose writers is a vulgar error. The distinction between philosophers and poets has been anticipated. Plato was essentially a poet—the truth and splendour of his imagery, and the melody of his language, are the most intense that it is possible to conceive. He rejected the harmony of the epic, dramatic, and lyrical forms, because he sought to kindle a harmony in thoughts divested of shape and action, and he forbore to invent any regular plan of rhythm which would include, under determinate forms, the varied pauses of his style. Cicero sought to imitate the cadence of his periods, but with little success. Lord Bacon was a poet.[2] His language has a sweet and majestic rhythm, which satisfies the sense, no less than the almost superhuman wisdom of his philosophy satisfies the intellect; it is a strain which distends, and then bursts the circumference of the reader's mind, and pours itself forth together with it into the universal element with which it has perpetual sympathy. All the authors of revolutions in opinion are not only necessarily poets as they are inventors, nor even as their words unveil the permanent analogy of things by images which participate in the life of truth; but as their periods are harmonious and rhythmical, and contain in themselves the elements of verse; being the echo of the eternal music. Nor are those supreme poets, who have employed traditional forms of rhythm on account of the form and action of their subjects, less capable of perceiving and teaching the truth of things, than those who have omitted that form. Shakespeare, Dante, and Milton (to confine ourselves to modern writers) are philosophers of the very loftiest power.

A poem is the very image of life expressed in its eternal truth. There is this difference between a story and a poem, that a story is a catalogue of detached facts, which have no other connexion than time, place, circumstance, cause and effect; the other is the creation of actions according to the unchangeable forms of human nature, as existing in the mind of the creator, which is itself the image of all other minds. The one is partial, and applies only to a definite period of time, and a certain combination of events which can never again recur; the other is universal, and contains within itself the germ of a relation to whatever motives or actions have place in the possible varieties of human nature. Time, which destroys the beauty and the use of the story of

---

[2] See the *Filum Labyrinthi*, and the Essay on Death particularly. [Shelley.]

particular facts, stripped of the poetry which should invest them, augments that of poetry, and for ever develops new and wonderful applications of the eternal truth which it contains. Hence epitomes have been called the moths of just history; they eat out the poetry of it. A story of particular facts is as a mirror which obscures and distorts that which should be beautiful: poetry is a mirror which makes beautiful that which is distorted.

The parts of a composition may be poetical, without the composition as a whole being a poem. A single sentence may be considered as a whole, though it may be found in the midst of a series of unassimilated portions; a single word even may be a spark of inextinguishable thought. And thus all the great historians, Herodotus, Plutarch, Livy, were poets; and although the plan of these writers, especially that of Livy, restrained them from developing this faculty in its highest degree, they made copious and ample amends for their subjection, by filling all the interstices of their subjects with living images.

Having determined what is poetry, and who are poets, let us proceed to estimate its effects upon society.

Poetry is ever accompanied with pleasure: all spirits on which it falls open themselves to receive the wisdom which is mingled with its delight. In the infancy of the world, neither poets themselves nor their auditors are fully aware of the excellence of poetry: for it acts in a divine and unapprehended manner, beyond and above consciousness; and it is reserved for future generations to contemplate and measure the mighty cause and effect in all the strength and splendour of their union. Even in modern times, no living poet ever arrived at the fullness of his fame; the jury which sits in judgment upon a poet, belonging as he does to all time, must be composed of his peers: it must be impanelled by Time from the selectest of the wise of many generations. A poet is a nightingale, who sits in darkness and sings to cheer its own solitude with sweet sounds; his auditors are as men entranced by the melody of an unseen musician, who feel that they are moved and softened, yet know not whence or why. The poems of Homer and his contemporaries were the delight of infant Greece; they were the elements of that social system which is the column upon which all succeeding civilization has reposed. Homer embodied the ideal perfection of his

age in human character; nor can we doubt that those who read
his verses were awakened to an ambition of becoming like to
Achilles, Hector, and Ulysses: the truth and beauty of friendship,
patriotism, and persevering devotion to an object, were unveiled
to the depths in these immortal creations: the sentiments of the
auditors must have been refined and enlarged by a sympathy
with such great and lovely impersonations, until from admiring
they imitated, and from imitation they identified themselves with
the objects of their admiration. Nor let it be objected, that these
characters are remote from moral perfection, and that they are
by no means to be considered as edifying patterns for general imitation. Every epoch, under names more or less specious, has
deified its peculiar errors; Revenge is the naked idol of the worship of a semi-barbarous age; and Self-deceit is the veiled image
of unknown evil, before which luxury and satiety lie prostrate.
But a poet considers the vices of his contemporaries as a temporary dress in which his creations must be arrayed, and which
cover without concealing the eternal proportions of their beauty.
An epic or dramatic personage is understood to wear them
around his soul, as he may the ancient armour or the modern
uniform around his body; whilst it is easy to conceive a dress
more graceful than either. The beauty of the internal nature
cannot be so far concealed by its accidental vesture, but that the
spirit of its form shall communicate itself to the very disguise,
and indicate the shape it hides from the manner in which it is
worn. A majestic form and graceful motions will express themselves through the most barbarous and tasteless costume. Few
poets of the highest class have chosen to exhibit the beauty of
their conceptions in its naked truth and splendour; and it is
doubtful whether the alloy of costume, habit, &c., be not necessary to temper this planetary music for mortal ears.

The whole objection, however, of the immorality of poetry
rests upon a misconception of the manner in which poetry acts
to produce the moral improvement of man. Ethical science ar-
ranges the elements which poetry has created, and propounds
schemes and proposes examples of civil and domestic life: nor is
it for want of admirable doctrines that men hate, and despise,
and censure, and deceive, and subjugate one another. But poetry
acts in another and diviner manner. It awakens and enlarges the

mind itself by rendering it the receptacle of a thousand unapprehended combinations of thought. Poetry lifts the veil from the hidden beauty of the world, and makes familiar objects be as if they were not familiar; it reproduces all that it represents, and the impersonations clothed in its Elysian light stand thenceforward in the minds of those who have once contemplated them as memorials of that gentle and exalted content which extends itself over all thoughts and actions with which it coexists. The great secret of morals is love; or a going out of our own nature, and an identification of ourselves with the beautiful which exists in thought, action, or person, not our own. A man, to be greatly good, must imagine intensely and comprehensively; he must put himself in the place of another and of many others; the pains and pleasures of his species must become his own. The great instrument of moral good is the imagination; and poetry administers to the effect by acting upon the cause. Poetry enlarges the circumference of the imagination by replenishing it with thoughts of ever new delight, which have the power of attracting and assimilating to their own nature all other thoughts, and which form new intervals and interstices whose void for ever craves fresh food. Poetry strengthens the faculty which is the organ of the moral nature of man, in the same manner as exercise strengthens a limb. A poet therefore would do ill to embody his own conceptions of right and wrong, which are usually those of his place and time, in his poetical creations, which participate in neither. By this assumption of the inferior office of interpreting the effect, in which perhaps after all he might acquit himself but imperfectly, he would resign a glory in a participation in the cause. There was little danger that Homer, or any of the eternal poets, should have so far misunderstood themselves as to have abdicated this throne of their widest dominion. Those in whom the poetical faculty, though great, is less intense, as Euripides, Lucan, Tasso, Spenser, have frequently affected a moral aim, and the effect of their poetry is diminished in exact proportion to the degree in which they compel us to advert to this purpose.

Homer and the cyclic poets were followed at a certain interval by the dramatic and lyrical poets of Athens, who flourished contemporaneously with all that is most perfect in the kindred expressions of the poetical faculty; architecture, painting, music, the dance, sculpture, philosophy, and, we may add, the forms of civil life. For although the scheme of Athenian society was deformed by many imperfections which the poetry existing in chivalry and Christianity has erased from the habits and institutions of modern Europe; yet never at any other period has so much energy, beauty, and virtue, been developed; never was blind strength and stubborn form so disciplined and rendered subject to the will of man, or that will less repugnant to the dictates of the beautiful and the true, as during the century which preceded the death of Socrates. Of no other epoch in the history of our species have we records and fragments stamped so visibly with the image of the divinity in man. But it is poetry alone, in form, in action, and in language, which has rendered this epoch memorable above all others, and the storehouse of examples to everlasting time. For written poetry existed at that epoch simultaneously with the other arts, and it is an idle inquiry to demand which gave and which received the light, which all, as from a common focus, have scattered over the darkest periods of succeeding time. We know no more of cause and effect than a constant conjunction of events: poetry is ever found to coexist with whatever other arts contribute to the happiness and perfection of man. I appeal to what has already been established to distinguish between the cause and the effect.

It was at the period here adverted to, that the drama had its birth; and however a succeeding writer may have equalled or surpassed those few great specimens of the Athenian drama which have been preserved to us, it is indisputable that the art itself never was understood or practised according to the true philosophy of it, as at Athens. For the Athenians employed language, action, music, painting, the dance, and religious institutions, to produce a common effect in the representation of the highest idealisms of passion and of power; each division in the art was made perfect in its kind by artists of the most consummate skill, and was disciplined into a beautiful proportion and unity one towards the other. On the modern stage a few only of the elements capable of expressing the image of the poet's conception are employed at once. We have tragedy without music and dancing; and music and dancing without the highest impersonations of which they are the fit accompaniment, and both

without religion and solemnity. Religious institution has indeed
been usually banished from the stage. Our system of divesting
the actor's face of a mask, on which the many expressions appropriated to his dramatic character might be moulded into one permanent and unchanging expression, is favourable only to a partial
and inharmonious effect; it is fit for nothing but a monologue,
where all the attention may be directed to some great master of
ideal mimicry. The modern practice of blending comedy with
tragedy, though liable to great abuse in point of practice, is undoubtedly an extension of the dramatic circle; but the comedy
should be as in King Lear, universal, ideal, and sublime. It is perhaps the intervention of this principle which determines the
balance in favour of King Lear against the Oedipus Tyrannus or
the Agamemnon; or, if you will, the trilogies with which they are
connected; unless the intense power of the choral poetry, especially that of the latter, should be considered as restoring the
equilibrium. King Lear, if it can sustain this comparison, may be
judged to be the most perfect specimen of the dramatic art existing in the world; in spite of the narrow conditions to which the
poet was subjected by the ignorance of the philosophy of the
drama which has prevailed in modern Europe. Calderon,[3] in his
religious Autos, has attempted to fulfill some of the high conditions of dramatic representation neglected by Shakespeare; such
as the establishing a relation between the drama and religion,
and the accommodating them to music and dancing; but he
omits the observation of conditions still more important, and more
is lost than gained by the substitution of the rigidly-defined and
ever-repeated idealisms of a distorted superstition for the living
impersonations of the truth of human passion.

But I digress.—The connexion of scenic exhibitions with the
improvement or corruption of the manners of men, has been universally recognized: in other words, the presence or absence of
poetry in its most perfect and universal form, has been found to
be connected with good and evil in conduct or habit. The corruption which has been imputed to the drama as an effect, begins,
when the poetry employed in its constitution ends: I appeal to

---

[3] Pedro Calderon de la Barca (1600–1681), Spanish dramatist and poet.
Shelley wrote of Calderon that he "excels all modern dramatists, with the
exception of Shakespeare."

the history of manners whether the periods of the growth of the one and the decline of the other have not corresponded with an exactness equal to any example of moral cause and effect.

The drama at Athens, or wheresoever else it may have approached to its perfection, ever co-existed with the moral and intellectual greatness of the age. The tragedies of the Athenian poets are as mirrors in which the spectator beholds himself, under a thin disguise of circumstance, stript of all but that ideal perfection and energy which every one feels to be the internal type of all that he loves, admires, and would become. The imagination is enlarged by a sympathy with pains and passions so mighty, that they distend in their conception the capacity of that by which they are conceived; the good affections are strengthened by pity, indignation, terror, and sorrow; and an exalted calm is prolonged from the satiety of this high exercise of them into the tumult of familiar life: even crime is disarmed of half its horror and all its contagion by being represented as the fatal consequence of the unfathomable agencies of nature; error is thus divested of its wilfulness; men can no longer cherish it as the creation of their choice. In a drama of the highest order there is little food for censure or hatred; it teaches rather self-knowledge and self-respect. Neither the eye nor the mind can see itself, unless reflected upon that which it resembles. The drama, so long as it continues to express poetry, is as a prismatic and many-sided mirror, which collects the brightest rays of human nature and divides and reproduces them from the simplicity of their elementary forms, and touches them with majesty and beauty, and multiplies all that it reflects, and endows it with the power of propagating its like wherever it may fall.

But in periods of the decay of social life, the drama sympathizes with that decay. Tragedy becomes a cold imitation of the forms of the great masterpieces of antiquity, divested of all harmonious accompaniment of the kindred arts; and often the very form misunderstood, or a weak attempt to teach certain doctrines, which the writer considers as moral truths; and which are usually no more than specious flatteries of some gross vice or weakness, with which the author, in common with his auditors, are infected. Hence what has been called the classical and domestic drama. Addison's "Cato" is a specimen of the one; and would it were not superfluous to cite examples of the other! To such purposes poetry cannot be made subservient. Poetry is a sword of lightning, ever unsheathed, which consumes the scabbard that would contain it. And thus we observe that all dramatic writings of this nature are unimaginative in a singular degree; they affect sentiment and passion, which, divested of imagination, are other names for caprice and appetite. The period in our own history of the grossest degradation of the drama is the reign of Charles II, when all forms in which poetry had been accustomed to be expressed became hymns to the triumph of kingly power over liberty and virtue. Milton stood alone illuminating an age unworthy of him. At such periods the calculating principle pervades all the forms of dramatic exhibition, and poetry ceases to be expressed upon them. Comedy loses its ideal universality; wit succeeds to humour; we laugh from self-complacency and triumph, instead of pleasure; malignity, sarcasm, and contempt, succeed to sympathetic merriment; we hardly laugh, but we smile. Obscenity, which is ever blasphemy against the divine beauty in life, becomes, from the very veil which it assumes, more active if less disgusting: it is a monster for which the corruption of society for ever brings forth new food, which it devours in secret.

The drama being that form under which a greater number of modes of expression of poetry are susceptible of being combined than any other, the connexion of poetry and social good is more observable in the drama than in whatever other form. And it is indisputable that the highest perfection of human society has ever corresponded with the highest dramatic excellence; and that the corruption or the extinction of the drama in a nation where it has once flourished, is a mark of a corruption of manners, and an extinction of the energies which sustain the soul of social life. But, as Machiavelli says of political institutions, that life may be preserved and renewed, if men should arise capable of bringing back the drama to its principles. And this is true with respect to poetry in its most extended sense: all language, institution and form, require not only to be produced but to be sustained: the office and character of a poet participates in the divine nature as regards providence, no less than as regards creation.

Civil war, the spoils of Asia, and the fatal predominance first

of the Macedonian, and then of the Roman arms, were so many
symbols of the extinction or suspension of the creative faculty in
Greece. The bucolic writers, who found patronage under the let-
tered tyrants of Sicily and Egypt, were the latest representatives
of its most glorious reign. Their poetry is intensely melodious;
like the odour of the tuberose, it overcomes and sickens the spirit
with excess of sweetness; whilst the poetry of the preceding age
was as a meadow-gale of June, which mingles the fragrance of
all the flowers of the field, and adds a quickening and harmonizing spirit of its own, which endows the sense with a power of
sustaining its extreme delight. The bucolic and erotic delicacy in
written poetry is correlative with that softness in statuary, music,
and the kindred arts, and even in manners and institutions, which
distinguished the epoch to which I now refer. Nor is it the
poetical faculty itself, or any misapplication of it, to which this
want of harmony is to be imputed. An equal sensibility to the influence of the senses and the affections is to be found in the
writings of Homer and Sophocles: the former, especially, has
clothed sensual and pathetic images with irresistible attractions.
Their superiority over these succeeding writers consists in the
presence of those thoughts which belong to the inner faculties of
our nature, not in the absence of those which are connected with
the external: their incomparable perfection consists in a harmony
of the union of all. It is not what the erotic poets have, but what
they have not, in which their imperfection consists. It is not inasmuch as they were poets, but inasmuch as they were not poets,
that they can be considered with any plausibility as connected
with the corruption of their age. Had that corruption availed so
as to extinguish in them the sensibility to pleasure, passion, and
natural scenery, which is imputed to them as an imperfection,
the last triumph of evil would have been achieved. For the end
of social corruption is to destroy all sensibility to pleasure; and
therefore it is corruption. It begins at the imagination and the
intellect as at the core, and distributes itself thence as a paralysing
venom, through the affections into the very appetites, until all
become a torpid mass in which hardly sense survives. At the approach of such a period, poetry ever addresses itself to those
faculties which are the last to be destroyed, and its voice is heard,
like the footsteps of Astraea, departing from the world. Poetry

ever communicates all the pleasure which men are capable of receiving: it is ever still the light of life; the source of whatever of beautiful or generous or true can have place in an evil time. It will readily be confessed that those among the luxurious citizens of Syracuse and Alexandria, who were delighted with the poems of Theocritus, were less cold, cruel, and sensual than the remnant of their tribe. But corruption must utterly have destroyed the fabric of human society before poetry can ever cease. The sacred links of that chain have never been entirely disjoined, which descending through the minds of many men is attached to those great minds, whence as from a magnet the invisible effluence is sent forth, which at once connects, animates, and sustains the life of all. It is the faculty which contains within itself the seeds at once of its own and of social renovation. And let us not circumscribe the effects of the bucolic and erotic poetry within the limits of the sensibility of those to whom it was addressed. They may have perceived the beauty of those immortal compositions, simply as fragments and isolated portions: those who are more finely organized, or born in a happier age, may recognize them as episodes to that great poem, which all poets, like the co-operating thoughts of one great mind, have built up since the beginning of the world.

The same revolutions within a narrower sphere had place in ancient Rome; but the actions and forms of its social life never seem to have been perfectly saturated with the poetical element. The Romans appear to have considered the Greeks as the selectest treasuries of the selectest forms of manners and of nature, and to have abstained from creating in measured language, sculpture, music, or architecture, anything which might bear a particular relation to their own condition, whilst it should bear a general one to the universal constitution of the world. But we judge from partial evidence, and we judge perhaps partially. Ennius, Varro, Pacuvius, and Accius, all great poets, have been lost. Lucretius is in the highest, and Virgil in a very high sense, a creator. The chosen delicacy of expressions of the latter, are as a mist of light which conceal from us the intense and exceeding truth of his conceptions of nature. Livy is instinct with poetry. Yet Horace, Catullus, Ovid, and generally the other great writers of the Virgilian age, saw man and nature in the mirror of Greece.

The institutions also, and the religion, of Rome were less poetical than those of Greece, as the shadow is less vivid than the substance. Hence poetry in Rome, seemed to follow, rather than accompany, the perfection of political and domestic society. The true poetry of Rome lived in its institutions; for whatever of beautiful, true, and majestic, they contained, could have sprung only from the faculty which creates the order in which they consist. The life of Camillus, the death of Regulus; the expectation of the senators, in their godlike state, of the victorious Gauls; the refusal of the republic to make peace with Hannibal, after the battle of Cannae, were not the consequences of a refined calculation of the probable personal advantage to result from such a rhythm and order in the shows of life, to those who were at once the poets and the actors of these immortal dramas. The imagination beholding the beauty of this order, created it out of itself according to its own idea; the consequence was empire, and the reward everlasting fame. These things are not the less poetry, *quia carent vate sacro*. They are the episodes of that cyclic poem written by Time upon the memories of men. The Past, like an inspired rhapsodist, fills the theatre of everlasting generations with their harmony.

At length the ancient system of religion and manners had fulfilled the circle of its evolutions. And the world would have fallen into utter anarchy and darkness, but that there were found poets among the authors of the Christian and chivalric systems of manners and religion, who created forms of opinion and action never before conceived; which, copied into the imaginations of men, become as generals to the bewildered armies of their thoughts. It is foreign to the present purpose to touch upon the evil produced by these systems: except that we protest, on the ground of the principles already established, that no portion of it can be attributed to the poetry they contain.

It is probable that the poetry of Moses, Job, David, Solomon, and Isaiah, had produced a great effect upon the mind of Jesus and his disciples. The scattered fragments preserved to us by the biographers of this extraordinary person, are all instinct with the most vivid poetry. But his doctrines seem to have been quickly distorted. As a certain period after the prevalence of a system of opinions founded upon those promulgated by him, the three forms into which Plato had distributed the faculties of mind underwent a sort of apotheosis, and became the object of the worship of the civilized world. Here it is to be confessed that 'Light seems to thicken,' and

> The crow makes wing to the rooky wood,
> Good things of day begin to droop and drowse,
> And night's black agents to their preys do rouse.[4]

But mark how beautiful an order has sprung from the dust and blood of this fierce chaos! how the world, as from a resurrection, balancing itself on the golden wings of knowledge and of hope, has reassumed its yet unwearied flight into the heaven of time. Listen to the music, unheard by outward ears, which is as a ceaseless and invisible wind, nourishing its everlasting course with strength and swiftness.

The poetry in the doctrines of Jesus Christ, and the mythology and institutions of the Celtic conquerors of the Roman empire, outlived the darkness and the convulsions connected with their growth and victory, and blended themselves in a new fabric of manners and opinion. It is an error to impute the ignorance of the dark ages to the Christian doctrines or the predominance of the Celtic nations. Whatever of evil their agencies may have contained sprang from the extinction of the poetical principle, connected with the progress of despotism and superstition. Men, from causes too intricate to be here discussed, had become insensible and selfish: their own will had become feeble, and yet they were its slaves, and thence the slaves of the will of others: lust, fear, avarice, cruelty, and fraud, characterized a race amongst whom no one was to be found capable of *creating* in form, language, or institution. The moral anomalies of such a state of society are not justly to be charged upon any class of events immediately connected with them, and those events are most entitled to our approbation which could dissolve it most expeditiously. It is unfortunate for those who cannot distinguish words from thoughts, that many of these anomalies have been incorporated into our popular religion.

It was not until the eleventh century that the effects of the

---

4 *Macbeth*, Act III, scene ii, ll. 50–52.

poetry of the Christian and chivalric systems began to manifest themselves. The principle of equality had been discovered and applied by Plato in his *Republic,* as the theoretical rule of the mode in which the materials of pleasure and of power produced by the common skill and labour of human beings, ought to be distributed among them. The limitations of this rule were asserted by him to be determined only by the sensibility of each, or the utility to result to all. Plato, following the doctrines of Timaeus and Pythagoras, taught also a moral and intellectual system of doctrine, comprehending at once the past, the present, and the future condition of man. Jesus Christ divulged the sacred and eternal truths contained in these views to mankind, and Christianity, in its abstract purity, became the exoteric expression of the esoteric doctrines of the poetry and wisdom of antiquity. The incorporation of the Celtic nations with the exhausted population of the south, impressed upon it the figure of the poetry existing in their mythology and institutions. The result was a sum of the action and reaction of all the causes included in it; for it may be assumed as a maxim that no nation or religion can supersede any other without incorporating into itself a portion of that which it supersedes. The abolition of personal and domestic slavery, and the emancipation of women from a great part of the degrading restraints of antiquity, were among the consequences of these events.

The abolition of personal slavery is the basis of the highest political hope that it can enter into the mind of man to conceive. The freedom of women produced the poetry of sexual love. Love became a religion, the idols of whose worship were ever present. It was as if the statues of Apollo and the Muses had been endowed with life and motion, and had walked forth among their worshippers; so that earth became peopled by the inhabitants of a diviner world. The familiar appearance and proceedings of life became wonderful and heavenly, and a paradise was created as out of the wrecks of Eden. And as this creation itself is poetry, so its creators were poets; and language was the instrument of their art: 'Galeotto fù il libro, e chi lo scrisse.' The Provençal Trouveurs, or inventors, preceded Petrarch, whose verses are as spells, which unseal the inmost enchanted fountains of the delight which is in the grief of love. It is impossible to feel them without be-

L

coming a portion of that beauty which we contemplate: it were superfluous to explain how the gentleness and the elevation of mind connected with these sacred emotions can render men more amiable, more generous and wise, and lift them out of the dull vapours of the little world of self. Dante understood the secret things of love even more than Petrarch. His *Vita Nuova* is an inexhaustible fountain of purity of sentiment and language: it is the idealized history of that period, and those intervals of his life which were dedicated to love. His apotheosis of Beatrice in Paradise, and the gradations of his own love and her loveliness, by which as by steps he feigns himself to have ascended to the throne of the Supreme Cause, is the most glorious imagination of modern poetry. The acutest critics have justly reversed the judgement of the vulgar, and the order of the great acts of the Divina Commedia, in the measure of the admiration which they accord to the Hell, Purgatory, and Paradise. The latter is a perpetual hymn of everlasting love. Love, which found a worthy poet in Plato alone of all the ancients, has been celebrated by a chorus of the greatest writers of the renovated world; and the music has penetrated the caverns of society, and its echoes still drown the dissonance of arms and superstition. At successive intervals, Ariosto, Tasso, Shakespeare, Spenser, Calderon, Rousseau, and the great writers of our own age, have celebrated the dominion of love, planting as it were trophies in the human mind of that sublimest victory over sensuality and force. The true relation borne to each other by the sexes into which human kind is distributed, has become less misunderstood; and if the error which confounded diversity with inequality of the powers of the two sexes has been partially recognized in the opinions and institutions of modern Europe, we owe this great benefit to the worship of which chivalry was the law, and poets the prophets.

The poetry of Dante may be considered as the bridge thrown over the stream of time, which unites the modern and ancient world. The distorted notions of invisible things which Dante and his rival Milton have idealized, are merely the mask and the mantle in which these great poets walk through eternity enveloped and disguised. It is a difficult question to determine how far they were conscious of the distinction which must have subsisted in their minds between their own creeds and that of the

people. Dante at least appears to wish to mark the full extent of
it by placing Riphaeus, whom Virgil calls *justissimus unus,* in
Paradise, and observing a most heretical caprice in his distribution of rewards and punishments. And Milton's poem contains
within itself a philosophical refutation of that system, of which,
by a strange and natural antithesis, it has been a chief popular
support. Nothing can exceed the energy and magnificence of the
character of Satan as expressed in *Paradise Lost.* It is a mistake
to suppose that he could ever have been intended for the popular
personification of evil. Implacable hate, patient cunning, and a
sleepless refinement of device to inflict the extremest anguish on
an enemy, these things are evil; and, although venial in a slave,
are not to be forgiven in a tyrant; although redeemed by much
that ennobles his defeat in one subdued, are marked by all that
dishonours his conquest in the victor. Milton's Devil as a moral
being is as far superior to his God, as one who perseveres in some
purpose which he has conceived to be excellent in spite of ad-
versity and torture, is to one who in the cold security of undoubted triumph inflicts the most horrible revenge upon his
enemy, not from any mistaken notion of inducing him to repent
of a perseverance in enmity, but with the alleged design of
exasperating him to deserve new torments. Milton has so far vio-
lated the popular creed (if this shall be judged to be a violation)
as to have alleged no superiority of moral virtue to his god over
his devil. And this bold neglect of a direct moral purpose is the
most decisive proof of the supremacy of Milton's genius. He
mingled as it were the elements of human nature as colours upon
a single pallet, and arranged them in the composition of his great
picture according to the laws of epic truth; that is, according to
the laws of that principle by which a series of actions of the external universe and of intelligent and ethical beings is calculated
to excite the sympathy of succeeding generations of mankind.
The *Divina Commedia* and *Paradise Lost* have conferred upon
modern mythology a systematic form; and when change and
time shall have added one more superstition to the mass of those
which have arisen and decayed upon the earth, commentators
will be learnedly employed in elucidating the religion of ancestral
Europe, only not utterly forgotten because it will have been
stamped with the eternity of genius.

Homer was the first and Dante the second epic poet: that is, the second poet, the series of whose creations bore a defined and intelligible relation to the knowledge and sentiment and religion of the age in which he lived, and of the ages which followed it: developing itself in correspondence with their development. For Lucretius had limed the wings of his swift spirit in the dregs of the sensible world; and Virgil, with a modesty that ill became his genius, had affected the fame of an imitator, even whilst he created anew all that he copied; and none among the flock of mockbirds, though their notes were sweet, Apollonius Rhodius, Quintus Calaber, Smyrnaeus Nonnus, Lucan, Statius, or Claudian, have sought even to fulfil a single condition of epic truth. Milton was the third epic poet. For if the title of epic in its highest sense be refused to the Aeneid, still less can it be conceded to the Orlando Furioso, the Gerusalemme Liberata, the Lusiad, or the Fairy Queen.

Dante and Milton were both deeply penetrated with the ancient religion of the civilized world; and its spirit exists in their poetry probably in the same proportion as its forms survived in the unreformed worship of modern Europe. The one preceded and the other followed the Reformation at almost equal intervals. Dante was the first religious reformer, and Luther surpassed him rather in the rudeness and acrimony, than in the boldness of his censures of papal usurpation. Dante was the first awakener of entranced Europe; he created a language, in itself music and persuasion, out of a chaos of inharmonious barbarisms. He was the congregator of those great spirits who presided over the resurrection of learning; the Lucifer of that starry flock which in the thirteenth century shone forth from republican Italy, as from a heaven, into the darkness of the benighted world. His very words are instinct with spirit; each is as a spark, a burning atom of inextinguishable thought; and many yet lie covered in the ashes of their birth, and pregnant with a lightning which has yet found no conductor. All high poetry is infinite; it is as the first acorn, which contained all oaks potentially. Veil after veil may be undrawn, and the inmost naked beauty of the meaning never exposed. A great poem is a fountain for ever overflowing with the waters of wisdom and delight; and after one person and one age has exhausted all its divine effluence which their peculiar relations enable them to share, another and yet another succeeds, and new relations are ever developed, the source of an unforeseen and an unconceived delight.

The age immediately succeeding to that of Dante, Petrarch, and Boccaccio, was characterized by a revival of painting, sculpture, and architecture. Chaucer caught the sacred inspiration, and the superstructure of English literature is based upon the materials of Italian invention.

But let us not be betrayed from a defence into a critical history of poetry and its influence on society. Be it enough to have pointed out the effects of poets, in the large and true sense of the word, upon their own and all succeeding times.

But poets have been challenged to resign the civic crown to reasoners and mechanists, on another plea. It is admitted that the exercise of the imagination is most delightful, but it is alleged that that of reason is more useful. Let us examine, as the grounds of this distinction, what is here meant by utility. Pleasure or good, in a general sense, is that which the consciousness of a sensitive and intelligent being seeks, and in which, when found, it acquiesces. There are two kinds of pleasure, one durable, universal and permanent; the other transitory and particular. Utility may either express the means of producing the former or the latter. In the former sense, whatever strengthens and purifies the affections, enlarges the imagination, and adds spirit to sense, is useful. But a narrower meaning may be assigned to the word utility, confining it to express that which banishes the importunity of the wants of our animal nature, the surrounding men with security of life, the dispersing the grosser delusions of superstition, and the conciliating such a degree of mutual forbearance among men as may consist with the motives of personal advantage.

Undoubtedly the promoters of utility, in this limited sense, have their appointed office in society. They follow the footsteps of poets, and copy the sketches of their creations into the book of common life. They make space, and give time. Their exertions are of the highest value, so long as they confine their administration of the concerns of the inferior powers of our nature within the limits due to the superior ones. But whilst the sceptic destroys gross superstitions, let him spare to deface, as some of the

French writers have defaced, the eternal truths charactered upon the imaginations of men. Whilst the mechanist abridges, and the political economist combines labour, let them beware that their speculations, for want of correspondence with those first principles which belong to the imagination, do not tend, as they have in modern England, to exasperate at once the extremes of luxury and of want. They have exemplified the saying, 'To him that hath, more shall be given; and from him that hath not, the little that he hath shall be taken away.' The rich have become richer, and the poor have become poorer; and the vessel of the state is driven between the Scylla and Charybdis of anarchy and despotism. Such are the effects which must ever flow from an unmitigated exercise of the calculating faculty.

It is difficult to define pleasure in its highest sense; the definition involving a number of apparent paradoxes. For, from an inexplicable defect of harmony in the constitution of human nature, the pain of the inferior is frequently connected with the pleasures of the superior portions of our being. Sorrow, terror, anguish, despair itself, are often the chosen expressions of an approximation to the highest good. Our sympathy in tragic fiction depends on this principle; tragedy delights by affording a shadow of the pleasure which exists in pain. This is the source also of the melancholy which is inseparable from the sweetest melody. The pleasure that is in sorrow is sweeter than the pleasure of pleasure itself. And hence the saying, 'It is better to go to the house of mourning, than to the house of mirth.' Not that this highest species of pleasure is necessarily linked with pain. The delight of love and friendship, the ecstasy of the admiration of nature, the joy of the perception and still more of the creation of poetry, is often wholly unalloyed.

The production and assurance of pleasure in this highest sense is true utility. Those who produce and preserve this pleasure are poets or poetical philosophers.

The exertions of Locke, Hume, Gibbon, Voltaire, Rousseau,[5] and their disciples, in favour of oppressed and deluded humanity, are entitled to the gratitude of mankind. Yet it is easy to calculate the degree of moral and intellectual improvement which the

---

[5] Although Rousseau has been thus classed, he was essentially a poet. The others, even Voltaire, were mere reasoners. [Shelley.]

world would have exhibited, had they never lived. A little more
nonsense would have been talked for a century or two; and perhaps a few more men, women, and children, burnt as heretics.
We might not at this moment have been congratulating each
other on the abolition of the Inquisition in Spain. But it exceeds
all imagination to conceive what would have been the moral condition of the world if neither Dante, Petrarch, Boccaccio, Chaucer, Shakespeare, Calderon, Lord Bacon, nor Milton, had ever
existed; if Raphael and Michael Angelo had never been born; if
the Hebrew poetry had never been translated; if a revival of the
study of Greek literature had never taken place; if no monuments of ancient sculpture had been handed down to us; and if
the poetry of the religion of the ancient world had been extinguished together with its belief. The human mind could never,
except by the intervention of these excitements, have been awakened to the invention of the grosser sciences, and that application
of analytical reasoning to the aberrations of society, which it is
now attempted to exalt over the direct expression of the inventive
and creative faculty itself.

We have more moral, political and historical wisdom, than we
know how to reduce into practice; we have more scientific and
economical knowledge than can be accomodated to the just distribution of the produce which it multiplies. The poetry in these
systems of thought, is concealed by the accumulation of facts and
calculating processes. There is no want of knowledge respecting
what is wisest and best in morals, government, and political econ-
omy, or at least what is wiser and better than what men now
practise and endure. But we let '*I dare not* wait upon *I would,*
like the poor cat in the adage.' [6] We want the creative faculty to
imagine that which we know; we want the generous impulse to
act that which we imagine; we want the poetry of life: our calcu-
lations have outrun conception; we have eaten more than we can
digest. The cultivation of those sciences which have enlarged the
limits of the empire of man over the external world, has, for want
of the poetical faculty, proportionally circumscribed those of the
internal world; and man, having enslaved the elements, remains
himself a slave. To what but a cultivation of the mechanical arts
in a degree disproportioned to the presence of the creative

[6] *Macbeth*, Act I, scene vii, ll. 44–45.

faculty, which is the basis of all knowledge, is to be attributed the abuse of all invention for abridging and combining labour, to the exasperation of the inequality of mankind? From what other cause has it arisen that the discoveries which should have lightened, have added a weight to the curse imposed on Adam? Poetry, and the principle of Self of which money is the visible incarnation, are the God and Mammon of the world.

The functions of the poetical faculty are two-fold; by one it creates new materials of knowledge and power and pleasure; by the other it engenders in the mind a desire to reproduce and arrange them according to a certain rhythm and order which may be called the beautiful and the good. The cultivation of poetry is never more to be desired than at periods when, from an excess of the selfish and calculating principle, the accumulation of the materials of external life exceed the quantity of the power of assimilating them to the internal laws of human nature. The body has then become too unwieldy for that which animates it.

Poetry is indeed something divine. It is at once the centre and circumference of knowledge; it is that which comprehends all science, and that to which all science must be referred. It is at the same time the root and blossom of all other systems of thought; it is that from which all spring, and that which adorns all; and that which, if blighted, denies the fruit and the seed, and withholds from the barren world the nourishment and the succession of the scions of the tree of life. It is the perfect and consummate surface and bloom of all things; it is as the odour and the colour of the rose to the texture of the elements which compose it, as the form and splendour of unfaded beauty to the secrets of anatomy and corruption. What were virtue, love, patriotism, friendship—what were the scenery of this beautiful universe which we inhabit; what were our consolations on this side of the grave—and what were our aspirations beyond it, if poetry did not ascend to bring light and fire from those eternal regions where the owl-winged faculty of calculation dare not ever soar? Poetry is not like reasoning, a power to be exerted according to the determination of the will. A man cannot say, 'I will compose poetry.' The greatest poet even cannot say it; for the mind in creation is as a fading coal, which some invisible influence, like an inconstant wind, awakens to transitory brightness; this power arises from within, like the colour of a flower which fades and changes as it is developed, and the conscious portions of our natures are unprophetic either of its approach or its departure. Could this influence be durable in its original purity and force, it is impossible to predict the greatness of the results; but when composition begins, inspiration is already on the decline, and the most glorious poetry that has ever been communicated to the world is probably a feeble shadow of the original conceptions of the poet. I appeal to the greatest poets of the present day, whether it is not an error to assert that the finest passages of poetry are produced by labour and study. The toil and the delay recommended by critics, can be justly interpreted to mean no more than a careful observation of the inspired moments, and an artificial connexion of the spaces between their suggestions, by the intertexture of conventional expressions; a necessity only imposed by the limitedness of the poetical faculty itself; for Milton conceived the Paradise Lost as a whole before he executed it in portions. We have his own authority also for the muse having 'dictated' to him the 'unpremeditated song'. And let this be an answer to those who would allege the fifty-six various readings of the first line of the Orlando Furioso. Compositions so produced are to poetry what mosaic is to painting. This instinct and intuition of the poetical faculty is still more observable in the plastic and pictorial arts; a great statue or picture grows under the power of the artist as a child in the mother's womb; and the very mind which directs the hands in formation is incapable of accounting to itself for the origin, the gradations, or the media of the process.

Poetry is the record of the best and happiest moments of the happiest and best minds. We are aware of evanescent visitations of thought and feeling, sometimes associated with place or person, sometimes regarding our own mind alone, and always arising unforeseen and departing unbidden, but elevating and delightful beyond all expression: so that even in the desire and regret they leave, there cannot but be pleasure, participating as it does in the nature of its object. It is as it were the interpenetration of a diviner nature through our own; but its footsteps are like those of a wind over the sea, which the morning calm erases, and whose traces remain only, as on the wrinkled sand which paves it. These and corresponding conditions of being are experienced principally by those of the most delicate sensibility and the most enlarged imagination; and the state of mind produced by them is at war with every base desire. The enthusiasm of virtue, love, patriotism, and friendship, is essentially linked with such emotions; and whilst they last, self appears as what it is, an atom to a universe. Poets are not only subject to these experiences as spirits of the most refined organization, but they can colour all that they combine with the evanescent hues of this ethereal world; a word, a trait in the representation of a scene or a passion, will touch the enchanted chord, and reanimate, in those who have ever experienced these emotions, the sleeping, the cold, the buried image of the past. Poetry thus makes immortal all that is best and most beautiful in the world; it arrests the vanishing apparitions which haunt the interlunations of life, and veiling them, or in language or in form, sends them forth among mankind, bearing sweet news of kindred joy to those with whom their sisters abide—abide, because there is no portal of expression from the caverns of the spirit which they inhabit into the universe of things. Poetry redeems from decay the visitations of the divinity in man.

Poetry turns all things to loveliness; it exalts the beauty of that which is most beautiful, and it adds beauty to that which is most deformed; it marries exultation and horror, grief and pleasure, eternity and change; it subdues to union under its light yoke, all irreconcilable things. It transmutes all that it touches, and every form moving within the radiance of its presence is changed by wondrous sympathy to an incarnation of the spirit which it breathes: its secret alchemy turns to potable gold the poisonous waters which flow from death through life; it strips the evil of familiarity from the world, and lays bare the naked and sleeping beauty, which is the spirit of its forms.

All things exist as they are perceived; at least in relation to the percipient. 'The mind is its own place, and of itself can make a heaven of hell, a hell of heaven.'[7] But poetry defeats the curse which binds us to be subjected to the accident of surrounding impressions. And whether it spreads its own figured curtain, or withdraws life's dark veil from before the scene of things, it equally creates for us a being within our being. It makes us the inhabitants of a world to which the familiar world is a chaos. It

[7] *Paradise Lost,* Book I, ll. 254–55.

reproduces the common universe of which we are portions and percipients, and it purges from our inward sight the film of familiarity which obscures from us the wonder of our being. It compels us to feel that which we perceive, and to imagine that which we know. It creates anew the universe, after it has been annihilated in our minds by the recurrence of impressions blunted by reiteration. It justifies the bold and true words of Tasso: *Non merita nome di creatore, se non Iddio ed il Poeta.* [None merits the name of creator except God and the poet.]

A poet, as he is the author to others of the highest wisdom, pleasure, virtue and glory, so he ought personally to be the happiest, the best, the wisest, and the most illustrious of men. As to his glory, let time be challenged to declare whether the fame of any other institutor of human life be comparable to that of a poet. That he is the wisest, the happiest, and the best, inasmuch as he is a poet, is equally incontrovertible: the greatest poets have been men of the most spotless virtue, of the most consummate prudence, and, if we would look into the interior of their lives, the most fortunate of men: and the exceptions, as they regard those who possessed the poetic faculty in a high yet inferior degree, will be found on consideration to confine rather than destroy the rule. Let us for a moment stoop to the arbitration of popular breath, and usurping and uniting in our own persons the incompatible characters of accuser, witness, judge, and executioner, let us decide without trial, testimony, or form, that certain motives of those who are 'there sitting where we dare not soar', are reprehensible. Let us assume that Homer was a drunkard, that Virgil was a flatterer, that Horace was a coward, that Tasso was a madman, that Lord Bacon was a peculator, that Raphael was a libertine, that Spenser was a poet laureate. It is inconsistent with this division of our subject to cite living poets, but posterity has done ample justice to the great names now referred to. Their errors have been weighed and found to have been dust in the balance; if their sins 'were as scarlet, they are now white as snow': they have been washed in the blood of the mediator and redeemer, time. Observe in what a ludicrous chaos the imputations of real or fictitious crime have been confused in the contemporary calumnies against poetry and poets; consider how little is as it appears—or appears, as it is; look to your own motives, and judge not, lest ye be judged.

Poetry, as has been said, differs in this respect from logic, that it is not subject to the control of the active powers of the mind, and that its birth and recurrence have no necessary connexion with the consciousness or will. It is presumptuous to determine that these are the necessary conditions of all mental causation, when mental effects are experienced insusceptible of being referred to them. The frequent recurrence of the poetical power, it is obvious to suppose, may produce in the mind a habit of order and harmony correlative with its own nature and with its effects upon other minds. But in the intervals of inspiration, and they may be frequent without being durable, a poet becomes a man, and is abandoned to the sudden reflux of the influences under which others habitually live. But as he is more delicately organized than other men, and sensible to pain and pleasure, both his own and that of others, in a degree unknown to them, he will avoid the one and pursue the other with an ardour proportioned to this difference. And he renders himself obnoxious to calumny, when he neglects to observe the circumstances under which these objects of universal pursuit and flight have disguised themselves in one another's garments.

But there is nothing necessarily evil in this error, and thus cruelty, envy, revenge, avarice, and the passions purely evil, have never formed any portion of the popular imputations on the lives of poets.

I have thought it most favourable to the cause of truth to set down these remarks according to the order in which they were suggested to my mind, by a consideration of the subject itself, instead of observing the formality of a polemical reply; but if the view which they contain be just, they will be found to involve a refutation of the arguers against poetry, so far at least as regards the first division of the subject. I can readily conjecture what should have moved the gall of some learned and intelligent writers who quarrel with certain versifiers; I, like them, confess myself unwilling to be stunned by the Theseids of the hoarse Codri of the day. Bavius and Maevius undoubtedly are, as they ever were, insufferable persons. But it belongs to a philosophical critic to distinguish rather than confound.

The first part of these remarks has related to poetry in its elements and principles; and it has been shown, as well as the narrow limits assigned them would permit, that what is called poetry in a restricted sense, has a common source with all other forms of order and of beauty, according to which the materials of human life are susceptible of being arranged, and which is poetry in a universal sense.

The second part will have for its object an application of these principles to the present state of the cultivation of poetry, and a defence of the attempt to idealize the modern forms of manners and opinions, and compel them into a subordination to the imaginative and creative faculty. For the literature of England, an energetic development of which has ever preceded or accompanied a great and free development of the national will, has arisen as it were from a new birth. In spite of the low-thoughted envy which would undervalue contemporary merit, our own will be a memorable age in intellectual achievements, and we live among such philosophers and poets as surpass beyond comparison any who have appeared since the last national struggle for civil and religious liberty. The most unfailing herald, companion, and follower of the awakening of a great people to work a beneficial change in opinion or institution, is poetry. At such periods there is an accumulation of the power of communicating and receiving intense and impassioned conceptions respecting man and nature. The persons in whom this power resides may often, as far as regards many portions of their nature, have little apparent correspondence with that spirit of good of which they are the ministers. But even whilst they deny and abjure they are yet compelled to serve, the power which is seated on the throne of their own soul. It is impossible to read the compositions of the most celebrated writers of the present day without being startled with the electric life which burns within their words. They measure the circumference and sound the depths of human nature with a comprehensive and all-penetrating spirit, and they are themselves perhaps the most sincerely astonished at its manifestations; for it is less their spirit than the spirit of the age. Poets are the hierophants of an unapprehended inspiration; the mirrors of the gigantic shadows which futurity casts upon the present; the words which express what they understand not; the trumpets which sing to battle, and feel not what they inspire; the influence which is moved not, but moves. Poets are the unacknowledged legislators of the world.

John Stuart Mill

[1806–1873]

❧❧❧

JOHN STUART MILL WAS THE eldest son of the utilitarian philosopher James Mill, who directed his education according to a rigid and comprehensive intellectual discipline. The son became a leading disciple of the father's school; but however much he depended on Bentham's principle of utility to unify his understanding of the world, he found that philosophy inadequate to redeem him from the despair into which he was plunged by a mental crisis, brought on by his unrelenting studies, in his twenty-first year. What did restore his capacity for delight was, as he records in his *Autobiography*, the poems of Wordsworth, in which he learned "what would be the perennial sources of happiness, when all the greater evils of life shall be removed." Mill read law but never practiced; successive positions in the India House gave him sufficient income and leisure to pursue his speculative studies. Mill's major writings are in logic, epistemology, and political philosophy; his best known works are his essay *On Liberty* (1859) and the posthumous *Autobiography* (1873). "What Is Poetry?" is one of two essays later reprinted together under the title "Thoughts on Poetry and its Varieties."

Mill's definition of poetry is a useful example of the course which Romantic theory had taken since Wordsworth's day. Starting from Wordsworth's assertion (see Preface to *Lyrical Ballads*, above, p. 24) that poetry is properly opposed, not to prose but to science, Mill goes a good deal farther than his source did in arguing a subjectivist, or expressive theory of poetry. Poetry, he says, is "the delineation of the deeper and more secret workings of human emotion"; it is therefore to be distinguished, not only from science, but from narrative and description. If its essence is a state of mind, it can also be distinguished from eloquence: as Mill puts it, in his most famous aphorism, "Eloquence is *heard*; poetry is *over*heard." Mill intended his essay as a defense of the truth of poetry against the attacks of the utilitarians. But in fact his argument that poetry is self-expression, and that the poet's audience is himself, leads in the opposite direction, toward art-for-art's-sake, and the aesthetic criticism of the end of the century.

BIBLIOGRAPHY. *Dissertations and Discussions,* 5 vols. (New York, 1874–82).

Emery E. Neff, *Carlyle and Mill, Mystic and Utilitarian* (New York, 1924); Leslie Stephen, *The English Utilitarians* (New York and London, 1900); Alba H. Warren, Jr., *English Poetic Theory 1825–1865* (Princeton, 1950).

TEXT. *Dissertations and Discussions,* vol. I.

WHAT IS POETRY?

[1833]

IT HAS OFTEN BEEN ASKED, What is Poetry? And many and various are the answers which have been returned. The vulgarest of all—one with which no person possessed of the faculties to which poetry addresses itself can ever have been satisfied—is that which confounds poetry with metrical composition; yet to this wretched mockery of a definition many have been led back by the failure of all their attempts to find any other that would distinguish what they have been accustomed to call poetry from much which they have known only under other names.

That, however, the word "poetry" imports something quite peculiar in its nature; something which may exist in what is called prose as well as in verse; something which does not even require the instrument of words, but can speak through the other audible symbols called musical sounds, and even through the visible ones which are the language of sculpture, painting, and architecture,—all this, we believe, is and must be felt, though perhaps indistinctly, by all upon whom poetry in any of its shapes produces any impression beyond that of tickling the ear. The distinction between poetry and what is not poetry, whether explained or not, is felt to be fundamental; and, where every one feels a difference, a difference there must be. All other appearances may be fallacious; but the appearance of a difference is a real difference. Appearances too, like other things, must have a cause; and that which can cause any thing, even an illusion, must be a reality. And hence, while a half-philosophy disdains the classifications and distinctions indicated by popular language, philosophy carried to its highest point frames new ones, but rarely sets aside the old, content with correcting and regularizing them. It cuts fresh channels for thought, but does not fill up such as it finds ready-made: it traces, on the contrary, more deeply, broadly, and distinctly, those into which the current has spontaneously flowed.

Let us then attempt, in the way of modest inquiry, not to coerce and confine Nature within the bounds of an arbitrary definition, but rather to find the boundaries which she herself has set, and erect a barrier round them; not calling mankind to account for having misapplied the word "poetry," but attempting to clear up the conception which they already attach to it, and to bring forward as a distinct principle that which, as a vague feeling, has really guided them in their employment of the term.

The object of poetry is confessedly to act upon the emotions;—and therein is poetry sufficiently distinguished from what Wordsworth affirms to be its logical opposite; namely, not prose, but matter of fact, or science. The one addresses itself to the belief; the other, to the feelings. The one does its work by convincing or persuading; the other, by moving. The one acts by presenting a proposition to the understanding; the other, by offering interesting objects of contemplation to the sensibilities.

This, however, leaves us very far from a definition of poetry. This distinguishes it from one thing; but we are bound to distinguish it from every thing. To bring thoughts or images before the mind, for the purpose of acting upon the emotions, does not belong to poetry alone. It is equally the province (for example) of the novelist: and yet the faculty of the poet and that of the novelist are as distinct as any other two faculties; as the faculties of the novelist and of the orator, or of the poet and the metaphysician. The two characters may be united, as characters the most disparate may; but they have no natural connection.

Many of the greatest poems are in the form of fictitious narratives; and, in almost all good serious fictions, there is true

poetry. But there is a radical distinction between the interest
felt in a story as such, and the interest excited by poetry; for the
one is derived from incident, the other from the representation
of feeling. In one, the source of the emotion excited is the exhibition of a state or states of human sensibility; in the other, of a
series of states of mere outward circumstances. Now, all minds
are capable of being affected more or less by representations of
the latter kind, and all, or almost all, by those of the former; yet
the two sources of interest correspond to two distinct and (as
respects their greatest development) mutually exclusive characters of mind.

At what age is the passion for a story, for almost any kind of
story, merely as a story, the most intense? In childhood. But
that also is the age at which poetry, even of the simplest description, is least relished and least understood; because the feelings
with which it is especially conversant are yet undeveloped, and,
not having been even in the slightest degree experienced, cannot
be sympathized with. In what stage of the progress of society,
again, is story-telling most valued, and the story-teller in greatest
request and honor? In a rude state like that of the Tartars and
Arabs at this day, and of almost all nations in the earliest ages.
But, in this state of society, there is little poetry except ballads,
which are mostly narrative,—that is, essentially stories,—and
derive their principal interest from the incidents. Considered as
poetry, they are of the lowest and most elementary kind: the
feelings depicted, or rather indicated, are the simplest our nature
has; such joys and griefs as the immediate pressure of some outward event excites in rude minds, which live wholly immersed in
outward things, and have never, either from choice or a force they
could not resist, turned themselves to the contemplation of the
world within. Passing now from childhood, and from the childhood of society, to the grown-up men and women of this most
grown-up and unchild-like age, the minds and hearts of greatest
depth and elevation are commonly those which take greatest
delight in poetry: the shallowest and emptiest, on the contrary,
are, at all events, not those least addicted to novel-reading. This
accords, too, with all analogous experience of human nature. The
sort of persons whom not merely in books, but in their lives, we
find perpetually engaged in hunting for excitement from without,

are invariably those who do not possess, either in the vigor of their
intellectual powers or in the depth of their sensibilities, that which
would enable them to find ample excitement nearer home. The
most idle and frivolous persons take a natural delight in fictitious
narrative: the excitement it affords is of the kind which comes
from without. Such persons are rarely lovers of poetry, though
they may fancy themselves so because they relish novels in verse.
But poetry, which is the delineation of the deeper and more
secret workings of human emotion, is interesting only to those
to whom it recalls what they have felt, or whose imagination it
stirs up to conceive what they could feel, or what they might
have been able to feel, had their outward circumstances been
different.

Poetry, when it is really such, is truth; and fiction also, if it is
good for any thing, is truth: but they are different truths. The
truth of poetry is to paint the human soul truly: the truth of
fiction is to give a true picture of life. The two kinds of knowledge
are different, and come by different ways,—come mostly to
different persons. Great poets are often proverbially ignorant of
life. What they know has come by observation of themselves:
they have found within them one highly delicate and sensitive
specimen of human nature, on which the laws of emotion are
written in large characters, such as can be read off without much
study. Other knowledge of mankind, such as comes to men of
the world by outward experience, is not indispensable to them
as poets: but, to the novelist, such knowledge is all in all; he has
to describe outward things, not the inward man; actions and
events, not feelings; and it will not do for him to be numbered
among those, who, as Madame Roland said of Brissot, know man,
but not *men*.

All this is no bar to the possibility of combining both elements,
poetry and narrative or incident, in the same work, and calling
it either a novel or a poem; but so may red and white combine
on the same human features or on the same canvas. There is
one order of composition which requires the union of poetry and
incident, each in its highest kind,—the dramatic. Even there,
the two elements are perfectly distinguishable, and may exist
of unequal quality and in the most various proportion. The
incidents of a dramatic poem may be scanty and ineffective,

though the delineation of passion and character may be of the
highest order, as in Goethe's admirable "Torquato Tasso;" or,
again, the story as a mere story may be well got up for effect, as
is the case with some of the most trashy productions of the
Minerva press: it may even be, what those are not, a coherent and
probable series of events, though there be scarcely a feeling
exhibited which is not represented falsely, or in a manner absolutely commonplace. The combination of the two excellences is
what renders Shakespeare so generally acceptable,—each sort of
readers finding in him what is suitable to their faculties. To the
many, he is great as a story-teller; to the few, as a poet.

In limiting poetry to the delineation of states of feeling, and
denying the name where nothing is delineated but outward
objects, we may be thought to have done what we promised to
avoid,—to have not found, but made, a definition in opposition
to the usage of language, since it is established by common consent that there is a poetry called descriptive. We deny the charge.
Description is not poetry because there is descriptive poetry,
no more than science is poetry because there is such a thing as a
didactic poem. But an object which admits of being described,
or a truth which may fill a place in a scientific treatise, may also
furnish an occasion for the generation of poetry, which we there-
upon choose to call descriptive or didactic. The poetry is not in
the object itself, nor in the scientific truth itself, but in the state
of mind in which the one and the other may be contemplated.
The mere delineation of the dimensions and colors of external
objects is not poetry, no more than a geometrical ground-plan
of St. Peter's or Westminster Abbey is painting. Descriptive
poetry consists, no doubt, in description, but in description of
things as they appear, not as they are; and it paints them, not in
their bare and natural lineaments, but seen through the medium
and arrayed in the colors of the imagination set in action by the
feelings. If a poet describes a lion, he does not describe him
as a naturalist would, nor even as a traveller would, who was
intent upon stating the truth, the whole truth, and nothing but
the truth. He describes him by imagery, that is, by suggesting the
most striking likenesses and contrasts which might occur to a
mind contemplating a lion, in the state of awe, wonder, or terror,
which the spectacle naturally excites, or is, on the occasion, sup-

posed to excite. Now, this is describing the lion professedly, but the state of excitement of the spectator really. The lion may be described falsely or with exaggeration, and the poetry be all the better: but, if the human emotion be not painted with scrupulous truth, the poetry is bad poetry; i.e., is not poetry at all, but a failure.

Thus far, our progress towards a clear view of the essentials of poetry has brought us very close to the last two attempts at a definition of poetry which we happen to have seen in print, both of them by poets, and men of genius. The one is by Ebenezer Elliott, the author of "Corn-law Rhymes," and other poems of still greater merit. "Poetry," says he, "is impassioned truth." The other is by a writer in "Blackwood's Magazine," and comes, we think, still nearer the mark. He defines poetry, "man's thoughts tinged by his feelings." There is in either definition a near approximation to what we are in search of. Every truth which a human being can enunciate, every thought, even every outward impression, which can enter into his consciousness, may become poetry, when shown through any impassioned medium; when invested with the coloring of joy, or grief, or pity, or affection, or admiration, or reverence, or awe, or even hatred or terror; and, unless so colored, nothing, be it as interesting as it may, is poetry. But both these definitions fail to discriminate between poetry and eloquence. Eloquence, as well as poetry, is impassioned truth; eloquence, as well as poetry, is thoughts colored by the feelings. Yet common apprehension and philosophic criticism alike recognize a distinction between the two: there is much that every one would call eloquence, which no one would think of classing as poetry. A question will sometimes arise, whether some particular author is a poet; and those who maintain the negative commonly allow, that, though not a poet, he is a highly eloquent writer. The distinction between poetry and eloquence appears to us to be equally fundamental with the distinction between poetry and narrative, or between poetry and description, while it is still farther from having been satisfactorily cleared up than either of the others.

Poetry and eloquence are both alike the expression or utterance of feeling: but, if we may be excused the antithesis, we should say that eloquence is *heard;* poetry is *over*heard. Eloquence sup-

poses an audience. The peculiarity of poetry appears to us to
lie in the poet's utter unconsciousness of a listener. Poetry is
feeling confessing itself to itself in moments of solitude, and
embodying itself in symbols which are the nearest possible representations of the feeling in the exact shape in which it exists in
the poet's mind. Eloquence is feeling pouring itself out to other
minds, courting their sympathy, or endeavoring to influence their
belief, or move them to passion or to action.

All poetry is of the nature of soliloquy. It may be said that
poetry which is printed on hot-pressed paper, and sold at a book-
seller's shop, is a soliloquy in full dress and on the stage. It is so;
but there is nothing absurd in the idea of such a mode of
soliloquizing. What we have said to ourselves we may tell to
others afterwards; what we have said or done in solitude we may
voluntarily reproduce when we know that other eyes are upon
us. But no trace of consciousness that any eyes are upon us must
be visible in the work itself. The actor knows that there is an
audience present; but, if he act as though he knew it, he acts ill.
A poet may write poetry, not only with the intention of printing
it, but for the express purpose of being paid for it. That it should
be poetry, being written under such influences, is less probable,
not, however, impossible; but no otherwise possible than if he can
succeed in excluding from his work every vestige of such look-
ings-forth into the outward and every-day world, and can express
his emotions exactly as he has felt them in solitude, or as he is
conscious that he should feel them, though they were to remain
for ever unuttered, or (at the lowest) as he knows that others feel
them in similar circumstances of solitude. But when he turns
round, and addresses himself to another person; when the act
of utterance is not itself the end, but a means to an end,—viz.,
by the feelings he himself expresses, to work upon the feelings,
or upon the belief or the will of another; when the expression of
his emotions, or of his thoughts tinged by his emotions, is tinged
also by that purpose, by that desire of making an impression upon
another mind,—then it ceases to be poetry, and becomes eloquence.

Poetry, accordingly, is the natural fruit of solitude and meditation; eloquence, of intercourse with the world. The persons who
have most feeling of their own, if intellectual culture has given

them a language in which to express it, have the highest faculty of poetry: those who best understand the feelings of others are the most eloquent. The persons and the nations who commonly excel in poetry are those whose character and tastes render them least dependent upon the applause or sympathy or concurrence of the world in general. Those to whom that applause, that sympathy, that concurrence, are most necessary, generally excel most in eloquence. And hence, perhaps, the French, who are the least poetical of all great and intellectual nations, are among the most eloquent; the French also being the most sociable, the vainest, and the least self-dependent.

If the above be, as we believe, the true theory of the distinction commonly admitted between eloquence and poetry, or even though it be not so, yet if, as we cannot doubt, the distinction above stated be a real *bonâ-fide* distinction, it will be found to hold, not merely in the language of words, but in all other language, and to intersect the whole domain of art. . . .

John Ruskin

[1819–1900]

᪥᪥᪥

RUSKIN'S WEALTHY PARENTS intended him for a career in the church, but before he was 20 he had indicated the direction that his future was to take by defending the paintings of Turner against critical attack. This defence became the nucleus of an extended study, *Modern Painters* (published in five volumes between 1843 and 1860), from which the essay included here is taken. Ruskin was a voluminous writer; his works include criticism of painting, architecture, literature, and politics, and tracts on aesthetics, science, theology, economics, and mythology. From 1869 to 1878, and from 1883 to 1884 he was Slade professor of art at Oxford.

Although Ruskin was, strictly speaking, a critic of the fine arts, he was by nature a moralist and a reformer. Ruskin preached first the necessity in art of "bringing everything to root in human passion or human life," and, in his writings after 1860, the need to reaffirm human values in an industrial society. Like Carlyle and like Arnold, he saw that the growing Victorian materialism (and its philosophical justification, Utilitarianism) was corrupting art and morality alike, and he attacked Victorian ugliness in a criticism which became increasingly social in its focus. But he was equally distrustful of art which should aspire to a purely aesthetic excellence; beauty and truth are not identical, and of the two, truth is the more important. Ruskin's moralistic bias led him to emphasize content rather than form, in pictures as well as in poems: "The picture which has the nobler and more numerous ideas," he wrote, "however awkwardly expressed, is a greater and a better picture than that which has the less noble and less numerous ideas, however beautifully expressed." It also led him to distrust the figurative, the decorative, the non-literal, and to argue "the love of natural objects for their own sake" as a truer foundation for art.

Ruskin's most famous critical term, the "pathetic fallacy," is a device for distinguishing truth from untruth in poetic description.

200

Descriptions are fallacies when they attribute qualities to things which are not there. (Ruskin offers this example from Kingsley's *Alton Locke:* "They rowed her in across the rolling foam—The cruel, crawling foam." "The foam," he observes, "is not cruel, neither does it crawl.") When the attribution expresses an "excited state of feelings" toward the object, the fallacy is pathetic, and the poet is justified in using it, though Ruskin still thinks the usage is a sign of "*some* degree of weakness in the character," and that a great poet would have gotten along without it. Fallacies which are not pathetic are morbid as well as untrue; they may be mere "wilful fancy" (as in Pope), or self-examining subjectivism (as in Byron and Shelley), but in either case Ruskin excluded them from the poetry of "true imaginative power."

BIBLIOGRAPHY. *Works*, ed. E. T. Cook and A. D. O. Wedderburn, 39 vols. (London, 1902–1912).

H. Ladd, *The Victorian Morality of Art. An Analysis of Ruskin's Aesthetic* (New York, 1932); Alba H. Warren, Jr., *English Poetic Theory 1825–1865* (Princeton, 1950).

TEXT. *Modern Painters*, vol. 3 (new edition, 1873).

OF THE PATHETIC FALLACY

[1856]

§ 1. GERMAN DULNESS, AND English affectation, have of late much multiplied among us the use of two of the most objectionable words that were ever coined by the troublesomeness of metaphysicians,—namely, "Objective," and "Subjective."

No words can be more exquisitely, and in all points, useless; and I merely speak of them that I may, at once and for ever, get them out of my way, and out of my reader's. But to get that done, they must be explained.

The word "Blue," say certain philosophers, means the sensation of colour which the human eye receives in looking at the open sky, or at a bell gentian.

Now, say they farther, as this sensation can only be felt when the eye is turned to the object, and as, therefore, no such sensation is produced by the object when nobody looks at it, therefore the thing, when it is not looked at, is not blue; and thus (say they) there are many qualities of things which depend as much on something else as on themselves. To be sweet, a thing must have a taster; it is only sweet while it is being tasted, and if the tongue had not the capacity of taste, then the sugar would not have the quality of sweetness.

And then they agree that the qualities of things which thus depend upon our perception of them, and upon our human nature as affected by them, shall be called Subjective; and the qualities of things which they always have, irrespective of any other nature, as roundness or squareness, shall be called Objective.

From these ingenious views the step is very easy to a farther opinion, that it does not much matter what things are in themselves, but only what they are to us; and that the only real truth of them is their appearance to, or effect upon, us. From which position, with a hearty desire for mystification, and much egotism, selfishness, shallowness, and impertinence, a philosopher may easily go so far as to believe, and say, that everything in the world depends upon his seeing or thinking of it, and that nothing, therefore, exists, but what he sees or thinks of.

§ 2. Now, to get rid of all these ambiguities and troublesome words at once, be it observed that the word "Blue" does *not* mean the *sensation* caused by a gentian on the human eye; but it means the *power* of producing that sensation: and this power is always there, in the thing, whether we are there to experience it or not, and would remain there though there were not left a man on the face of the earth. Precisely in the same way gunpowder has a power of exploding. It will not explode if you put no match to it. But it has always the power of so exploding, and is therefore called an explosive compound, which it very positively and assuredly is, whatever philosophy may say to the contrary.

In like manner, a gentian does not produce the sensation of blueness if you don't look at it. But it has always the power of doing so; its particles being everlastingly so arranged by its Maker. And, therefore, the gentian and the sky are always verily blue, whatever philosophy may say to the contrary; and if you do not see them blue when you look at them, it is not their fault, but yours.[1]

§ 3. Hence I would say to these philosophers: If, instead of using the sonorous phrase, "It is objectively so," you will use the plain old phrase, "It *is* so," and if instead of the sonorous phrase, "It is subjectively so," you will say, in plain old English, "It does so," or "It seems so to me," you will, on the whole, be more intelligible to your fellow-creatures; and besides, if you find that a thing which generally "does so" to other people (as a gentian looks blue to most men), does *not* so to you, on any particular occasion, you will not fall into the impertinence of saying, that the thing is not so, or did not so, but you will say simply (what you will be all the better for speedily finding out), that something is the matter with you. If you find that you cannot explode the gunpowder, you will not declare that all gunpowder is subjective, and all explosion imaginary, but you will simply suspect and declare yourself to be an ill-made match. Which, on the whole, though there may be a distant chance of a mistake about it, is, nevertheless, the wisest conclusion you can come to until further experiment.[2]

[1] It is quite true, that in all qualities involving sensation, there may be a doubt whether different people receive the same sensation from the same thing (compare Part II. sect. i. ch. v. § 6); but, though this makes such facts not distinctly explicable, it does not alter the facts themselves. I derive a certain sensation, which I call sweetness, from sugar. That is a fact. Another person feels a sensation, which *he* also calls sweetness, from sugar. That is also a fact. The sugar's power to produce these two sensations, which we suppose to be, and which are, in all probability, very nearly the same in both of us, and, on the whole, in the human race, is its sweetness. [Ruskin's note.]

[2] In fact (for I may as well, for once, meet our German friends in their own style), all that has been subjected to us on the subject seems object to this great objection; that the subjection of all things (subject to no exceptions) to senses which are, in us, both subject and object, and objects of perpetual contempt, cannot but make it our ultimate object to subject ourselves to the senses, and to remove whatever objections existed to such subjection. So that, finally, that which is the subject of examination or object of attention, uniting thus in itself the characters of subness and obness (so that, that which has no obness in it should be called sub-subjective, or a sub-subject, and that which has no subness in it should be called upper or ober-objective, or an ob-object); and we also, who suppose ourselves the objects of every arrangement, and are certainly the subjects of every sensual impression, thus uniting in ourselves, in an obverse or adverse manner, the characters of obness and

§ 4. Now, therefore, putting these tiresome and absurd words quite out of our way, we may go on at our ease to examine the point in question,—namely, the difference between the ordinary, proper, and true appearances of things to us; and the extraordinary, or false appearances, when we are under the influence of emotion, or contemplative fancy; [3] false appearances, I say, as being entirely unconnected with any real power or character in the object, and only imputed to it by us.

For instance—

> The spendthrift crocus, bursting through the mould
> Naked and shivering, with his cup of gold.[4]

This is very beautiful, and yet very untrue. The crocus is not a spendthrift, but a hardy plant; its yellow is not gold, but saffron. How is it that we enjoy so much the having it put into our heads that it is anything else than a plain crocus?

It is an important question. For, throughout our past reasonings about art, we have always found that nothing could be good or useful, or ultimately pleasurable, which was untrue. But here is something pleasurable in written poetry, which is nevertheless *un*true. And what is more, if we think over our favourite poetry, we shall find it full of this kind of fallacy, and that we like it all the more for being so.

§ 5. It will appear also, on consideration of the matter, that this fallacy is of two principal kinds. Either, as in this case of the crocus, it is the fallacy of wilful fancy, which involves no real expectation that it will be believed; or else it is a fallacy caused by an excited state of the feelings, making us, for the time, more or less irrational. Of the cheating of the fancy we shall have to speak presently; but in this chapter, I want to examine the na-

---

subness, must both become metaphysically dejected or rejected, nothing remaining in *us* objective, but subjectivity, and the very objectivity of the object being lost in the abyss of this subjectivity of the Human.

There is, however, some meaning in the above sentence, if the reader cares to make it out; but in a pure German sentence of the highest style there is often none whatever. [Ruskin.]

[3] Contemplative, in the sense explained in Part III. sec. ii. chap. iv. [of *Modern Painters*—Ruskin's note].

[4] Holmes (Oliver Wendell), quoted by Miss Mitford in her *Recollections of a Literary Life*. [Ruskin.]

ture of the other error, that which the mind admits when affected strongly by emotion. Thus, for instance, in Alton Locke,—

> They rowed her in across the rolling foam—
> The cruel, crawling foam.

The foam is not cruel, neither does it crawl. The state of mind which attributes to it these characters of a living creature is one in which the reason is unhinged by grief. All violent feelings have the same effect. They produce in us a falseness in all our impressions of external things, which I would generally characterize as the "pathetic fallacy."

§ 6. Now we are in the habit of considering this fallacy as eminently a character of poetical description, and the temper of mind in which we allow it, as one eminently poetical, because passionate. But I believe, if we look well into the matter, that we shall find the greatest poets do not often admit this kind of falseness,—that it is only the second order of poets who much delight in it.[5]

---

[5] I admit two orders of poets, but no third; and by these two orders I mean the creative (Shakespeare, Homer, Dante), and Reflective or Perceptive (Wordsworth, Keats, Tennyson). But both of these must be *first-rate* in their range, though their range is different; and with poetry second-rate in *quality* no one ought to be allowed to trouble mankind. There is quite enough of the best,—much more than we can ever read or enjoy in the length of a life; and it is a literal wrong or sin in any person to encumber us with inferior work. I have no patience with apologies made by young pseudo-poets, "that they believe there is *some* good in what they have written: that they hope to do better in time," etc. *Some* good! If there is not *all* good, there is no good. If they ever hope to do better, why do they trouble us now? Let them rather courageously burn all they have done, and wait for the better days. There are few men, ordinarily educated, who in moments of strong feeling could not strike out a poetical thought, and afterwards polish it so as to be presentable. But men of sense know better than so to waste their time; and those who sincerely love poetry, know the touch of the master's hand on the chords too well to fumble among them after him. Nay, more than this, all inferior poetry is an injury to the good, inasmuch as it takes away the freshness of rhymes, blunders upon and gives a wretched commonalty to good thoughts; and, in general, adds to the weight of human weariness in a most woful and culpable manner. There are few thoughts likely to come across ordinary men, which have not already been expressed by greater men in the best possible way; and it is a wiser, more generous, more noble thing to remember and point out the perfect words, than to invent poorer ones, wherewith to encumber temporarily the world. [Ruskin.]

Thus, when Dante describes the spirits falling from the bank of Acheron "as dead leaves flutter from a bough," he gives the most perfect image possible of their utter lightness, feebleness, passiveness, and scattering agony of despair, without, however, for an instant losing his own clear perception that *these* are souls, and *those* are leaves; he makes no confusion of one with the other. But when Coleridge speaks of

> The one red leaf, the last of its clan,
> That dances as often as dance it can,[6]

he has a morbid, that is to say, a so far false, idea about the leaf; he fancies a life in it, and will, which there are not; confuses its powerlessness with choice, its fading death with merriment, and the wind that shakes it with music. Here, however, there is some beauty, even in the morbid passage; but take an instance in Homer and Pope. Without the knowledge of Ulysses, Elpenor, his youngest follower, has fallen from an upper chamber in the Circean palace, and has been left dead, unmissed by his leader or companions, in the haste of their departure. They cross the sea to the Cimmerian land; and Ulysses summons the shades from Tartarus. The first which appears is that of the lost Elpenor. Ulysses, amazed, and in exactly the spirit of bitter and terrified lightness which is seen in Hamlet,[7] addresses the spirit with the simple, startled words:—

"Elpenor! How camest thou under the shadowy darkness? Hast thou come faster on foot than I in my black ship?"

Which Pope renders thus:—

> O, say, what angry power Elpenor led
> To glide in shades, and wander with the dead?
> How could thy soul, by realms and seas disjoined,
> Outfly the nimble sail, and leave the lagging wind?

I sincerely hope the reader finds no pleasure here, either in the nimbleness of the sail, or the laziness of the wind! And yet

[6] *Cristabel*, Part I.
[7] "Well said, old mole! canst work i' the ground so fast?" [Ruskin.]

how is it that these conceits are so painful now, when they have been pleasant to us in the other instances?

§ 7. For a very simple reason. They are not a *pathetic* fallacy at all, for they are put into the mouth of the wrong passion—a passion which never could possibly have spoken them—agonized curiosity. Ulysses wants to know the facts of the matter; and the very last thing his mind could do at the moment would be to pause, or suggest in any wise what was *not* a fact. The delay in the first three lines, and conceit in the last, jar upon us instantly like the most frightful discord in music. No poet of true imaginative power could possibly have written the passage. It is worth while comparing the way a similar question is put by the exquisite sincerity of Keats:—

> He wept, and his bright tears
> Went trickling down the golden bow he held.
> Thus, with half-shut, suffused eyes, he stood;
> While from beneath some cumbrous boughs hard by
> With solemn step an awful goddess came,
> And there was purport in her looks for him,
> Which he with eager guess began to read
> Perplex'd, the while melodiously he said,
> 'How camest thou over the unfooted sea?' [Ruskin.
> The quotation is from *Hyperion*, book III.]

Therefore we see that the spirit of truth must guide us in some sort, even in our enjoyment of fallacy. Coleridge's fallacy has no discord in it, but Pope's has set our teeth on edge. Without farther questioning, I will endeavour to state the main bearings of this matter.

§ 8. The temperament which admits the pathetic fallacy, is, as I said above, that of a mind and body in some sort too weak to deal fully with what is before them or upon them; borne away, or over-clouded, or over-dazzled by emotion; and it is a more or less noble state, according to the force of the emotion which has induced it. For it is no credit to a man that he is not morbid or inaccurate in his perceptions, when he has no strength of feeling to warp them; and it is in general a sign of higher capacity and stand in the ranks of being, that the emotions should be strong enough to vanquish, partly, the intellect, and make it believe what they choose. But it is still a grander condition when the intellect also rises, till it is strong enough to assert its rule against, or together with, the utmost efforts of the passions; and the whole man stands in an iron glow, white hot, perhaps, but still strong, and in no wise evaporating; even if he melts, losing none of his weight.

So, then, we have the three ranks: the man who perceives rightly, because he does not feel, and to whom the primrose is very accurately the primrose, because he does not love it. Then, secondly, the man who perceives wrongly, because he feels, and to whom the primrose is anything else than a primrose: a star, or a sun, or a fairy's shield, or a forsaken maiden. And then, lastly, there is the man who perceives rightly in spite of his feelings, and to whom the primrose is for ever nothing else than itself—a little flower apprehended in the very plain and leafy fact of it, whatever and how many soever the associations and passions may be that crowd around it. And, in general, these three classes may be rated in comparative order, as the men who are not poets at all, and the poets of the second order, and the poets of the first; only however great a man may be, there are always some subjects which *ought* to throw him off his balance; some, by which his poor human capacity of thought should be conquered, and brought into the inaccurate and vague state of perception, so that the language of the highest inspiration becomes broken, obscure, and wild in metaphor, resembling that of the weaker man, overborne by weaker things.

§ 9. And thus, in full, there are four classes: the men who feel nothing, and therefore see truly; the men who feel strongly, think weakly, and see untruly (second order of poets); the men who feel strongly, think strongly, and see truly (first order of poets); and the men who, strong as human creatures can be, are yet submitted to influences stronger than they, and see in a sort untruly, because what they see is inconceivably above them. This last is the usual condition of prophetic inspiration.

§ 10. I separate these classes, in order that their character may be clearly understood; but of course they are united each to the other by imperceptible transitions, and the same mind, according to the influences to which it is subjected, passes at different times into the various states. Still, the difference between the great and less man is, on the whole, chiefly in this point of *alterability*. That is to say, the one knows too much, and perceives and feels too much of the past and future, and of all things beside and around that which immediately affects him, to be in any wise shaken by it. His mind is made up; his thoughts have an accustomed current; his ways are steadfast; it is not this or that new sight which will at once unbalance him. He is tender to impression at the surface, like a rock with deep moss upon it; but there is too much mass of him to be moved. The smaller man, with the same degree of sensibility, is at once carried off his feet; he wants to do something he did not want to do before; he views all the universe in a new light through his tears; he is gay or enthusiastic, melancholy or passionate, as things come and go to him. Therefore the high creative poet might even be thought, to a great extent, impassive (as shallow people think Dante stern), receiving indeed all feelings to the full, but having a great centre of reflection and knowledge in which he stands serene, and watches the feeling, as it were, from afar off.

Dante, in his most intense moods, has entire command of himself, and can look around calmly, at all moments, for the image or the word that will best tell what he sees to the upper or lower world. But Keats and Tennyson, and the poets of the second order, are generally themselves subdued by the feelings under which they write, or, at least, write as choosing to be so; and therefore admit certain expressions and modes of thought which are in some sort diseased or false.

§ 11. Now so long as we see that the *feeling* is true, we pardon, or are even pleased by, the confessed fallacy of sight which it induces: we are pleased, for instance, with those lines of Kingsley's above quoted, not because they fallaciously describe foam, but because they faithfully describe sorrow. But the moment the mind of the speaker becomes cold, that moment every such expression becomes untrue, as being for ever untrue in the external facts. And there is no greater baseness in literature than the habit of using these metaphorical expressions in cool blood. An inspired writer, in full impetuosity of passion, may speak wisely and truly of "raging waves of the sea foaming out their own shame"; but it is only the basest writer who cannot speak of the sea without talking of "raging waves," "remorseless floods," "ravenous billows," etc.; and it is one of the signs of the highest power in a writer to check all such habits of thought, and to keep his eyes fixed firmly on the *pure fact*, out of which if any feeling comes to him or his reader, he knows it must be a true one.

To keep to the waves, I forget who it is who represents a man in despair desiring that his body may be cast into the sea,

> Whose changing mound, and foam that passed away,
> Might mock the eyes that questioned where I lay.

Observe, there is not here a single false, or even overcharged, expression. "Mound" of the sea wave is perfectly simple and true; "changing" is as familiar as may be; "foam that passed away," strictly literal; and the whole line descriptive of the reality with a degree of accuracy which I know not any other verse, in the range of poetry, that altogether equals. For most people have not a distinct idea of the clumsiness and massiveness of a large wave. The word "wave" is used too generally of ripples and breakers, and bendings in light drapery or grass: it does not by itself convey a perfect image. But the word "mound" is heavy, large, dark, definite; there is no mistaking the kind of wave meant, nor missing the sight of it. Then the term "changing" has a peculiar force also. Most people think of waves as rising and falling. But if they look at the sea carefully, they will perceive that the waves do not rise and fall. They change. Change both place and form, but they do not fall; one wave goes on, and on, and still on; now lower, now higher, now tossing its mane like a horse, now building itself together like a wall, now shaking, now steady, but still the same wave, till at last it seems struck by something, and changes, one knows not how,—becomes another wave.

The close of the line insists on this image, and paints it still more perfectly,—"foam that passed away." Not merely melting, disappearing, but passing on, out of sight, on the career of the wave. Then, having put the absolute ocean fact as far as he may before our eyes, the poet leaves us to feel about it as we may, and to trace for ourselves the opposite fact,—the image of the green mounds that do not change, and the white and written stones that do not pass away; and thence to follow out also the associated images of the calm life with the quiet grave, and the despairing life with the fading foam—

> Let no man move his bones.
> As for Samaria, her king is cut off like the foam upon the water.[8]

[8] 2 Kings 23:18; Hosea 10:7.

But nothing of this is actually told or pointed out, and the expressions, as they stand, are perfectly severe and accurate, utterly uninfluenced by the firmly governed emotion of the writer. Even the word "mock" is hardly an exception, as it may stand merely for "deceive" or "defeat," without implying any impersonation of the waves.

§ 12. It may be well, perhaps, to give one or two more instances to show the peculiar dignity possessed by all passages, which thus limit their expression to the pure fact, and leave the hearer to gather what he can from it. Here is a notable one from the *Iliad*. Helen, looking from the Scæan gate of Troy over the Grecian host, and telling Priam the names of its captains, says at last:—

"I see all the other dark-eyed Greeks; but two I cannot see,—Castor and Pollux,—whom one mother bore with me. Have they not followed from fair Lacedæmon, or have they indeed come in their sea-wandering ships, but now will not enter into the battle of men, fearing the shame and the scorn that is in Me?"

Then Homer:—

"So she spoke. But them, already, the life-giving earth possessed, there in Lacedæmon, in the dear fatherland." [9]

Note, here, the high poetical truth carried to the extreme. The poet has to speak of the earth in sadness, but he will not let that sadness affect or change his thoughts of it. No; though Castor and Pollux be dead, yet the earth is our mother still, fruitful, life-giving. These are the facts of the thing. I see nothing else than these. Make what you will of them.

§ 13. Take another very notable instance from Casimir de la Vigne's terrible ballad, "La Toilette de Constance." I must quote a few lines out of it here and there, to enable the reader who has not the book by him, to understand its close.

> *Vite, Anna, vite; au miroir,*
> *Plus vite, Anna. L'heure s'avance,*
> *Et je vais au bal ce soir*
> *Chez l'ambassadeur de France.*

[10] *Iliad* III, 243.

Y pensez-vous? ils sont fanés, ces nœuds;
   Ils sont d'hier; mon Dieu, comme tout passe!
Que du réseau qui retient mes cheveux
   Les glands d'azur retombent avec grâce.
Plus haut! Plus bas! Vous ne comprenez rien!
   Que sur mon front ce saphir étincelle:
Vous me piquez, maladroite. Ah, c'est bien,
   Bien,—chère Anna! Je t'aime, je suis belle.

Celui qu'en vain je voudrais oublier . . .
   (Anna, ma robe) il y sera, j'espère.
(Ah, fi! profane, est-ce là mon collier?
   Quoi! ces grains d'or bénits par le Saint-Père!)
Il y sera; Dieu, s'il pressait ma main,
   En y pensant à peine je respire:
Frère Anselmo doit m'entendre demain,
   Comment ferai-je, Anna, pour tout lui dire? . . . .

     Vite! un coup d'œil au miroir,
       Le dernier.—J'ai l'assurance
     Qu'on va m'adorer ce soir
       Chez l'ambassadeur de France.

Près du foyer, Constance s'admirait.
   Dieu! sur sa robe il vole une étincelle!
Au feu! Courez! Quand l'espoir l'enivrait
   Tout perdre ainsi! Quoi! Mourir,—et si belle!
L'horrible feu ronge avec volupté
   Ses bras, son sein, et l'entoure, et s'élève,
Et sans pitié dévore sa beauté,
   Ses dix-huit ans, hélas, et son doux rêve!

     Adieu, bal, plaisir, amour!
       On disait, Pauvre Constance!
     Et on dansait, jusqu'au jour,
       Chez l'ambassadeur de France."

Yes, that is the fact of it. Right or wrong, the poet does not say. What you may think about it, he does not know. He has nothing to do with that. There lie the ashes of the dead girl in her chamber. There they danced, till the morning, at the Ambassador's of France. Make what you will of it.

If the reader will look through the ballad, of which I have quoted only about the third part, he will find that there is not, from beginning to end of it, a single poetical (so called) expression, except in one stanza. The girl speaks as simple prose as may be; there is not a word she would not have actually used as she was dressing. The poet stands by, impassive as a statue, recording her words just as they come. At last the doom seizes her, and in the very presence of death, for an instant, his own emotions conquer him. He records no longer the facts only, but the facts as they seem to him. The fire gnaws with *voluptuousness—without pity.* It is soon past. The fate is fixed for ever; and he retires into his pale and crystalline atmosphere of truth. He closes all with the calm veracity,

"They said, 'Poor Constance!' "

§ 14. Now in this there is the exact type of the consummate poetical temperament. For, be it clearly and constantly remembered, that the greatness of a poet depends upon the two facilities, acuteness of feeling, and command of it. A poet is great, first in proportion to the strength or his passion, and then, that strength being granted, in proportion to his government of it; there being, however, always a point beyond which it would be inhuman and monstrous if he pushed this government, and, therefore, a point at which all feverish and wild fancy becomes just and true. Thus the destruction of the kingdom of Assyria cannot be contemplated firmly by a prophet of Israel. The fact is too great, too wonderful. It overthrows him, dashes him into a confused element of dreams. All the world is, to his stunned thought, full of strange voices. "Yea, the fir-trees rejoice at thee, and the cedars of Lebanon, saying, 'Since thou art gone down to the grave, no feller is come up against us.' " [10] So, still more, the thought of the presence of Deity cannot be borne without this great astonishment. "The mountains and the hills shall break forth before you into singing, and all the trees of the field shall clap their hands." [11]

§ 15. But by how much this feeling is noble when it is justified by the strength of its cause, by so much it is ignoble when there

[10] Isaiah 14:8.
[11] Isaiah 55:12.

is not cause enough for it; and beyond all other ignobleness is
the mere affectation of it, in hardness of heart. Simply bad writing may almost always, as above noticed, be known by its adoption of these fanciful metaphorical expressions as a sort of current
coin; yet there is even a worse, at least a more harmful condition
of writing than this, in which such expressions are not ignorantly
and feelinglessly caught up, but, by some master, skilful in handling, yet insincere, deliberately wrought out with chill and
studied fancy; as if we should try to make an old lava-stream
look red hot again, by covering it with dead leaves, or white-
hot, with hoar-frost.

When Young is lost in veneration, as he dwells on the character of truly good and holy man, he permits himself for a moment
to be overborne by the feeling so far as to exclaim—

> Where shall I find him? angels, tell me where.
> You know him; he is near you; point him out.
> Shall I see glories beaming from his brow,
> Or trace his footsteps by the rising flowers? [12]

This emotion has a worthy cause, and is thus true and right.
But now hear the cold-hearted Pope say to a shepherd girl—

> Where'er you walk, cool gales shall fan the glade;
> Trees, where you sit, shall crowd into a shade;
> Your praise the birds shall chant in every grove,
> And winds shall waft it to the powers above.
> But would you sing, and rival Orpheus' strain,
> The wondering forests soon should dance again;
> The moving mountains hear the powerful call,
> And headlong streams hang, listening, in their fall. [13]

This is not, nor could it for a moment be mistaken for, the
language of passion. It is simple falsehood, uttered by hypocrisy;
definite absurdity, rooted in affectation, and coldly asserted in
the teeth of nature and fact. Passion will indeed go far in deceiv-
ing itself; but it must be a strong passion, not the simple wish of

[12] *Night Thoughts,* II, 345.
[13] *Pastorals:* "Summer." Ruskin omits four lines after the first couplet.

a lover to tempt his mistress to sing. Compare a very closely parallel passage in Wordsworth, in which the lover has lost his mistress:

> Three years had Barbara in her grave been laid,
> When thus his moan he made:—
>
> 'Oh, move, thou cottage, from behind yon oak,
>   Or let the ancient tree uprooted lie,
> That in some other way yon smoke
>   May mount into the sky.
>
> If still behind yon pine-tree's ragged bough,
>   Headlong, the waterfall must come,
>   Oh, let it, then, be dumb—
> Be anything, sweet stream, but that which thou art now.' [14]

Here is a cottage to be moved, if not a mountain, and a waterfall to be silent, if it is not to hang listening: but with what different relation to the mind that contemplates them! Here, in the extremity of its agony, the soul cries out wildly for relief, which at the same moment it partly knows to be impossible, but partly believes possible, in a vague impression that a miracle *might* be wrought to give relief even to a less sore distress,—that nature is kind, and God is kind, and that grief is strong: it knows not well what *is* possible to such grief. To silence a stream, to move a cottage wall,—one might think it could do as much as that!

§ 16. I believe these instances are enough to illustrate the main point I insist upon respecting the pathetic fallacy,—that so far as it *is* a fallacy, it is always the sign of a morbid state of mind, and comparatively of a weak one. Even in the most inspired prophet it is a sign of the incapacity of his human sight or thought to bear what has been revealed to it. In ordinary poetry, if it is found in the thoughts of the poet himself, it is at once a sign of his belonging to the inferior school; if in the thoughts of the characters imagined by him, it is right or wrong according to the genuineness of the emotion from which it springs; always, however, implying necessarily *some* degree of weakness in the character.

[14] " 'Tis said, That some have died for love." Ruskin again misquotes slightly.

Take two most exquisite instances from master hands. The Jessy of Shenstone, and the Ellen of Wordsworth, have both been betrayed and deserted. Jessy, in the course of her most touching complaint, says:

> If through the garden's flowery tribes I stray,
>   Where bloom the jasmines that could once allure,
> 'Hope not to find delight in us,' they say,
>   'For we are spotless, Jessy; we are pure.' [15]

Compare this with some of the words of Ellen:

> 'Ah, why,' said Ellen, sighing to herself,
> 'Why do not words, and kiss, and solemn pledge,
> And nature, that is kind in woman's breast,
> And reason, that in man is wise and good,
> And fear of Him Who is a righteous Judge,—
> Why do not these prevail for human life,
> To keep two hearts together, that began
> Their springtime with one love, and that have need
> Of mutual pity and forgiveness sweet
> To grant, or be received; while that poor bird—
> O, come and hear him! Thou who hast to me
> Been faithless, hear him;—though a lowly creature,
> One of God's simple children that yet know not
> The Universal Parent, *how* he sings!
> As if he wished the firmament of heaven
> Should listen, and give back to him the voice
> Of his triumphant constancy and love;
> The proclamation that he makes, how far
> His darkness doth transcend our fickle light.' [16]

The perfection of both these passages, as far as regards truth and tenderness of imagination in the two poets, is quite insuperable. But of the two characters imagined, Jessy is weaker than Ellen, exactly in so far as something appears to her to be in nature which is not. The flowers do not really reproach her. God meant them to comfort her, not to taunt her; they would do so if she saw them rightly.

[15] William Shenstone (1714–1763), "Elegy XXVI, Describing the sorrow of an ingenuous mind, on the melancholy event of a licentious amour."
[16] *The Excursion,* Book VI, 869–887.

Ellen, on the other hand, is quite above the slightest erring emotion. There is not the barest film of fallacy in all her thoughts. She reasons as calmly as if she did not feel. And, although the singing of the bird suggests to her the idea of its desiring to be heard in heaven, she does not for an instant admit any veracity in the thought. "As if," she says,—"I know he means nothing of the kind; but it does verily seem as if." The reader will find, by examining the rest of the poem, that Ellen's character is throughout consistent in this clear though passionate strength.

It then being, I hope, now made clear to the reader in all respects that the pathetic fallacy is powerful only so far as it is pathetic, feeble so far as it is fallacious, and, therefore, that the dominion of Truth is entire, over this, as over every other natural and just state of the human mind, we may go on to the subject for the dealing with which this prefatory inquiry became necessary; and why necessary, we shall see forthwith.[17]

[17] I cannot quit this subject without giving two more instances, both exquisite, of the pathetic fallacy, which I have just come upon, in *Maud:*

For a great speculation had fail'd;
And ever he mutter'd and madden'd, and ever wann'd with despair;
And out he walk'd, when the wind like a broken worldling wail'd,
And the *flying gold of the ruin'd woodlands drove thro' the air.*

There has fallen a splendid tear
From the passion-flower at the gate.
The red rose cries, 'She is near, she is near!'
And the white rose weeps, 'She is late.'
The larkspur listens, 'I hear, I hear!'
And the lily whispers, 'I wait.'

[Ruskin's note.]

George Eliot

[1819–1880]

GEORGE ELIOT (her real name was Mary Ann Evans) was born on a Warwickshire farm, and lived there and in the nearby town of Coventry until she was thirty. In Coventry she moved among the local intelligentsia, and published her first book, a translation of Strauss' *Life of Jesus*. After the death of her father in 1849 she traveled for a time on the Continent, and eventually settled in London, where she was for several years assistant editor of the *Westminster Review*. She contributed critical articles to the *Review*, and translated Feuerbach's *Essence of Christianity* (1854), but it was not until 1858, when she was nearly forty, that her first work of fiction, *Scenes of Clerical Life*, appeared under the pen name of "George Eliot." During the following two decades she wrote seven novels, as well as two volumes of poetry and one of essays (*Impressions of Theophrastus Such*, 1879).

Like Wordsworth and Ruskin, George Eliot was a moralist in her view of art, but her treatment of the idea was different in two ways: she applied it to the novel, a form which had had little serious critical attention in the nineteenth century, and she extended it to include social and political reform. In her reviews and letters she insisted again and again that art should perform its moral function by enlarging men's sympathies, and she was scathingly critical of "silly novels by women novelists" which taught nothing. But at the same time she was aware of the danger of this principle, and she insisted that the novel must achieve its moral end by "aesthetic teaching," and not by preaching. (Her exchange of letters with Frederic Harrison, the English Positivist, is extremely interesting on this point: see Haight, *Letters*, vol. IV.) For George Eliot, the best defence against preaching is a scrupulous concern for the realities of existence: "Art," she says, "is the nearest thing to life," and if it *is* near, it is moral. In her concern for fiction containing true pictures of human life, she is the first articulate English realist, and her criticism, scattered and fragmentary though it is, is evidence that the novel was being thought of as a serious art form in

England at the same time that Flaubert was thinking seriously about it in France.

BIBLIOGRAPHY. *Essays* (New York, 1884); *Letters,* ed. Gordon Haight, 7 vols. (New Haven, 1954–5).

Barbara Hardy, *The Novels of George Eliot* (London, 1958); Richard Stang, *Theory of the Novel in England, 1850–1870* (New York, 1959).

TEXT. *Essays.*

from

THE NATURAL HISTORY OF GERMAN LIFE

[1856]

IT IS AN INTERESTING branch of psychological observation to note the images that are habitually associated with abstract or collective terms,—what may be called the picture-writing of the mind, which it carries on concurrently with the more subtle symbolism of language. Perhaps the fixity or variety of these associated images would furnish a tolerably fair test of the amount of concrete knowledge and experience which a given word represents in the minds of two persons who use it with equal familiarity. The word *railways,* for example, will probably call up, in the mind of a man who is not highly locomotive, the image either of a Bradshaw,[1] or of the station with which he is most familiar, or of an indefinite length of tram-road; he will alternate between these three images, which represent his stock of concrete acquaintance with railways. But suppose a man to have had successively the experience of a navvy, an engineer, a traveller, a railway director and shareholder, and a landed proprietor in treaty with a railway company, and it is probable that the range of images which would by turns present themselves to his mind at the mention of the *word* railways, would include all the essential facts in the existence and relations of the *thing.* Now it is possible for the first-mentioned

[1] A British railway time-table.

personage to entertain very expanded views as to the multiplication of railways in the abstract, and their ultimate function in civilization. He may talk of a vast network of railways stretching over the globe, of future lines in Madagascar, and elegant refreshment-rooms in the Sandwich Islands, with none the less glibness because his distinct conceptions on the subject do not extend beyond his one station and his indefinite length of tramroad. But it is evident that if we want a railway to be made, or its affairs to be managed, this man of wide views and narrow observation will not serve our purpose.

Probably, if we could ascertain the images called up by the terms "the people," "the masses," "the proletariat," "the peasantry," by many who theorize on those bodies with eloquence, or who legislate without eloquence, we should find that they indicate almost as small an amount of concrete knowledge, that they are as far from completely representing the complex facts summed up in the collective term, as the railway images of our non-locomotive gentleman. How little the real characteristics of the working-classes are known to those who are outside them, how little their natural history has been studied, is sufficiently disclosed by our art as well as by our political and social theories. Where, in our picture-exhibitions, shall we find a group of true peasantry? What English artist even attempts to rival in truthfulness such studies of popular life as the pictures of Teniers or the ragged boys of Murillo? [2] Even one of the greatest painters of the pre-eminently realistic school,[3] while, in his picture of "The Hireling Shepherd," he gave us a landscape of marvellous truthfulness, placed a pair of peasants in the foreground who were not much more real than the idyllic swains and damsels of our chimney-ornaments. Only a total absence of acquaintance and sympathy with our peasantry could give a moment's popularity to such a picture as "Cross-Purposes," where we have a peasant-girl who looks as if she knew L. E. L.'s [4] poems by heart, and English rustics, whose costume seems to indicate that they are meant for ploughmen, with exotic features that remind us of a handsome *primo tenore*.

[2] David Teniers (1610–90), Flemish genre painter; Bartolome Murillo (1617–82), Spanish painter.
[3] Holman Hunt (1827–1910), Pre-Raphaelite painter.
[4] Letitia Elizabeth Landon (1802–38), English poet and novelist.

Rather than such cockney sentimentality as this, as an education for the taste and sympathies, we prefer the most crapulous group of boors that Teniers ever painted. But even those among our painters, who aim at giving the rustic type of features, who are far above the effeminate feebleness of the "Keepsake" style, treat their subjects under the influence of traditions and prepossessions rather than of direct observation. The notion that peasants are joyous, that the typical moment to represent a man in a smock-frock is when he is cracking a joke and showing a row of sound teeth, that cottage matrons are usually buxom and village children necessarily rosy and merry, are prejudices difficult to dislodge from the artistic mind, which looks for its subjects into literature instead of life. The painter is still under the influence of idyllic literature, which has always expressed the imagination of the cultivated and town-bred, rather than the truth of rustic life. Idyllic ploughmen are jocund when they drive their team afield; idyllic shepherds make bashful love under hawthorn bushes; idyllic villagers dance in the checkered shade, and refresh themselves, not immoderately, with spicy nut-brown ale. But no one who has seen much of actual ploughmen thinks them jocund; no one who is well acquainted with the English peasantry can pronounce them merry. The slow gaze, in which no sense of beauty beams, no humor twinkles, the slow utterance, and the heavy slouching walk, remind one rather of that melancholy animal the camel, than of the sturdy countryman, with striped stockings, red waistcoat, and hat aside, who represents the traditional English peasant. Observe a company of haymakers. When you see them at a distance, tossing up the forkfuls of hay in the golden light, while the wagon creeps slowly with its increasing burden over the meadow, and the bright-green space, which tells of work done, gets larger and larger, you pronounce the scene "smiling," and you think these companions in labor must be as bright and cheerful as the picture to which they give animation. Approach nearer, and you will certainly find that haymaking time is a time for joking, especially if there are women among the laborers; but the coarse laugh that bursts out every now and then, and expresses the triumphant taunt, is as far as possible from your conception of idyllic merriment. That delicious effervescence of the mind which we call fun, has no equivalent for the northern

peasant, except tipsy revelry; the only realm of fancy and imagination for the English clown exists at the bottom of the third
quart-pot.

The conventional countryman of the stage, who picks up
pocket-books and never looks into them, and who is too simple
even to know that honesty has its opposite, represents the still
lingering mistake, that an unintelligible dialect is a guarantee for
ingenuousness, and that slouching shoulders indicate an upright
disposition. It is quite true that a thresher is likely to be innocent
of any adroit arithmetical cheating, but he is not the less likely
to carry home his master's corn in his shoes and pocket; a reaper is
not given to writing begging-letters, but he is quite capable of
cajoling the dairymaid into filling his small-beer bottle with ale.
The selfish instincts are not subdued by the sight of buttercups,
nor is integrity in the least established by that classic rural
occupation, sheep-washing. To make men moral, something more
is requisite than to turn them out to grass.

Opera peasants, whose unreality excites Mr. Ruskin's indignation, are surely too frank an idealization to be misleading; and
since popular chorus is one of the most effective elements of the
opera, we can hardly object to lyric rustics in elegant lace bodices
and picturesque motley, unless we are prepared to advocate a
chorus of colliers in their pit costumes, or a ballet of char-women
and stocking-weavers. But our social novels profess to represent
the people as they are, and the unreality of their representations
is a grave evil. The greatest benefit we owe to the artist, whether
painter, poet, or novelist, is the extension of our sympathies. Appeals founded on generalizations and statistics require a sympathy
ready-made, a moral sentiment already in activity; but a picture
of human life such as a great artist can give, surprises even the
trivial and the selfish into that attention to what is apart from
themselves, which may be called the raw material of moral
sentiment. When Scott takes us into Luckie Mucklebackit's [5]
cottage, or tells the story of "The Two Drovers;" when Wordsworth sings to us the reveries of "Poor Susan;" when Kingsley
shows us Alton Locke gazing yearningly over the gate which
leads from the highway into the first wood he ever saw; when

[5] In Scott's *The Antiquary* (1816).

Hornung[6] paints a group of chimney-sweepers,—more is done towards linking the higher classes with the lower, towards obliterating the vulgarity of exclusiveness, than by hundreds of sermons and philosophical dissertations. Art is the nearest thing to life; it is a mode of amplifying experience and extending our contact with our fellow-men beyond the bounds of our personal lot. All the more sacred is the task of the artist when he undertakes to paint the life of the people. Falsification here is far more pernicious than in the more artificial aspects of life. It is not so very serious that we should have false ideas about evanescent fashions, about the manners and conversation of beaux and duchesses; but it *is* serious that our sympathy with the perennial joys and struggles, the toil, the tragedy, and the humor in the life of our more heavily-laden fellow-men, should be perverted, and turned towards a false object instead of the true one.

This perversion is not the less fatal because the misrepresentation which gives rise to it has what the artist considers a moral end. The thing for mankind to know is, not what are the motives and influences which the moralist thinks *ought* to act on the laborer or the artisan, but what are the motives and influences which *do* act on him. We want to be taught to feel, not for the heroic artisan or the sentimental peasant, but for the peasant in all his coarse apathy, and the artisan in all his suspicious selfishness.

We have one great novelist[7] who is gifted with the utmost power of rendering the external traits of our town population; and if he could give us their psychological character—their conception of life, and their emotions—with the same truth as their idiom and manners, his books would be the greatest contribution Art has ever made to the awakening of social sympathies. But while he can copy Mrs. Plornish's colloquial style,[8] with the delicate accuracy of a sun-picture, while there is the same startling inspiration in his description of the gestures and phrases of Boots, as in the speeches of Shakespeare's mobs or numskulls, he scarcely ever passes from the humorous and external to the emotional and tragic, without becoming as transcendent in his un-

6 Joseph Hornung (1792–1870), Swiss historical and genre painter.
7 Charles Dickens.
8 A poor woman in *Little Dorrit* (1857–8).

reality as he was a moment before in his artistic truthfulness. But for the precious salt of his humor, which compels him to reproduce external traits that serve in some degree as a corrective to his frequently false psychology, his preternaturally virtuous poor children and artisans, his melodramatic boatmen and courtesans, would be as obnoxious as Eugène Sue's [9] idealized proletaires, in encouraging the miserable fallacy, that high morality and refined sentiment can grow out of harsh social relations, ignorance, and want; or that the working-classes are in a condition to enter at once into a millennial state of *altruism,* wherein every one is caring for every one else, and no one for himself.

If we need a true conception of the popular character to guide our sympathies rightly, we need it equally to check our theories, and direct us in their application. The tendency created by the spendid conquests of modern generalization, to believe that all social questions are merged in economical science, and that the relations of men to their neighbors may be settled by algebraic equations; the dream that the uncultured classes are prepared for a condition which appeals principally to their moral sensibilities; the aristocratic dilettanteism which attempts to restore the "good old times" by a sort of idyllic masquerading, and to grow feudal fidelity and veneration as we grow prize turnips, by an artificial system of culture,—none of these diverging mistakes can co-exist with a real knowledge of the people, with a thorough study of their habits, their ideas, their motives. The landholder, the clergyman, the mill-owner, the mining-agent, have each an opportunity for making precious observations on different sections of the working-classes, but unfortunately their experience is too often not registered at all, or its results are too scattered to be available as a source of information and stimulus to the public mind generally. If any man of sufficient moral and intellectual breadth, whose observations would not be vitiated by a foregone conclusion or by a professional point of view, would devote himself to studying the natural history of our social classes, especially of the small shopkeepers, artisans, and peasantry,—the degree in which they are influenced by local conditions, their maxims and habits, the points of view from which they regard their religious

[9] French novelist (1804–57).

teachers, and the degree in which they are influenced by religious doctrines, the interaction of the various classes on each other, and what are the tendencies in their position towards disintegration or towards development,—and if, after all this study, he would give us the result of his observations in a book well nourished with specific facts, his work would be a valuable aid to the social and political reformer. . . .

Matthew Arnold

[1822–1888]

ARNOLD WAS EDUCATED at Rugby, where his father was a famous headmaster, and at Oxford. He won prizes for his poetry at both institutions, and continued as a poet after he left Oxford (four volumes of verse appeared between 1849 and 1853). In 1851 he was appointed an Inspector of Schools, and this post was his principal occupation for 25 years. From 1857 to 1867 he was Professor of Poetry at Oxford, though he continued to perform his duties as school inspector. During his tenure as Professor of Poetry, Arnold turned to the writing of prose; in the decades that followed he wrote widely on literary, social, religious, and educational subjects, in an unceasing crusade against the Philistinism of the British public. A government pension allowed him to retire in 1886; he died two years later.

It is impossible to see Arnold apart from Victorian culture. Because he believed that art and society shape each other, and because he saw his own time as a cultural chaos, he devoted his critical energies to encouraging the conditions under which a creative, civilized culture could flourish. He was, as T. S. Eliot has written, "a propagandist for criticism," but this remark is just only if we remember that for Arnold *criticism* meant something vaster than literary judgment: it meant "simply to know the best that is known and thought in the world, and by in its turn making this known, to create a current of true and fresh ideas." It was, therefore, directed toward the evaluation and dissemination of ideas, and its standards of judgment were cultural and moral. In this sense, books like *Culture and Anarchy* are certainly "propaganda," but not pejoratively so.

For support of his didactic theory of poetry, Arnold turned to classical authority; but unlike eighteenth-century neo-classicism, Arnold's is colored by the intervening Romantic movement, and is best understood as a counter-attack on Romantic subjectivism, "the dialogue of the mind with itself." Arnold argued, in his first critical essay, the 1853 Preface, that subjective art is not moral because it does not emerge in action, and for this reason he suppressed (rather melodra-

226

matically) his "Empedocles on Etna" on the grounds that the poem did not embody an answer to the question of how to live.

The same moral bias appears in Arnold's later criticism. We find it, for example, in "The Study of Poetry," in the two famous prescriptions: that poetry must be a "criticism of life," and that the best must have "high seriousness" (a test which Shakespeare passes, but which Chaucer fails). By criticism of life Arnold seems to mean that literature should provide the materials for moral judgment and action; "high seriousness" means the employment of serious moral subjects, and of a tone appropriate to them. This combination of moral direction and "higher truth" suggests a function for poetry very like that traditionally served by religion, and Arnold is one of the first to propose that poetry might serve, in the modern world, as a surrogate for religion. Later poets (Thomas Hardy and Wallace Stevens, for example) have maintained this position, though it has been attacked by T. S. Eliot.

Arnold's weaknesses are those of any thorough-going moralist-critic: he is more often prosecuting attorney than judge, he is inclined to solemnity, and he is blind to works which do not advance his principles (for example, the poems of Keats). Yet in spite of these weaknesses, he has his place in English criticism with those few great critics— Samuel Johnson and T. S. Eliot are among them—who attempted a re-evaluation of the literary tradition for their own time.

BIBLIOGRAPHY. *Works*, 15 vols. (London, 1903); *Complete Prose Works*, ed. R. H. Super (Ann Arbor, Mich., 1961—[in progress]); *Letters, 1848–88*, ed. G. W. E. Russell (London, 1895); *Letters to Arthur Hugh Clough*, ed. H. F. Lowry (New York, 1932); *Essays, Letters, and Reviews*, ed. Fraser Neiman (Cambridge, Mass., 1960).

E. K. Brown, *Matthew Arnold, A Study in Conflict* (Chicago, 1948); Vincent Buckley, *Poetry and Morality* (London, 1959); T. S. Eliot, "Arnold and Pater," *Selected Essays* (New York, 1932) and "Matthew Arnold," *The Use of Poetry and the Use of Criticism* (Cambridge, Mass., 1933); Geoffrey Tillotson, "Matthew Arnold: The Critic and the Advocate," in *Criticism and the Nineteenth Century* (London, 1951); Lionel Trilling, *Matthew Arnold* (2nd. ed., New York, 1959).

TEXTS. *Culture and Anarchy* (3rd ed., New York, 1882); *Irish Essays and Others* (London, 1882); *Essays in Criticism, Second Series* (London, 1888).

preface to

POEMS *

[1853]

IN TWO SMALL VOLUMES of Poems, published anonymously, one
in 1849, the other in 1852, many of the poems which compose the
present volume have already appeared. The rest are now published for the first time.

I have, in the present collection, omitted the poem from which
the volume published in 1852 took its title.[1] I have done so, not
because the subject of it was a Sicilian Greek born between two
and three thousand years ago, although many persons would
think this a sufficient reason. Neither have I done so because I
had, in my own opinion, failed in the delineation which I intended to effect. I intended to delineate the feelings of one of
the last of the Greek religious philosophers, one of the family
of Orpheus and Musæus, having survived his fellows, living on
into a time when the habits of Greek thought and feeling had
begun fast to change, character to dwindle, the influence of the
Sophists to prevail. Into the feelings of a man so situated there
entered much that we are accustomed to consider as exclusively
modern; how much, the fragments of Empedocles himself which
remain to us are sufficient at least to indicate. What those who
are familiar only with the great monuments of early Greek genius
suppose to be its exclusive characteristics, have disappeared; the
calm, the cheerfulness, the disinterested objectivity have disappeared; the dialogue of the mind with itself has commenced;
modern problems have presented themselves; we hear already
the doubts, we witness the discouragement, of Hamlet and of
Faust.

The representation of such a man's feelings must be interesting,

* This is the preface to the first edition of *Poems*.

[1] "Empedocles on Etna."

if consistently drawn. We all naturally take pleasure, says Aristotle,[2] in any imitation or representation whatever: this is the basis of our love of poetry; and we take pleasure in them, he adds, because all knowledge is naturally agreeable to us; not to the philosopher only, but to mankind at large. Every representation, therefore, which is consistently drawn may be supposed to be interesting, inasmuch as it gratifies this natural interest in knowledge of all kinds. What is *not* interesting, is that which does not add to our knowledge of any kind; that which is vaguely conceived and loosely drawn; a representation which is general, indeterminate, and faint, instead of being particular, precise, and firm.

Any accurate representation may therefore be expected to be interesting; but, if the representation be a poetical one, more than this is demanded. It is demanded, not only that it shall interest, but also that it shall inspirit and rejoice the reader; that it shall convey a charm, and infuse delight. For the Muses, as Hesiod says,[3] were born that they might be 'a forgetfulness of evils, and a truce from cares:' and it is not enough that the poet should add to the knowledge of men, it is required of him also that he should add to their happiness. 'All art,' says Schiller,[4] 'is dedicated to Joy, and there is no higher and no more serious problem, than how to make men happy. The right art is that alone, which creates the highest enjoyment.'

A poetical work, therefore, is not yet justified when it has been shown to be an accurate, and therefore interesting representation; it has to be shown also that it is a representation from which men can derive enjoyment. In presence of the most tragic circumstances, represented in a work of art, the feeling of enjoyment, as is well known, may still subsist; the representation of the most utter calamity, of the liveliest anguish, is not sufficient to destroy it; the more tragic the situation, the deeper becomes the enjoyment; and the situation is more tragic in proportion as it becomes more terrible.

What then are the situations, from the representation of which, though accurate, no poetical enjoyment can be derived? They are

[2] *Poetics* 4. 1–5.
[3] *Theogony*, 55.
[4] Preface to *Die Braut von Messina*.

those in which the suffering finds no vent in action; in which a continuous state of mental distress is prolonged, unrelieved by incident, hope, or resistance; in which there is everything to be endured, nothing to be done. In such situations there is inevitably something morbid, in the description of them something monotonous. When they occur in actual life, they are painful, not tragic; the representation of them in poetry is painful also.

To this class of situations, poetically faulty as it appears to me, that of Empedocles, as I have endeavoured to represent him, belongs; and I have therefore excluded the poem from the present collection.

And why, it may be asked, have I entered into this explanation respecting a matter so unimportant as the admission or exclusion of the poem in question? I have done so, because I was anxious to avow that the sole reason for its exclusion was that which has been stated above; and that it has not been excluded in deference to the opinion which many critics of the present day appear to entertain against subjects chosen from distant times and countries: against the choice, in short, of any subjects but modern ones.

'The poet,' it is said [5] and by an intelligent critic, 'the poet who would really fix the public attention must leave the exhausted past, and draw his subjects from matters of present import, and *therefore* both of interest and novelty.'

Now this view I believe to be completely false. It is worth examining, inasmuch as it is a fair sample of a class of critical dicta everywhere current at the present day, having a philosophical form and air, but no real basis in fact; and which are calculated to vitiate the judgment of readers of poetry, while they exert, so far as they are adopted, a misleading influence on the practice of those who make it.

What are the eternal objects of poetry, among all nations, and at all times? They are actions; human actions; possessing an inherent interest in themselves, and which are to be communicated in an interesting manner by the art of the poet. Vainly will the latter imagine that he has everything in his own power; that he can make an intrinsically inferior action equally delightful with a

[5] In the *Spectator* of April 2, 1853. The words quoted were not used with reference to poems of mine. [Arnold's note.]

more excellent one by his treatment of it. He may indeed compel us to admire his skill, but his work will possess, within itself, an incurable defect.

The poet, then, has in the first place to select an excellent action; and what actions are the most excellent? Those, certainly, which most powerfully appeal to the great primary human affections: to those elementary feelings which subsist permanently in the race, and which are independent of time. These feelings are permanent and the same; that which interests them is permanent and the same also. The modernness or antiquity of an action, therefore, has nothing to do with its fitness for poetical representation; this depends upon its inherent qualities. To the elementary part of our nature, to our passions, that which is great and passionate is eternally interesting; and interesting solely in proportion to its greatness and to its passion. A great human action of a thousand years ago is more interesting to it than a smaller human action of to-day, even though upon the representation of this last the most consummate skill may have been expended, and though it has the advantage of appealing by its modern language, familiar manners, and contemporary allusions, to all our transient feelings and interests. These, however, have no right to demand of a poetical work that it shall satisfy them; their claims are to be directed elsewhere. Poetical works belong to the domain of our permanent passions; let them interest these, and the voice of all subordinate claims upon them is at once silenced.

Achilles, Prometheus, Clytemnestra, Dido,—what modern poem presents personages as interesting, even to us moderns, as these personages of an 'exhausted past'? We have the domestic epic dealing with the details of modern life which pass daily under our eyes; we have poems representing modern personages in contact with the problems of modern life, moral, intellectual, and social; these works have been produced by poets the most distinguished of their nation and time; yet I fearlessly assert that Hermann and Dorothea, Childe Harold, Jocelyn, The Excursion,[6] leave the reader cold in comparison with the effect produced upon him by the latter books of the Iliad, by the Oresteia, or by the episode of Dido. And why is this? Simply because in the three last-named

[6] By Goethe, Byron, Lamartine, Wordsworth.

cases the action is greater, the personages nobler, the situations more intense: and this is the true basis of the interest in a poetical work, and this alone.

It may be urged, however, that past actions may be interesting in themselves, but that they are not to be adopted by the modern poet, because it is impossible for him to have them clearly present to his own mind, and he cannot therefore feel them deeply, nor represent them forcibly. But this is not necessarily the case. The externals of a past action, indeed, he cannot know with the precision of a contemporary; but his business is with its essentials. The outward man of Œdipus or of Macbeth, the houses in which they lived, the ceremonies of their courts, he cannot accurately figure to himself; but neither do they essentially concern him. His business is with their inward man; with their feelings and behaviour in certain tragic situations, which engage their passions as men; these have in them nothing local and casual; they are as accessible to the modern poet as to a contemporary.

The date of an action, then, signifies nothing; the action itself, its selection and construction, this is what is all-important. This the Greeks understood far more clearly than we do. The radical difference between their poetical theory and ours consists, as it appears to me, in this: that, with them, the poetical character of the action in itself, and the conduct of it, was the first consideration; with us, attention is fixed mainly on the value of the separate thoughts and images which occur in the treatment of an action. They regarded the whole; we regard the parts. With them, the action predominated over the expression of it; with us, the expression predominates over the action. Not that they failed in expression, or were inattentive to it; on the contrary, they are the highest models of expression, the unapproached masters of the *grand style*. But their expression is so excellent because it is so admirably kept in its right degree of prominence; because it is so simple and so well subordinated; because it draws its force directly from the pregnancy of the matter which it conveys. For what reason was the Greek tragic poet confined to so limited a range of subjects? Because there are so few actions which unite in themselves, in the highest degree, the conditions of excellence: and it was not thought that on any but an excellent subject could an excellent poem be constructed. A few actions, therefore, emi-

nently adapted for tragedy, maintained almost exclusive possession of the Greek tragic stage. Their significance appeared inexhaustible; they were as permanent problems, perpetually offered
to the genius of every fresh poet. This too is the reason of what
appears to us moderns a certain baldness of expression in Greek
tragedy; of the triviality with which we often reproach the remarks of the chorus, where it takes part in the dialogue: that the
action itself, the situation of Orestes, or Merope, or Alcmæon,
was to stand the central point of interest, unforgotten, absorbing,
principal; that no accessories were for a moment to distract the
spectator's attention from this; that the tone of the parts was to be
perpetually kept down, in order not to impair the grandiose effect
of the whole. The terrible old mythic story on which the drama
was founded stood, before he entered the theatre, traced in its
bare outlines upon the spectator's mind; it stood in his memory,
as a group of statuary, faintly seen, at the end of a long and dark
vista: then came the poet, embodying outlines, developing situations, not a word wasted, not a sentiment capriciously thrown in:
stroke upon stroke, the drama proceeded: the light deepened upon
the group; more and more it revealed itself to the riveted gaze
of the spectator: until at last, when the final words were spoken,
it stood before him in broad sunlight, a model of immortal
beauty.

This was what a Greek critic demanded; this was what a Greek
poet endeavoured to effect. It signified nothing to what time an action belonged. We do not find that the Persæ occupied a particularly high rank among the dramas of Æschylus, because it represented a matter of contemporary interest; this was not what a
cultivated Athenian required. He required that the permanent elements of his nature should be moved; and dramas of which the
action, though taken from a long-distant mythic time, yet was calculated to accomplish this in a higher degree than that of the
Persæ, stood higher in his estimation accordingly. The Greeks felt,
no doubt, with their exquisite sagacity of taste, that an action of
present times was too near them, too much mixed up with what
was accidental and passing, to form a sufficiently grand, detached,
and self-subsistent object for a tragic poem. Such objects belonged
to the domain of the comic poet, and of the lighter kinds of poetry.
For the more serious kinds, for *pragmatic* poetry, to use an excel-

lent expression of Polybius, they were more difficult and severe in the range of subjects which they permitted. Their theory and practice alike, the admirable treatise of Aristotle, and the unrivalled works of their poets, exclaim with a thousand tongues— 'All depends upon the subject; choose a fitting action, penetrate yourself with the feeling of its situations; this done, everything else will follow.'

But for all kinds of poetry alike there was one point on which they were rigidly exacting: the adaptability of the subject to the kind of poetry selected, and the careful construction of the poem.

How different a way of thinking from this is ours! We can hardly at the present day understand what Menander meant, when he told a man who enquired as to the progress of his comedy that he had finished it, not having yet written a single line, because he had constructed the action of it in his mind. A modern critic would have assured him that the merit of his piece depended on the brilliant things which arose under his pen as he went along. We have poems which seem to exist merely for the sake of single lines and passages; not for the sake of producing any total impression. We have critics who seem to direct their attention merely to detached expressions, to the language about the action, not to the action itself. I verily think that the majority of them do not in their hearts believe that there is such a thing as a total impression to be derived from a poem at all, or to be demanded from a poet; they think the term a commonplace of metaphysical criticism. They will permit the poet to select any action he pleases, and to suffer that action to go as it will, provided he gratifies them with occasional bursts of fine writing, and with a shower of isolated thoughts and images. That is, they permit him to leave their poetical sense ungratified, provided that he gratifies their rhetorical sense and their curiosity. Of his neglecting to gratify these, there is little danger. He needs rather to be warned against the danger of attempting to gratify these alone; he needs rather to be perpetually reminded to prefer his action to everything else; so to treat this, as to permit its inherent excellences to develop themselves, without interruption from the intrusion of his personal peculiarities; most fortunate, when he most entirely succeeds in effacing himself, and in enabling a noble action to subsist as it did in nature.

But the modern critic not only permits a false practice, he absolutely prescribes false aims.—'A true allegory of the state of one's own mind in a representative history,' the poet is told, 'is perhaps the highest thing that one can attempt in the way of poetry.' And accordingly he attempts it. An allegory of the state of one's own mind, the highest problem of an art which imitates actions! No assuredly, it is not, it never can be so: no great poetical work has ever been produced with such an aim. Faust itself, in which something of the kind is attempted, wonderful passages as it contains, and in spite of the unsurpassed beauty of the scenes which relate to Margaret, Faust itself, judged as a whole, and judged strictly as a poetical work, is defective: its illustrious author, the greatest poet of modern times, the greatest critic of all times, would have been the first to acknowledge it; he only defended his work, indeed, by asserting it to be 'something incommensurable.'

The confusion of the present times is great, the multitude of voices counselling different things bewildering, the number of existing works capable of attracting a young writer's attention and of becoming his models, immense. What he wants is a hand to guide him through the confusion, a voice to prescribe to him the aim which he should keep in view, and to explain to him that the value of the literary works which offer themselves to his attention is relative to their power of helping him forward on his road towards this aim. Such a guide the English writer at the present day will nowhere find. Failing this, all that can be looked for, all indeed that can be desired, is, that his attention should be fixed on excellent models; that he may reproduce, at any rate, something of their excellence, by penetrating himself with their works and by catching their spirit, if he cannot be taught to produce what is excellent independently.

Foremost among these models for the English writer stands Shakespeare: a name the greatest perhaps of all poetical names; a name never to be mentioned without reverence. I will venture, however, to express a doubt, whether the influence of his works, excellent and fruitful for the readers of poetry, for the great majority, has been of unmixed advantage to the writers of it. Shakespeare indeed chose excellent subjects; the world could afford no better than Macbeth, or Romeo and Juliet, or Othello; he had no theory respecting the necessity of choosing subjects of present import, or the paramount interest attaching to allegories of the state of one's own mind; like all great poets, he knew well what constituted a poetical action; like them, wherever he found such an action, he took it; like them, too, he found his best in past times. But to these general characteristics of all great poets he added a special one of his own; a gift, namely, of happy, abundant, and ingenious expression, eminent and unrivalled: so eminent as irresistibly to strike the attention first in him, and even to throw into comparative shade his other excellences as a poet. Here has been the mischief. These other excellences were his fundamental excellences *as a poet;* what distinguishes the artist from the mere amateur, says Goethe, is *Architectonicè* in the highest sense; that power of execution, which creates, forms, and constitutes: not the profoundness of single thoughts, not the richness of imagery, not the abundance of illustration. But these attractive accessories of a poetical work being more easily seized than the spirit of the whole, and these accessories being possessed by Shakespeare in an unequalled degree, a young writer having recourse to Shakespeare as his model runs great risk of being vanquished and absorbed by them, and, in consequence, of reproducing, according to the measure of his power, these, and these alone. Of this preponderating quality of Shakespeare's genius, accordingly, almost the whole of modern English poetry has, it appears to me, felt the influence. To the exclusive attention on the part of his imitators to this it is in a great degree owing, that of the majority of modern poetical works the details alone are valuable, the composition worthless. In reading them one is perpetually reminded of that terrible sentence on a modern French poet:—*Il dit tout ce qu'il veut, mais malheureusement il n'a rien à dire.* [He says all that he wants to, but unfortunately he has nothing to say.]

Let me give an instance of what I mean. I will take it from the works of the very chief among those who seem to have been formed in the school of Shakespeare: of one whose exquisite genius and pathetic death render him for ever interesting. I will take the poem of Isabella, or the Pot of Basil, by Keats. I choose this rather than the Endymion, because the latter work (which a modern critic has classed with the Fairy Queen!) although undoubtedly there blows through it the breath of genius, is yet as a whole so utterly incoherent, as not strictly to merit the name of a poem at all. The poem of Isabella, then is a perfect treasure-house of graceful and felicitous words and images; almost in every stanza there occurs one of those vivid and picturesque turns of expression, by which the object is made to flash upon the eye of the mind, and which thrill the reader with a sudden delight. This one short poem contains, perhaps, a greater number of happy single expressions which one could quote than all the extant tragedies of Sophocles. But the action, the story? The action in itself is an excellent one; but so feebly is it conceived by the poet, so loosely constructed, that the effect produced by it, in and for itself, is absolutely null. Let the reader, after he has finished the poem of Keats, turn to the same story in the De-cameron: he will then feel how pregnant and interesting the same action has become in the hands of a great artist, who above all things delineates his object; who subordinates expression to that which it is designed to express.

I have said that the imitators of Shakespeare, fixing their atten-tion on his wonderful gift of expression, have directed their imi-tation to this, neglecting his other excellences. These excellences, the fundamental excellences of poetical art, Shakespeare no doubt possessed them,—possessed many of them in a splendid degree; but it may perhaps be doubted whether even he himself did not sometimes give scope to his faculty of expression to the prejudice of a higher poetical duty. For we must never forget that Shake-speare is the great poet he is from his skill in discerning and firmly conceiving an excellent action, from his power of intensely feeling a situation, of intimately associating himself with a character; not from his gift of expression, which rather even leads him astray, degenerating sometimes into a fondness for curiosity of expres-sion, into an irritability of fancy, which seems to make it impos-sible for him to say a thing plainly, even when the press of the action demands the very directest language, or its level character the very simplest. Mr. Hallam,[7] than whom it is impossible to find a saner and more judicious critic, has had the courage (for at the present day it needs courage) to remark, how extremely and

[7] Henry Hallam (1777–1859), British historian and critic.

faultily difficult Shakespeare's language often is. It is so: you may find main scenes in some of his greatest tragedies, King Lear for instance, where the language is so artificial, so curiously tortured, and so difficult, that every speech has to be read two or three times before its meaning can be comprehended. This over-curiousness of expression is indeed but the excessive employment of a wonderful gift,—of the power of saying a thing in a happier way than any other man; nevertheless, it is carried so far that one understands what M. Guizot [8] meant, when he said that Shakespeare appears in his language to have tried all styles except that of simplicity. He has not the severe and scrupulous self-restraint of the ancients, partly, no doubt, because he had a far less cultivated and exacting audience. He has indeed a far wider range than they had, a far richer fertility of thought; in this respect he rises above them. In his strong conception of his subject, in the genuine way in which he is penetrated with it, he resembles them, and is unlike the moderns. But in the accurate limitation of it, the conscientious rejection of superfluities, the simple and rigorous development of it from the first line of his work to the last, he falls below them, and comes nearer to the moderns. In his chief works, besides what he has of his own, he has the elementary soundness of the ancients; he has their important action and their large and broad manner; but he has not their purity of method. He is therefore a less safe model; for what he has of his own is personal, and inseparable from his own rich nature; it may be imitated and exaggerated, it cannot be learned or applied as an art. He is above all suggestive; more valuable, therefore, to young writers as men than as artists. But clearness of arrangement, rigour of development, simplicity of style,—these may to a certain extent be learned; and these may, I am convinced, be learned best from the ancients, who, although infinitely less suggestive than Shakespeare, are thus, to the artist, more instructive.

What then, it will be asked, are the ancients to be our sole models? the ancients with their comparatively narrow range of experience and their widely different circumstances? Not certainly, that which is narrow in the ancients, nor that in which we can no longer sympathise. An action like the action of the

---

[8] François Guizot (1787–1874), French historian and statesman.

Antigone of Sophocles, which turns upon the conflict between the heroine's duty to her brother's corpse and that to the laws of her country, is no longer one in which it is possible that we should feel a deep interest. I am speaking too, it will be remembered, not of the best sources of intellectual stimulus for the general reader, but of the best models of instruction for the individual writer. This last may certainly learn of the ancients, better than anywhere else, three things which it is vitally important for him to know:—the all-importance of the choice of a subject; the necessity of accurate construction; and the subordinate character of expression. He will learn from them how unspeakably superior is the effect of the one moral impression left by a great action treated as a whole, to the effect produced by the most striking single thought or by the happiest image. As he penetrates into the spirit of the great classical works, as he becomes gradually aware of their intense significance, their noble simplicity, and their calm pathos, he will be convinced that it is this effect, unity and profoundness of moral impression, at which the ancient poets aimed; that it is this which constitutes the grandeur of their works, and which makes them immortal. He will desire to direct his own efforts towards producing the same effect. Above all, he will deliver himself from the jargon of modern criticism, and escape the danger of producing poetical works conceived in the spirit of the passing time, and which partake of its transitoriness.

The present age makes great claims upon us: we owe it service, it will not be satisfied without our admiration. I know not how it is, but their commerce with the ancients appears to me to produce, in those who constantly practice it, a steadying and composing effect upon their judgment, not of literary works only, but of men and events in general. They are like persons who have had a very weighty and impressive experience: they are more truly than others under the empire of facts; and more independent of the language current among those with whom they live. They wish neither to applaud nor to revile their age; they wish to know what it is, what it can give them, and whether this is what they want. What they want, they know very well; they want to educe and cultivate what is best and noblest in themselves; they know, too, that this is no easy task—χαλεπὸν, as Pittacus said, χαλεπὸν ἐσθλὸν ἔμμεναι [it is hard to be excellent]—and they ask them-

selves sincerely whether their age and its literature can assist
them in the attempt. If they are endeavouring to practise any
art, they remember the plain and simple proceedings of the old
artists, who attained their grand results by penetrating themselves with some noble and significant action, not by inflating
themselves with a belief in the pre-eminent importance and
greatness of their own times. They do not talk of their mission,
nor of interpreting their age, nor of the coming poet; all of this,
they know, is the mere delilirium of vanity; their business is not
to praise their age, but to afford to the men who live in it the
highest pleasure which they are capable of feeling. If asked to
afford this by means of subjects drawn from the age itself, they
ask what special fitness the present age has for supplying them.
They are told that it is an era of progress, an age commissioned
to carry out the great ideas of industrial development and social
amelioration. They reply that with all this they can do nothing;
that the elements they need for the exercise of their art are great
actions, calculated powerfully and delightfully to affect what is
permanent in the human soul; that so far as the present age can
supply such actions, they will gladly make use of them; but that
an age wanting in moral grandeur can with difficulty supply such,
and an age of spiritual discomfort with difficulty be powerfully
and delightfully affected by them.

A host of voices will indignantly rejoin that the present age is
inferior to the past neither in moral grandeur nor in spiritual
health. He who possesses the discipline I speak of will content
himself with remembering the judgments passed upon the present age, in this respect, by the men of strongest head and widest
culture whom it has produced; by Goethe and by Niebuhr.[9] It will
be sufficient for him that he knows the opinions held by these two
great men respecting the present age and its literature; and that
he feels assured in his own mind that their aims and demands
upon life were such as he would wish, at any rate, his own to be;
and their judgment as to what is impeding and disabling such as
he may safely follow. He will not, however, maintain a hostile
attitude towards the false pretensions of his age; he will content
himself with not being overwhelmed by them. He will esteem

[9] Barthold Georg Niebuhr (1776–1831), German historian.

himself fortunate if he can succeed in banishing from his mind all feelings of contradiction, and irritation, and impatience; in order to delight himself with the contemplation of some noble action of a heroic time, and to enable others, through his representation of it, to delight in it also.

I am far indeed from making any claim, for myself, that I possess this discipline; or for the following poems, that they breathe its spirit. But I say, that in the sincere endeavour to learn and practise, amid the bewildering confusion of our times, what is sound and true in poetical art, I seemed to myself to find the only sure guidance, the only solid footing, among the ancients. They, at any rate, knew what they wanted in art, and we do not. It is this uncertainty which is disheartening, and not hostile criticism. How often have I felt this when reading words of disparagement or of cavil: that it is the uncertainty as to what is really to be aimed at which makes our difficulty, not the dissatisfaction of the critic, who himself suffers from the same uncertainty! *Nom me tua fervida terrent Dicta; . . . Dii me terrent, et Jupiter hostis.* [Your hot words do not terrify me. The gods terrify me, and Jupiter if he is my enemy. *Aeneid* XII, 894–5.]

Two kinds of *dilettanti,* says Goethe, there are in poetry: he who neglects the indispensable mechanical part, and thinks he has done enough if he shows spirituality and feeling; and he who seeks to arrive at poetry merely by mechanism, in which he can acquire an artisan's readiness, and is without soul and matter. And he adds, that the first does most harm to art, and the last to himself. If we must be *dilettanti:* if it is impossible for us, under the circumstances amidst which we live, to think clearly, to feel nobly, and to delineate firmly: if we cannot attain to the mastery of the great artists;—let us, at least, have so much respect for our art as to prefer it to ourselves. Let us not bewilder our successors; let us transmit to them the practice of poetry, with its boundaries and wholesome regulative laws, under which excellent works may again, perhaps, at some future time, be produced, not yet fallen into oblivion through our neglect, not yet condemned and cancelled by the influence of their eternal enemy, caprice.

SWEETNESS AND LIGHT *

[1869]

THE DISPARAGERS OF CULTURE make its motive curiosity; sometimes, indeed, they make its motive mere exclusiveness and vanity. The culture which is supposed to plume itself on a smattering of Greek and Latin is a culture which is begotten by nothing so intellectual as curiosity; it is valued either out of sheer vanity and ignorance, or else as an engine of social and class distinction, separating its holder, like a badge or title, from other people who have not got it. No serious man would call this *culture*, or attach any value to it, as culture, at all. To find the real ground for the very differing estimate which serious people will set upon culture, we must find some motive for culture in the terms of which may lie a real ambiguity; and such a motive the word *curiosity* gives us.

I have before now pointed out that we English do not, like the foreigners, use this word in a good sense as well as in a bad sense.[1] With us the word is always used in a somewhat disapproving sense. A liberal and intelligent eagerness about the things of the mind may be meant by a foreigner when he speaks of curiosity, but with us the word always conveys a certain notion of frivolous and unedifying activity. In the *Quarterly Review,* some little time ago, was an estimate of the celebrated French critic, M. Sainte-Beuve, and a very inadequate estimate it in my judgment was. And its inadequacy consisted chiefly in this: that in our English way it left out of sight the double sense really involved in the word *curiosity*, thinking enough was said to stamp M. Sainte-Beuve with blame if it was said that he was impelled in his operations as a critic by curiosity, and omitting either to perceive that M. Sainte-Beuve himself, and many other people with him, would consider that this was praiseworthy and not blameworthy, or to point out why it ought really to be ac-

* FROM *Culture and Anarchy*, 1869.

[1] See Arnold's "The Function of Criticism at the Present Time" (1864).

counted worthy of blame and not of praise. For as there is a curiosity about intellectual matters which is futile, and merely a disease, so there is certainly a curiosity,—a desire after the things of the mind simply for their own sakes and for the pleasure of seeing them as they are,—which is, in an intelligent being, natural and laudable. Nay, and the very desire to see things as they are, implies a balance and regulation of mind which is not often attained without fruitful effort, and which is the very opposite of the blind and diseased impulse of mind which is what we mean to blame when we blame curiosity. Montesquieu [2] says: "The first motive which ought to impel us to study is the desire to augment the excellence of our nature, and to render an intelligent being yet more intelligent." This is the true ground to assign for the genuine scientific passion, however manifested, and for culture, viewed simply as a fruit of this passion; and it is a worthy ground, even though we let the term *curiosity* stand to describe it.

But there is of culture another view, in which not solely the scientific passion, the sheer desire to see things as they are, natural and proper in an intelligent being, appears as the ground of it. There is a view in which all the love of our neighbour, the impulses towards action, help, and beneficence, the desire for removing human error, clearing human confusion, and diminishing human misery, the noble aspiration to leave the world better and happier than we found it,—motives eminently such as are called social,—come in as part of the grounds of culture, and the main and pre-eminent part. Culture is then properly described not as having its origin in curiosity, but as having its origin in the love of perfection; it is *a study of perfection.* It moves by the force, not merely or primarily of the scientific passion for pure knowledge, but also of the moral and social passion for doing good. As, in the first view of it, we took for its worthy motto Montesquieu's words: "To render an intelligent being yet more intelligent!" so, in the second view of it, there is no better motto which it can have than these words of Bishop Wilson: "To make reason and the will of God prevail!" [3]

[2] Charles de Montesquieu (1689–1755), French philosopher of history and government.
[3] Thomas Wilson (1663–1755), Anglican bishop and author of *Maxims of Piety and Christianity.*

Only, whereas the passion for doing good is apt to be over-hasty in determining what reason and the will of God say, because its turn is for acting rather than thinking and it wants to be beginning to act; and whereas it is apt to take its own conceptions, which proceed from its own state of development and share in all the imperfections and immaturities of this, for a basis of action; what distinguishes culture is, that it is possessed by the scientific passion as well as by the passion of doing good; that it demands worthy notions of reason and the will of God, and does not readily suffer its own crude conceptions to substitute themselves for them. And knowing that no action or institution can be salutary and stable which is not based on reason and the will of God, it is not so bent on acting and instituting, even with the great aim of diminishing human error and misery ever before its thoughts, but that it can remember that acting and instituting are of little use, unless we know how and what we ought to act and to institute.

This culture is more interesting and more far-reaching than that other, which is founded solely on the scientific passion for knowing. But it needs times of faith and ardour, times when the intellectual horizon is opening and widening all around us, to flourish in. And is not the close and bounded intellectual horizon within which we have long lived and moved now lifting up, and are not new lights finding free passage to shine in upon us? For a long time there was no passage for them to make their way in upon us, and then it was of no use to think of adapting the world's action to them. Where was the hope of making reason and the will of God prevail among people who had a routine which they had christened reason and the will of God, in which they were inextricably bound, and beyond which they had no power of looking? But now the iron force of adhesion to the old routine,—social, political, religious,—has wonderfully yielded; the iron force of exclusion of all which is new has wonderfully yielded. The danger now is, not that people should obstinately refuse to allow anything but their old routine to pass for reason and the will of God, but either that they should allow some novelty or other to pass for these too easily, or else that they should underrate the importance of them altogether, and think it enough to follow action for its own sake, without troubling themselves to make reason and the will of God prevail therein. Now, then, is the moment for culture to be of service, culture which believes in making reason and the will of God prevail, believes in perfection, is the study and pursuit of perfection, and is no longer debarred, by a rigid invincible exclusion of whatever is new, from getting acceptance for its ideas, simply because they are new.

The moment this view of culture is seized, the moment it is regarded not solely as the endeavour to see things as they are, to draw towards a knowledge of the universal order which seems to be intended and aimed at in the world, and which it is a man's happiness to go along with or his misery to go counter to,—to learn, in short, the will of God,—the moment, I say, culture is considered not merely as the endeavour to *see* and *learn* this, but as the endeavour, also, to make it *prevail*, the moral, social, and beneficent character of culture becomes manifest. The mere endeavour to see and learn the truth for our own personal satisfaction is indeed a commencement for making it prevail, a preparing the way for this, which always serves this, and is wrongly, therefore, stamped with blame absolutely in itself and not only in its caricature and degeneration. But perhaps it has got stamped with blame, and disparaged with the dubious title of curiosity, because in comparison with this wider endeavour of such great and plain utility it looks selfish, petty and unprofitable.

And religion, the greatest and most important of the efforts by which the human race has manifested its impulse to perfect itself,—religion, that voice of the deepest human experience,— does not only enjoin and sanction the aim which is the great aim of culture, the aim of setting ourselves to ascertain what perfection is and to make it prevail; but also, in determining generally in what human perfection consists, religion comes to a conclusion identical with that which culture,—culture seeking the determination of this question through *all* the voices of human experience which have been heard upon it, of art, science, poetry, philosophy, history, as well as of religion, in order to give a greater fulness and certainty to its solution,— likewise reaches. Religion says: *The kingdom of God is within you;* and culture, in like manner, places human perfection in an *internal* condition, in the growth and predominance of our humanity proper, as distinguished from our animality. It places it in the ever-increasing efficacy and in the general harmonious expansion of those gifts of thought and feeling, which make the peculiar dignity, wealth, and happiness of human nature. As I have said on a former occasion: "It is in making endless additions to itself, in the endless expansion of its powers, in endless growth in wisdom and beauty, that the spirit of the human race finds its ideal. To reach this ideal, culture is an indispensable aid, and that is the true value of culture." Not a having and a resting, but a growing and a becoming, is the character of perfection as culture conceives it; and here, too, it coincides with religion.

And because men are all members of one great whole, and the sympathy which is in human nature will not allow one member to be indifferent to the rest or to have a perfect welfare independent of the rest, the expansion of our humanity, to suit the idea of perfection which culture forms, must be a *general* expansion. Perfection, as culture conceives it, is not possible while the individual remains isolated. The individual is required, under pain of being stunted and enfeebled in his own development if he disobeys, to carry others along with him in his march towards perfection, to be continually doing all he can to enlarge and increase the volume of the human stream sweeping thitherward. And here, once more, culture lays on us the same obligation as religion, which says, as Bishop Wilson has admirably put it, that "to promote the kingdom of God is to increase and hasten one's own happiness."

But, finally, perfection,—as culture from a thorough disinterested study of human nature and human experience learns to conceive it,—is a harmonious expansion of all the powers which make the beauty and worth of human nature, and is not consistent with the over-development of any one power at the expense of the rest. Here culture goes beyond religion, as religion is generally conceived by us.

If culture, then, is a study of perfection, and of harmonious perfection, general perfection, and perfection which consists in becoming something rather than in having something, in an inward condition of the mind and spirit, not in an outward set of circumstances,—it is clear that culture, instead of being the frivolous and useless thing which Mr. Bright, and Mr. Frederic Harrison,[4] and many other Liberals are apt to call it, has a very important function to fulfil for mankind. And this function is particularly important in our modern world, of which the whole civilisation is, to a much greater degree than the civilisation of Greece and Rome, mechanical and external, and tends constantly to become more so. But above all in our own country has culture a weighty part to perform, because here that mechanical character, which civilisation tends to take everywhere, is shown in the most eminent degree. Indeed nearly all the characters of perfection, as culture teaches us to fix them, meet in this country with some powerful tendency which thwarts them and sets them at defiance. The idea of perfection as an *inward* condition of the mind and spirit is at variance with the mechanical and material civilisation in esteem with us, and nowhere, as I have said, so much in esteem as with us. The idea of perfection as a *general* expansion of the human family is at variance with our strong individualism, our hatred of all limits to the unrestrained swing of the individual's personality, our maxim of "every man for himself." Above all, the idea of perfection as a *harmonious* expansion of human nature is at variance with our want of flexibility, with our inaptitude for seeing more than one side of a thing, with our intense energetic absorption in the particular pursuit we happen to be following. So culture has a rough task to achieve in this country. Its preachers have, and are likely long to have, a hard time of it, and they will much oftener be regarded, for a great while to come, as elegant or spurious Jeremiahs, than as friends and benefactors. That, however, will not prevent their doing in the end good service if they persevere. And meanwhile, the mode of action they have to pursue, and the sort of habits they must fight against, ought to be made quite clear for every one to see, who may be willing to look at the matter attentively and dispassionately.

Faith in machinery is, I said, our besetting danger; often in machinery most absurdly disproportioned to the end which this machinery, if it is to do any good at all, is to serve; but always

---

[4] John Bright (1811–89), Frederic Harrison (1831–1923), representatives of political and intellectual liberalism.

in machinery, as if it had a value in and for itself. What is freedom but machinery? what is population but machinery? what is coal but machinery? what are railroads but machinery? what is wealth but machinery? what are, even, religious organisations but machinery? Now almost every voice in England is accustomed to speak of these things as if they were precious ends in themselves, and therefore had some of the characters of perfection indisputably joined to them. I have before now noticed Mr. Roebuck's [5] stock argument for proving the greatness and happiness of England as she is, and for quite stopping the mouths of all gainsayers. Mr. Roebuck is never weary of reiterating this argument of his, so I do not know why I should be weary of noticing it. "May not every man in England say what he likes?"—Mr. Roebuck perpetually asks; and that, he thinks, is quite sufficient, and when every man may say what he likes, our aspirations ought to be satisfied. But the aspirations of culture, which is the study of perfection, are not satisfied, unless what men say, when they may say what they like, is worth saying,—has good in it, and more good than bad. In the same way the *Times,* replying to some foreign strictures on the dress, looks, and behaviour of the English abroad, urges that the English ideal is that every one should be free to do and to look just as he likes. But culture indefatigably tries, not to make what each raw person may like the rule by which he fashions himself; but to draw ever nearer to a sense of what is indeed beautiful, graceful, and becoming, and to get the raw person to like that.

And in the same way with respect to railroads and coal. Every one must have observed the strange language current during the late discussions as to the possible failure of our supplies of coal. Our coal, thousands of people were saying, is the real basis of our national greatness; if our coal runs short, there is an end of the greatness of England. But what *is* greatness?—culture makes us ask. Greatness is a spiritual condition worthy to excite love, interest, and admiration; and the outward proof of possessing greatness is that we excite love, interest, and admiration. If England were swallowed up by the sea to-morrow,

[5] John Arthur Roebuck (1801–1879), a Liberal reformer and Member of Parliament, was a frequent target of Arnold's ridicule.

which of the two, a hundred years hence, would most excite
the love, interest, and admiration of mankind,—would most,
therefore, show the evidences of having possessed greatness,—
the England of the last twenty years, or the England of Elizabeth, of a time of splendid spiritual effort, but when our coal,
and our industrial operations depending on coal, were very
little developed? Well, then, what an unsound habit of mind
it must be which makes us talk of things like coal or iron as
constituting the greatness of England, and how salutary a friend
is culture, bent on seeing things as they are, and thus dissipating delusions of this kind and fixing standards of perfection that
are real!

Wealth, again, that end to which our prodigious works for
material advantage are directed,—the commonest of commonplaces tells us how men are always apt to regard wealth as a
precious end in itself; and certainly they have never been so
apt thus to regard it as they are in England at the present time.
Never did people believe anything more firmly, than nine Englishmen out of ten at the present day believe that our greatness
and welfare are proved by our being so very rich. Now, the use
of culture is that it helps us, by means of its spiritual standard
of perfection, to regard wealth as but machinery, and not only
to say as a matter of words that we regard wealth as but machinery, but really to perceive and feel that it is so. If it were
not for this purging effect wrought upon our minds by culture,
the whole world, the future as well as the present, would inevitably belong to the Philistines. The people who believe most
that our greatness and welfare are proved by our being very
rich, and who most give their lives and thoughts to becoming
rich, are just the very people whom we call Philistines. Culture
says: "Consider these people, then, their way of life, their habits,
their manners, the very tones of their voice; look at them attentively; observe the literature they read, the things which give
them pleasure, the words which come forth out of their mouths,
the thoughts which make the furniture of their minds; would any
amount of wealth be worth having with the condition that one
was to become just like these people by having it?" And thus
culture begets a dissatisfaction which is of the highest possible
value in stemming the common tide of men's thoughts in a

wealthy and industrial community, and which saves the future, as one may hope, from being vulgarised, even if it cannot save the present.

Population, again, and bodily health and vigour, are things which are nowhere treated in such an unintelligent, misleading, exaggerated way as in England. Both are really machinery; yet how many people all around us do we see rest in them and fail to look beyond them! Why, one has heard people, fresh from reading certain articles of the *Times* on the Registrar-General's returns of marriages and births in this country, who would talk of our large English families in quite a solemn strain, as if they had something in itself beautiful, elevating, and meritorious in them; as if the British Philistine would have only to present himself before the Great Judge with his twelve children, in order to be received among the sheep as a matter of right!

But bodily health and vigour, it may be said, are not to be classed with wealth and population as mere machinery; they have a more real and essential value. True; but only as they are more intimately connected with a perfect spiritual condition than wealth or population are. The moment we disjoin them from the idea of a perfect spiritual condition, and pursue them, as we do pursue them, for their own sake and as ends in themselves, our worship of them becomes as mere worship of machinery, as our worship of wealth or population, and as unintelligent and vulgarising a worship as that is. Every one with anything like an adequate idea of human perfection has distinctly marked this subordination to higher and spiritual ends of the cultivation of bodily vigour and activity. "Bodily exercise profiteth little; but godliness is profitable unto all things," says the author of the Epistle to Timothy. And the utilitarian Franklin says just as explicitly:—"Eat and drink such an exact quantity as suits the constitution of thy body, *in reference to the services of the mind.*" [6] But the point of view of culture, keeping the mark of human perfection simply and broadly in view, and not assigning to this perfection, as religion or utilitarianism assigns to it, a special and limited character, this point of view,

---

[6] *I Timothy* 4:8; *Poor Richard's Almanack,* December, 1742.

I say, of culture is best given by these words of Epictetus [7]: "It is a sign of ἀφυΐα," says he,—that is, of a nature not finely tempered,—"to give yourselves up to things which relate to the body; to make, for instance, a great fuss about exercise, a great fuss about eating, a great fuss about drinking, a great fuss about walking, a great fuss about riding. All these things ought to be done merely by the way: the formation of the spirit and character must be our real concern." This is admirable; and, indeed, the Greek word εὐφυΐα, a finely tempered nature, gives exactly the notion of perfection as culture brings us to conceive it: a harmonious perfection, a perfection in which the characters of beauty and intelligence are both present, which unites "the two noblest of things,"—as Swift, who of one of the two, at any rate, had himself all too little, most happily calls them in his *Battle of the Books*,—"the two noblest of things, *sweetness and light*." The εὐφυής is the man who tends towards sweetness and light; the ἀφυής, on the other hand, is our Philistine. The immense spiritual significance of the Greeks is due to their having been inspired with this central and happy idea of the essential character of human perfection; and Mr. Bright's misconception of culture, as a smattering of Greek and Latin, comes itself, after all, from this wonderful significance of the Greeks having affected the very machinery of our education, and is in itself a kind of homage to it.

In thus making sweetness and light to be characters of perfection, culture is of like spirit with poetry, follows one law with poetry. Far more than on our freedom, our population, and our industrialism, many amongst us rely upon our religious organisations to save us. I have called religion a yet more important manifestation of human nature than poetry, because it has worked on a broader scale for perfection, and with greater masses of men. But the idea of beauty and of a human nature perfect on all its sides, which is the dominant idea of poetry, is a true and invaluable idea, though it has not yet had the success that the idea of conquering the obvious faults of our animality, and of a human nature perfect on the moral side,—

[7] Greek Stoic philosopher (60?–120? A.D.); the quotation is from his *Encheirodion*, Ch. 41.

which is the dominant idea of religion,—has been enabled to have; and it is destined, adding to itself the religious idea of a devout energy, to transform and govern the other.

The best art and poetry of the Greeks, in which religion and poetry are one, in which the idea of beauty and of a human nature perfect on all sides adds to itself a religious and devout energy, and works in the strength of that, is on this account of such surpassing interest and instructiveness for us, though it was,—as, having regard to the human race in general, and, indeed, having regard to the Greeks themselves, we must own,— a premature attempt, an attempt which for success needed the moral and religious fibre in humanity to be more braced and developed than it had yet been. But Greece did not err in having the idea of beauty, harmony, and complete human perfection, so present and paramount. It is impossible to have this idea too present and paramount; only, the moral fibre must be braced too. And we, because we have braced the moral fibre, are not on that account in the right way, if at the same time the idea of beauty, harmony, and complete human perfection, is wanting or misapprehended amongst us; and evidently it *is* wanting or misapprehended at present. And when we rely as we do on our religious organisations, which in themselves do not and cannot give us this idea, and think we have done enough if we make them spread and prevail, then, I say, we fall into our common fault of overvaluing machinery.

Nothing is more common than for people to confound the inward peace and satisfaction which follows the subduing of the obvious faults of our animality with what I may call absolute inward peace and satisfaction,—the peace and satisfaction which are reached as we draw near to complete spiritual perfection, and not merely to moral perfection, or rather to relative moral perfection. No people in the world have done more and struggled more to attain this relative moral perfection than our English race has. For no people in the world has the command to *resist the devil,* to *overcome the wicked one,* in the nearest and most obvious sense of those words, had such a pressing force and reality. And we have had our reward, not only in the great worldly prosperity which our obedience to this command has brought us, but also, and far more, in great inward

peace and satisfaction. But to me few things are more pathetic
than to see people, on the strength of the inward peace and
satisfaction which their rudimentary efforts towards perfection
have brought them, employ, concerning their incomplete perfection and the religious organisations within which they have
found it, language which properly applies only to complete
perfection, and is a far-off echo of the human soul's prophecy
of it. Religion itself, I need hardly say, supplies them in abundance with this grand language. And very freely do they use it;
yet it is really the severest possible criticism of such an incomplete perfection as alone we have yet reached through our religious organisation. . . .

The pursuit of perfection, then, is the pursuit of sweetness
and light. He who works for sweetness and light, works to
make reason and the will of God prevail. He who works for
machinery, he who works for hatred, works only for confusion.
Culture looks beyond machinery, culture hates hatred; culture
has one great passion, the passion for sweetness and light. It has
one even yet greater!—the passion for making them *prevail.*
It is not satisfied till we *all* come to a perfect man; it knows that
the sweetness and light of the few must be imperfect until the
raw and unkindled masses of humanity are touched with sweetness and light. If I have not shrunk from saying that we must
work for sweetness and light, so neither have I shrunk from
saying that we must have a broad basis, must have sweetness
and light for as many as possible. Again and again I have insisted how those are the happy moments of humanity, how
those are the marking epochs of a people's life, how those are
the flowering times for literature and art and all the creative
power of genius, when there is a *national* glow of life and
thought, when the whole of society is in the fullest measure
permeated by thought, sensible to beauty, intelligent and alive.
Only it must be *real* thought and *real* beauty; *real* sweetness
and *real* light. Plenty of people will try to give the masses, as
they call them, an intellectual food prepared and adapted in the
way they think proper for the actual condition of the masses.
The ordinary popular literature is an example of this way of
working on the masses. Plenty of people will try to indoctrinate
the masses with the set of ideas and judgments constituting the

creed of their own profession or party. Our religious and political organisations give an example of this way of working on the masses. I condemn neither way; but culture works differently. It does not try to teach down to the level of inferior classes; it does not try to win them for this or that sect of its own, with ready-made judgments and watchwords. It seeks to do away with classes; to make the best that has been thought and known in the world current everywhere; to make all men live in an atmosphere of sweetness and light, where they may use ideas, as it uses them itself, freely,—nourished, and not bound by them.

This is the *social idea;* and the men of culture are the true apostles of equality. The great men of culture are those who have had a passion for diffusing, for making prevail, for carrying from one end of society to the other, the best knowledge, the best ideas of their time; who have laboured to divest knowledge of all that was harsh, uncouth, difficult, abstract, professional, exclusive; to humanise it, to make it efficient outside the clique of the cultivated and learned, yet still remaining the *best* knowledge and thought of the time, and a true source, therefore, of sweetness and light. Such a man was Abelard [8] in the Middle Ages, in spite of all his imperfections; and thence the boundless emotion and enthusiasm which Abelard excited. Such were Lessing and Herder [9] in Germany, at the end of the last century; and their services to Germany were in this way inestimably precious. Generations will pass, and literary monuments will accumulate, and works far more perfect than the works of Lessing and Herder will be produced in Germany; and yet the names of these two men will fill a German with a reverence and enthusiasm such as the names of the most gifted masters will hardly awaken. And why? Because they *humanised* knowledge; because they broadened the basis of life and intelligence; because they worked powerfully to diffuse sweetness and light, to make reason and the will of God prevail. With Saint Augustine they said: "Let us not leave Thee alone to make in the secret of thy knowledge, as thou didst before the creation

---

[8] Peter Abelard (1079–1142), scholastic philosopher. One of his "imperfections" was his love for his student Heloise.

[9] G. E. Lessing (1729–81), German critic and playwright; J. G. Herder (1744–1803), German poet and philosopher.

of the firmament, the division of light from darkness; let the
children of thy spirit, placed in their firmament, make their
light shine upon the earth, mark the division of night and day,
and announce the revolution of the times; for the old order is
passed, and the new arises; the night is spent, the day is come
forth; and thou shalt crown the year with thy blessing, when
thou shalt send forth labourers into thy harvest sown by other
hands than theirs; when thou shalt send forth new labourers
to new seed-times, whereof the harvest shall be not yet."

from

THE STUDY OF POETRY

[1880]

"THE FUTURE OF POETRY is immense, because in poetry, where it
is worthy of its high destinies, our race, as time goes on, will
find an ever surer and surer stay. There is not a creed which
is not shaken, not an accredited dogma which is not shown to
be questionable, not a received tradition which does not threaten
to dissolve. Our religion has materialised itself in the fact, in
the supposed fact; it has attached its emotion to the fact, and
now the fact is failing it. But for poetry the idea is everything; the rest is a world of illusion, of divine illusion. Poetry
attaches its emotion to the idea; the idea *is* the fact. The strongest part of our religion to-day is its unconscious poetry."

Let me be permitted to quote these words of my own, as ut-
tering the thought which should, in my opinion, go with us and
govern us in all our study of poetry. In the present work it
is the course of one great contributory stream to the world-
river of poetry that we are invited to follow. We are here invited to trace the stream of English poetry. But whether we set
ourselves, as here, to follow only one of the several streams that
make the mighty river of poetry, or whether we seek to know
them all, our governing thought should be the same. We should
conceive of poetry worthily, and more highly than it has been

the custom to conceive of it. We should conceive of it as capable of higher uses, and called to higher destinies, than those which in general men have assigned to it hitherto. More and more mankind will discover that we have to turn to poetry to interpret life for us, to console us, to sustain us. Without poetry, our science will appear incomplete; and most of what now passes with us for religion and philosophy will be replaced by poetry. Science, I say, will appear incomplete without it. For finely and truly does Wordsworth call poetry "the impassioned expression which is in the countenance of all science"; and what is a countenance without its expression? Again, Wordsworth finely and truly calls poetry "the breath and finer spirit of all knowledge": our religion, parading evidences such as those on which the popular mind relies now; our philosophy, pluming itself on its reasonings about causation and finite and infinite being; what are they but the shadows and dreams and false shows of knowledge? The day will come when we shall wonder at ourselves for having trusted to them, for having taken them seriously; and the more we perceive their hollowness, the more we shall prize "the breath and finer spirit of knowledge" offered to us by poetry.

But if we conceive thus highly of the destinies of poetry, we must also set our standard for poetry high, since poetry, to be capable of fulfilling such high destinies, must be poetry of a high order of excellence. We must accustom ourselves to a high standard and to a strict judgment. Sainte-Beuve [1] relates that Napoleon one day said, when somebody was spoken of in his presence as a charlatan: "Charlatan as much as you please; but where is there *not* charlatanism?"—"Yes," answers Sainte-Beuve, "in politics, in the art of governing mankind, that is perhaps true. But in the order of thought, in art, the glory, the eternal honor is that charlatanism shall find no entrance; herein lies the inviolableness of that noble portion of man's being." It is admirably said, and let us hold fast to it. In poetry, which is thought and art in one, it is the glory, the eternal honour, that charlatanism shall find no entrance; that this noble sphere be kept inviolate and inviolable. Charlatanism is for confusing or obliterating the distinctions between excellent and inferior,

[1] Charles Sainte-Beuve (1804–1869), French critic much admired, and frequently quoted by Arnold.

sound and unsound or only half-sound, true and untrue or only half-true. It is charlatanism, conscious or unconscious, whenever we confuse or obliterate these. And in poetry, more than anywhere else, it is unpermissible to confuse or obliterate them. For in poetry the distinction between excellent and inferior, sound and unsound or only half-sound, true and untrue or only half-true, is of paramount importance. It is of paramount importance because of the high destinies of poetry. In poetry, as a criticism of life under the conditions fixed for such a criticism by the laws of poetic truth and poetic beauty, the spirit of our race will find, we have said, as time goes on and as other helps fail, its consolation and stay. But the consolation and stay will be of power in proportion to the power of the criticism of life. And the criticism of life will be of power in proportion as the poetry conveying it is excellent rather than inferior, sound rather than unsound or half-sound, true rather than untrue or half-true.

The best poetry is what we want; the best poetry will be found to have a power of forming, sustaining, and delighting us, as nothing else can. A clearer, deeper sense of the best in poetry, and of the strength and joy to be drawn from it, is the most precious benefit which we can gather from a poetical collection such as the present. And yet in the very nature and conduct of such a collection there is inevitably something which tends to obscure in us the consciousness of what our benefit should be, and to distract us from the pursuit of it. We should therefore steadily set it before our minds at the outset, and should compel ourselves to revert constantly to the thought of it as we proceed.

Yes; constantly in reading poetry, a sense for the best, the really excellent, and of the strength and joy to be drawn from it, should be present in our minds and should govern our estimate of what we read. But this real estimate, the only true one, is liable to be superseded, if we are not watchful, by two other kinds of estimate, the historic estimate and the personal estimate, both of which are fallacious. A poet or a poem may count to us historically, they may count to us on grounds personal to ourselves, and they may count to us really. They may count to us historically. The course of development of a na-

tion's language, thought, and poetry, is profoundly interesting;
and by regarding a poet's work as a stage in this course of development we may easily bring ourselves to make it of more importance as poetry than in itself it really is, we may come to
use a language of quite exaggerated praise in criticising it; in
short, to overrate it. So arises in our poetic judgments the
fallacy caused by the estimate which we may call historic. Then,
again, a poet or a poem may count to us on grounds personal to ourselves. Our personal affinities, likings, and circumstances, have great power to sway our estimate of this or that
poet's work, and to make us attach more importance to it as
poetry than in itself it really possesses, because to us it is, or
has been, of high importance. Here also we overrate the object
of our interest, and apply to it a language of praise which is
quite exaggerated. And thus we get the source of a second
fallacy in our poetic judgments—the fallacy caused by an estimate which we may call personal.

Both fallacies are natural. It is evident how naturally the
study of the history and development of a poetry may incline
a man to pause over reputations and works once conspicuous
but now obscure, and to quarrel with a careless public for skipping, in obedience to mere tradition and habit, from one famous
name or work in its national poetry to another, ignorant of
what it misses, and of the reason for keeping what it keeps,
and of the whole process of growth in its poetry. The French
have become diligent students of their own early poetry, which
they long neglected; the study makes many of them dissatisfied
with their so-called classical poetry, the court-tragedy of the
seventeenth century, a poetry which Pellisson [2] long ago re-
proached with its want of the true poetic stamp, with its *politesse
stérile et rampante,* but which nevertheless has reigned in France
as absolutely as if it had been the perfection of classical poetry
indeed. The dissatisfaction is natural; yet a lively and accomplished critic, M. Charles d'Héricault, the editor of Clément
Marot, goes too far when he says that "the cloud of glory playing round a classic is a mist as dangerous to the future of a literature as it is intolerable for the purposes of history." "It hin-

[2] Paul Pellisson (1624–1693), French critic.

ders," he goes on, "it hinders us from seeing more than one single point, the culminating and exceptional point; the summary, fictitious and arbitrary, of a thought and of a work. It substitutes a halo for a physiognomy, it puts a statue where there was once a man, and hiding from us all trace of the labour, the attempts, the weaknesses, the failures, it claims not study but veneration; it does not show us how the thing is done, it imposes upon us a model. Above all, for the historian this creation of classic personages is inadmissible; for it withdraws the poet from his time, from his proper life, it breaks historical relationships, it blinds criticism by conventional admiration, and renders the investigation of literary origins unacceptable. It gives us a human personage no longer, but a God seated immovable amidst His perfect work, like Jupiter on Olympus; and hardly will it be possible for the young student, to whom such work is exhibited at such a distance from him, to believe that it did not issue ready made from that divine head."

All this is brilliantly and tellingly said, but we must plead for a distinction. Everything depends on the reality of a poet's classic character. If he is a dubious classic, let us sift him; if he is a false classic, let us explode him. But if he is a real classic, if his work belongs to the class of the very best (for this is the true and right meaning of the word *classic, classical*), then the great thing for us is to feel and enjoy his work as deeply as ever we can, and to appreciate the wide difference between it and all work which has not the same high character. This is what is salutary, this is what is formative; this is the great benefit to be got from the study of poetry. Everything which interferes with it, which hinders it, is injurious. True, we must read our classic with open eyes, and not with eyes blinded with superstition; we must perceive when his work comes short, when it drops out of the class of the very best, and we must rate it, in such cases, at its proper value. But the use of this negative criticism is not in itself, it is entirely in its enabling us to have a clearer sense and a deeper enjoyment of what is truly excellent. To trace the labour, the attempts, the weaknesses, the failures of a genuine classic, to acquaint oneself with his time and his life and his historical relationships, is mere literary dilettantism unless it has that clear sense and deeper enjoyment

for its end. It may be said that the more we know about a classic
the better we shall enjoy him; and, if we lived as long as
Methuselah and had all of us heads of perfect clearness and
wills of perfect steadfastness, this might be true in fact as it is
plausible in theory. But the case here is much the same as the
case with the Greek and Latin studies of our schoolboys. The
elaborate philological groundwork which we require them to
lay is in theory an admirable preparation for appreciating the
Greek and Latin authors worthily. The more thoroughly we
lay the groundwork, the better we shall be able, it may be
said, to enjoy the authors. True, if time were not so short, and
schoolboys' wits not so soon tired and their power of attention
exhausted; only, as it is, the elaborate philological preparation
goes on, but the authors are little known and less enjoyed. So
with the investigator of "historic origins" in poetry. He ought
to enjoy the true classic all the better for his investigations; he
often is distracted from the enjoyment of the best, and with the
less good he overbusies himself, and is prone to overrate it in
proportion to the trouble which it has cost him.

The idea of tracing historic origins and historical relationships cannot be absent from a compilation like the present.
And naturally the poets to be exhibited in it will be assigned to
those persons for exhibition who are known to prize them
highly, rather than to those who have no special inclination
towards them. Moreover the very occupation with an author,
and the business of exhibiting him, disposes us to affirm and
amplify his importance. In the present work, therefore, we are
sure of frequent temptation to adopt the historic estimate, or
the personal estimate, and to forget the real estimate; which
latter, nevertheless, we must employ if we are to make poetry
yield us its full benefit. So high is that benefit, the benefit of
clearly feeling and of deeply enjoying the really excellent, the
truly classic in poetry, that we do well, I say, to set it fixedly
before our minds as our object in studying poets and poetry, and
to make the desire of attaining it the one principle to which, as
the *Imitation* [3] says, whatever we may read or come to know,
we always return. *Cum multa legeris et cognoveris, ad unum*

[3] *The Imitation of Christ,* a medieval religious work, generally attributed
to Thomas à Kempis (1380?–1471), German churchman.

semper oportet redire principium. [When one has read and learned much, he must always return to the one principle.]

The historic estimate is likely in especial to affect our judgment and our language when we are dealing with ancient poets; the personal estimate when we are dealing with poets our contemporaries, or at any rate modern. The exaggerations due to the historic estimate are not in themselves, perhaps, of very much gravity. Their report hardly enters the general ear; probably they do not always impose even on the literary men who adopt them. But they lead to a dangerous abuse of language. So we hear Caedmon [4] amongst our own poets, compared to Milton. I have already noticed the enthusiasm of one accomplished French critic for "historic origins." Another eminent French critic, M. Vitet, comments upon that famous document of the early poetry of his nation, the *Chanson de Roland.* It is indeed a most interesting document. The *joculator* or *jongleur* Taillefer, who was with William the Conqueror's army at Hastings, marched before the Norman troops, so said the tradition, singing "of Charlemagne and of Roland and of Oliver, and of the vassals who died at Roncevaux"; and it is suggested that in the *Chanson de Roland* by one Turoldus or Théroulde, a poem preserved in a manuscript of the twelfth century in the Bodleian Library at Oxford, we have certainly the matter, perhaps even some of the words, of the chant which Taillefer sang. The poem has vigor and freshness; it is not without pathos. But M. Vitet is not satisfied with seeing in it a document of some poetic value, and of very high historic and linguistic value; he sees in it a grand and beautiful work, a monument of epic genius. In its general design he finds the grandiose conception, in its details he finds the constant union of simplicity with greatness, which are the marks, he truly says, of the genuine epic, and distinguish it from the artificial epic of literary ages. One thinks of Homer; this is the sort of praise which is given to Homer, and justly given. Higher praise there cannot well be, and it is the praise due to epic poetry of the highest order only, and to no other. Let us try, then, the *Chanson de Roland* at its best. Roland, mortally wounded, lays

---

[4] English poet who flourished about 670; he was the first to write religious verse in the vernacular.

himself down under a pine-tree, with his face turned towards Spain and the enemy—

> *De plusurs choses à remembrer li prist,*
> *De tantes teres cume li bers cunquist,*
> *De dulce France, des humes de sun lign,*
> *De Charlemagne sun seignor ki l'nurrit.*[5]

That is primitive work, I repeat, with an undeniable poetic quality of its own. It deserves such praise, and such praise is sufficient for it. But now turn to Homer—

> Ὣς φάτο· τοὺς δ'ἤδη κατέχεν φυσίζοος αἶα
> ἐν Λακεδαίμονι αὖθι φίλη ἐν πατρίδι γαίη[6]

We are here in another world, another order of poetry altogether; here is rightly due such supreme praise as that which M. Vitet gives to the *Chanson de Roland.* If our words are to have any meaning, if our judgments are to have any solidity, we must not heap that supreme praise upon poetry of an order immeasurably inferior.

Indeed there can be no more useful help for discovering what poetry belongs to the class of the truly excellent, and can therefore do us most good, than to have always in one's mind lines and expressions of the great masters, and to apply them as a touchstone to other poetry. Of course we are not to require this other poetry to resemble them; it may be very dissimilar. But if we have any tact we shall find them, when we have lodged them well in our minds, an infallible touchstone for detecting the presence or absence of high poetic quality, and also the degree of this quality, in all other poetry which we may place beside them. Short passages, even single lines, will serve our turn quite sufficiently. Take the two lines which I have just quoted from Homer,

---

[5] "Then began he to call many things to remembrance,—all the lands which his valor conquered and pleasant France, and the men of his lineage, and Charlemagne his liege lord who nourished him."—*Chanson de Roland,* iii, 939–942. [Arnold's note.]

[6] "So said she; they long since in Earth's soft arms were reposing, There, in their own dear land, their fatherland, Lacedaemon." *Iliad,* iii, 243, 244 (translated by Dr. Hawtrey). [Arnold.]

the poet's comment on Helen's mention of her brothers;—or take his

> ῏Α δειλώ, τί σφῶϊ δόμεν Πηλῆϊ ἄνακτι
> Θνητᾷ; ὑμεῖς δ' ἐστὸν ἀγήρω τ' ἀθανάτω τε.
> ἦ ἵνα δυστήνοισι μετ' ἀνδράσιν ἄλγε' ἔχητον; [7]

the address of Zeus to the horses of Peleus;—or take finally his

> Καὶ σέ, γέρον, τὸ πρὶν μὲν ἀκούομεν ὄλβιον εἶναι [8]

the words of Achilles to Priam, a suppliant before him. Take that incomparable line and a half of Dante, Ugolino's tremendous words—

> *Io no piangeva; sì dentro impietrai.*
> *Piangevan elli . . .*[9]

take the lovely words of Beatrice to Virgil—

> *Io son fatta da Dio, sua merce, tale,*
> *Che la vostra miseria non mi tange,*
> *Nè fiamma d'esto incendio non m'assale . . .*[10]

take the simple, but perfect, single line—

> *In la sua volontade è nostra pace.*[11]

Take of Shakespeare a line or two of Henry the Fourth's expostulation with sleep—

---

[7] "Ah, unhappy pair, why gave we you to King Peleus, to a mortal? but ye are without old age, and immortal. Was it that with men born to misery ye might have sorrow?"—*Iliad*, xvii, 443–445. [Arnold.]

[8] "Nay, and thou too, old man, in former days wast, as we hear, happy." —*Iliad*, xxiv, 543.

[9] "I wailed not, so of stone grew I within;—*they* wailed."—*Inferno*, xxxiii, 39–40. [Arnold.]

[10] "Of such sort hath God, thanked be His mercy, made me, that your misery toucheth me not, neither doth the flame of this fire strike me."—*Inferno*, ii, 91–93. [Arnold.]

[11] "In his will is our peace."—*Paradiso*, iii, 85.

> Wilt thou upon the high and giddy mast
> Seal up the ship-boy's eyes, and rock his brains
> In cradle of the rude imperious surge . . .[12]

and take, as well, Hamlet's dying request to Horatio—

> If thou didst ever hold me in thy heart,
> Absent thee from felicity awhile,
> And in this harsh world draw thy breath in pain
> To tell my story . . .[13]

Take of Milton that Miltonic passage—

> Darken'd so, yet shone
> Above them all the archangel; but his face
> Deep scars of thunder had intrench'd, and care
> Sat on his faded cheek . . .[14]

add two such lines as—

> And courage never to submit or yield
> And what is else not to be overcome . . .[15]

and finish with the exquisite close to the loss of Proserpine, the loss

> . . . which cost Ceres all that pain
> To seek her through the world.[16]

These few lines, if we have tact and can use them, are enough even of themselves to keep clear and sound our judgments about poetry, to save us from fallacious estimates of it, to conduct us to a real estimate.

The specimens I have quoted differ widely from one another, but they have in common this: the possession of the very highest poetical quality. If we are thoroughly penetrated by their

[12] *Henry IV*, Part II, Act III, scene 1, ll. 18–20.
[13] *Hamlet,* Act V, scene 2, ll. 357–60.
[14] *Paradise Lost,* I, 599–602.
[15] *Ibid.,* 108–109.
[16] *Ibid.,* IV, 271–2

power, we shall find that we have acquired a sense enabling
us, whatever poetry may be laid before us, to feel the degree
in which a high poetical quality is present or wanting there.
Critics give themselves great labor to draw out what in the abstract constitutes the characters of a high quality of poetry. It is
much better simply to have recourse to concrete examples;—
to take specimens of poetry of the high, the very highest quality,
and to say: The characters of a high quality of poetry are what
is expressed *there*. They are far better recognized by being felt
in the verse of the master, than by being perused in the prose
of the critic. Nevertheless if we are urgently pressed to give some
critical account of them, we may safely, perhaps, venture on laying down, not indeed how and why the characters arise, but
where and in what they arise. They are in the matter and sub
stance of the poetry, and they are in its manner and style. Both
of these, the substance and matter on the one hand, the style
and manner on the other, have a mark, an accent, of high beauty,
worth, and power. But if we are asked to define this mark and
accent in the abstract, our answer must be: No, for we should
thereby be darkening the question, not clearing it. The mark and
accent are as given by the substance and matter of that poetry,
by the style and manner of that poetry, and of all other poetry
which is akin to it in quality.

Only one thing we may add as to the substance and matter
of poetry, guiding ourselves by Aristotle's profound observation
that the superiority of poetry over history consists in its possessing
a higher truth and a higher seriousness (φιλοσοφώτερον καί
σπουδαιότερον). Let us add, therefore, to what we have said, this:
that the substance and matter of the best poetry acquire their
special character from possessing, in an eminent degree, truth
and seriousness. We may add yet further, what is in itself evident, that to the style and manner of the best poetry their special
character, their accent, is given by their diction, and, even yet
more, by their movement. And though we distinguish between
the two characters, the two accents, of superiority, yet they are
nevertheless vitally connected one with the other. The superior
character of truth and seriousness, in the matter and substance
of the best poetry, is inseparable from the superiority of diction
and movement marking its style and manner. The two superiori-

ties are closely related, and are in steadfast proportion one to the other. So far as high poetic truth and seriousness are wanting to a poet's manner and substance, so far also, we may be sure, will a high poetic stamp of diction and movement be wanting to his style and manner. In proportion as this high stamp of diction and movement, again, is absent from a poet's style and manner, we shall find, also, that high poetic truth and seriousness are absent from his substance and matter. . . .

George Meredith

[1828–1909]

◈

MEREDITH WAS TRAINED for the bar but gave up law for a career in literature which included at various times work as an editor and as a publisher's reader, as well as the prolific production of novels, short stories, poetry, and critical essays. His philosophical turn of mind and his eccentric, difficult style kept his work from attracting a large popular audience; at the time of his death he had acquired a considerable following among intellectuals, but even this reputation has declined.

On the Idea of Comedy was delivered as a lecture in the same year that Meredith published his best, and most comic, novel, *The Egoist*. Both novel and essay take an essentially classical view of comedy— that its function is to correct and to civilize society through an appeal to "thoughtful laughter"—and it is not surprising to find that Meredith's examples are drawn from the classical and neo-classical periods, from Attic, French neo-classical, and English Restoration plays.

Meredith's comic world is a restricted one—he excludes from it not only the Puritan enemies of laughter but also the "hypergelasts," the belly-laughers. What are left are those cultivated and informed men and women who are capable of detecting ridicule of those they love without loving them less. The test is intellectual, not (as in Hazlitt) psychological; and the form is, in the end, only a sub-division of comedy—the comedy of manners.

If Meredith is the principal English writer on comedy after Hazlitt, this is mainly by default: English criticism of the last hundred years has not concerned itself with genre criticism. *On the Idea of Comedy* is interesting, particularly in relation to Meredith's own novels, but it is neither as rigorous nor as comprehensive as the great work of the seventeenth and eighteenth centuries.

BIBLIOGRAPHY. *Works*, 29 vols. (New York, 1910–12); *Essay on Comedy*, ed. Lane Cooper (Ithaca, 1956).

J. W. Beach, *The Comic Spirit of George Meredith* (New York, 1911); Norman Kelvin, *Troubled Eden: Nature and Society in the*

Works of George Meredith (Stanford, 1961); J. B. Priestley, *George Meredith* (New York, 1926).

TEXT. *An Essay on Comedy* (New York, 1897).

from

ON THE IDEA OF COMEDY AND THE USES OF THE COMIC SPIRIT

[1877]

GOOD COMEDIES ARE SUCH rare productions, that notwithstanding the wealth of our literature in the Comic element, it would not occupy us long to run over the English list. If they are brought to the test I shall propose, very reputable Comedies will be found unworthy of their station, like the ladies of Arthur's Court when they were reduced to the ordeal of the mantle.

There are plain reasons why the Comic poet is not a frequent apparition; and why the great Comic poet remains without a fellow. A society of cultivated men and women is required, wherein ideas are current, and the perceptions quick, that he may be supplied with matter and an audience. The semi-barbarism of merely giddy communities, and feverish emotional periods, repel him; and also a state of marked social inequality of the sexes; nor can he whose business is to address the mind be understood where there is not a moderate degree of intellectual activity.

Moreover, to touch and kindle the mind through laughter demands, more than sprightliness, a most subtle delicacy. That must be a natal gift in the Comic poet. The substance he deals with will show him a startling exhibition of the dyer's hand, if he is without it. People are ready to surrender themselves to witty thumps on the back, breast, and sides; all except the head: and it is there that he aims. He must be subtle to penetrate. A corresponding acuteness must exist to welcome him. The necessity for the two conditions will explain how it is that we count him during centuries in the singular number. . . .

In our prose literature we have had delightful Comic writers. Besides Fielding and Goldsmith, there is Miss Austen, whose *Emma* and Mr. Elton might walk straight into a comedy, were the plot arranged for them. Galt's neglected novels have some characters and strokes of shrewd comedy. In our poetic literature the comic is delicate and graceful above the touch of Italian and French. Generally, however, the English elect excel in satire, and they are noble humorists. The national disposition is for hard-hitting, with a moral purpose to sanction it; or for a rosy, sometimes a larmoyant [tearful], geniality, not unmanly in its verging upon tenderness, and with a singular attraction for thickheadedness, to decorate it with asses' ears and the most beautiful sylvan haloes. But the comic is a different spirit.

You may estimate your capacity for Comic perception by being able to detect the ridicule of them you love without loving them less; and more by being able to see yourself somewhat ridiculous in dear eyes, and accepting the correction their image of you proposes.

Each one of an affectionate couple may be willing, as we say, to die for the other, yet unwilling to utter the agreeable word at the right moment; but if the wits were sufficiently quick for them to perceive that they are in a comic situation, as affectionate couples must be when they quarrel, they would not wait for the moon or the almanac, or a Dorine, to bring back the flood-tide of tender feelings, that they should join hands and lips.

If you detect the ridicule, and your kindliness is chilled by it, you are slipping into the grasp of Satire.

If, instead of falling foul of the ridiculous person with a satiric rod, to make him writhe and shriek aloud, you prefer to sting him under a semi-caress, by which he shall in his anguish be rendered dubious whether indeed anything has hurt him, you are an engine of Irony.

If you laugh all around him, tumble him, roll him about, deal him a smack, and drop a tear on him, own his likeness to you, and yours to your neighbor, spare him as little as you shun, pity him as much as you expose, it is a spirit of Humor that is moving you.

The Comic, which is the perceptive, is the governing spirit, awakening and giving aim to these powers of laughter, but it

is not to be confounded with them; it enfolds a thinner form of
them, differing from satire in not sharply driving into the quiver-
ing sensibilities, and from humor in not comforting them and
tucking them up, or indicating a broader than the range of this
bustling world to them.

Fielding's Jonathan Wild presents a case of this peculiar distinction, when that man of eminent greatness remarks upon the
unfairness of a trial in which the condemnation has been brought
about by twelve men of the opposite party; for it is not satiric,
it is not humorous; yet it is immensely comic to hear a guilty
villain protesting that his own 'party' should have a voice in the
Law. It opens an avenue into villains' ratiocination.¹ And the
Comic is not canceled though we should suppose Jonathan to be
giving play to his humour. (I may have dreamed this, or had it
suggested to me, for, on referring to *Jonathan Wild*, I do not find
it.) Apply the case to the man of deep wit, who is ever certain
of his condemnation by the opposite party, and then it ceases to
be comic, and will be satiric.

The look of Fielding upon Richardson is essentially comic. His
method of correcting the sentimental writer is a mixture of the
comic and the humorous. Parson Adams is a creation of humor.
But both the conception and the presentation of Alceste and of
Tartuffe, of Célimène and Philaminte, are purely comic, addressed
to the intellect; there is no humor in them, and they refresh the
intellect they quicken to detect their comedy, by force of the contrast they offer between themselves and the wiser world about
them—that is to say, society, or that assemblage of minds whereof
the Comic spirit has its origin.

Byron had splendid powers of humor, and the most poetic
satire that we have example of, fusing at times to hard irony.
He had no strong comic sense, or he would not have taken an anti-
social position, which is directly opposed to the Comic; and in his
philosophy, judged by philosophers, he is a comic figure by reason
of his deficiency. '*Sobald er philosophirt ist er ein Kind,*' [The

¹ The exclamation of Lady Booby, when Joseph defends himself: '*Your
virtue!* I shall never survive it!' etc., is another instance.—Joseph Andrews.
Also that of Miss Mathews in her narrative to Booth: 'But such are the
friendships of women.'—Amelia. [Meredith's note.]

moment he reflects he is a child] Goethe says of him. Carlyle sees him in this comic light, treats him in the humorous manner.

The satirist is a moral agent, often a social scavenger, working on a storage of bile.

The ironist is one thing or another, according to his caprice. Irony is the humor of satire; it may be savage, as in Swift, with a moral object, or sedate, as in Gibbon, with a malicious. The foppish irony fretting to be seen, and the irony which leers, that you shall not mistake its intention, are failures in satiric effort pretending to the treasures of ambiguity.

The humorist of mean order is a refreshing laugher, giving tone to the feelings, and sometimes allowing the feelings to be too much for him; but the humorist of high has an embrace of contrasts beyond the scope of the Comic poet.

Heart and mind laugh out at Don Quixote, and still you brood on him. The juxtaposition of the knight and squire is a Comic conception, the opposition of their natures most humorous. They are as different as the two hemispheres in the time of Columbus, yet they touch, and are bound in one, by laughter. The knight's great aims and constant mishaps, his chivalrous valiancy exercised on absurd objects, his good sense along the high road of the craziest of expeditions, the compassion he plucks out of derision, and the admirable figure he preserves while stalking through the frantically grotesque and burlesque assailing him, are in the loftiest moods of humor, fusing the Tragic sentiment with the Comic narrative. The stroke of the great humorist is world-wide, with lights of tragedy in his laughter.

Taking a living great, though not creative, humorist [2] to guide our description: the skull of Yorick is in his hands in our seasons of festival; he sees visions of primitive man capering preposterously under the gorgeous robes of ceremonial. Our souls must be on fire when we wear solemnity, if we would not press upon his shrewdest nerve. Finite and infinite flash from one to the other with him, lending him a two-edged thought that peeps out of his peacefullest lines by fits, like the lantern of the fire-

---

[2] Thomas Carlyle (1795–1881); Meredith is referring particularly to Carlyle's *Sartor Resartus,* which deals with an imaginary Philosophy of Clothes.

watcher at windows, going the rounds at night. The comport-
ment and performances of men in society are to him, by the
vivid comparison with their mortality, more grotesque than
respectable. But ask yourself: 'Is he always to be relied on for
justness?' He will fly straight as the emissary eagle back to Jove
at the true Hero. He will also make as determined a swift descent
upon the man of his wilful choice, whom we cannot distinguish
as a true one. This vast power of his, built up of the feelings and
the intellect in union, is often wanting in proportion and in discretion. Humorists touching upon history or society are given
to be capricious. They are, as in the case of Sterne, given to be
sentimental; for with them the feelings are primary, as with
singers. Comedy, on the other hand, is an interpretation of the
general mind, and is for that reason of necessity kept in restraint.
The French lay marked stress on *mesure et goût*, and they own
how much they owe to Molière for leading them in simple justness and taste. We can teach them many things; they can teach us
in this.

The Comic poet is in the narrow field, or enclosed square, of
the society he depicts; and he addresses the still narrower en-
closure of men's intellects, with reference to the operation of the
social world upon their characters. He is not concerned with
beginnings or endings or surroundings, but with what you are
now weaving. To understand his work and value it, you must
have a sober liking of your kind, and a sober estimate of our
civilized qualities. The aim and business of the Comic poet are
misunderstood, his meaning is not seized nor his point of view
taken, when he is accused of dishonoring our nature and being
hostile to sentiment, tending to spitefulness and making an unfair use of laughter. Those who detect irony in Comedy do so
because they choose to see it in life. Poverty, says the satirist, 'has
nothing harder in itself than that it makes men ridiculous.' But
poverty is never ridiculous to Comic perception until it attempts
to make its rags conceal its bareness in a forlorn attempt at de-
cency, or foolishly to rival ostentation. Caleb Balderstone [3] in
his endeavor to keep up the honor of a noble household in a state
of beggary, is an exquisitely comic character. In the case of 'poor

---

[3] A faithful servant in Sir Walter Scott's *The Bride of Lammermoor*.

relatives,' on the other hand, it is the rich, whom they perplex, that are really comic; and to laugh at the former, not seeing the comedy of the latter, is to betray dulness of vision. Humorist and Satirist frequently hunt together as Ironists in pursuit of the grotesque, to the exclusion of the Comic. That was an affecting moment in the history of the Prince Regent, when the First Gentleman of Europe burst into tears at a sarcastic remark of Beau Brummell's on the cut of his coat. Humor, Satire, Irony, pounce on it altogether as their common prey. The Comic Spirit eyes, but does not touch, it. Put into action, it would be farcical. It is too gross for Comedy.

Incidents of a kind casting ridicule on our unfortunate nature, instead of our conventional life, provoke derisive laughter, which thwarts the Comic idea. But derision is foiled by the play of the intellect. Most of doubtful causes in contest are open to Comic interpretation, and any intellectual pleading of a doubtful cause contains germs of an Idea of Comedy.

The laughter of satire is a blow in the back or the face. The laughter of Comedy is impersonal and of unrivaled politeness, nearer a smile—often no more than a smile. It laughs through the mind, for the mind directs it; and it might be called the humor of the mind.

One excellent test of the civilization of a country, as I have said, I take to be the flourishing of the Comic idea and Comedy; and the test of true Comedy is that it shall awaken thoughtful laughter.

Gerard Manley Hopkins

[1844–1889]

❧❦❧

HOPKINS' FAME AND INFLUENCE are posthumous. His career as a poet was almost completely private, for, as a Jesuit, he had renounced all desire for literary renown. Doubtless the conflict between his passionate and sensuous nature and the strict vows of his profession account for both the intensity of the verse which he "charged with the grandeur of God" and the intransigence with which he rejected contemporary metrics and poetic diction. Hopkins showed early promise in both writing and drawing (two of his brothers were artists). He entered Balliol College, Oxford, in 1863, and was influenced not only by Ruskin and Pater but also by the Oxford Movement. In 1866 he was received into the Roman Catholic Church by John Henry (later Cardinal) Newman. When he joined the Society of Jesus in 1868 Hopkins destroyed much of his early poetry and for eight years did not write again. After his ordination as a priest in 1877 he found poetry compatible with his vocation. He served in a number of English and Scottish Jesuit establishments in several capacities, including teacher of Classics. In 1884 he was appointed professor of Classics in University College, Dublin. He died of enteric fever in 1889.

It was his friend and correspondent Robert Bridges, the poet laureate, who first in anthologies, then in a volume in 1918, introduced Hopkins' poetry to the world. This poetry was carefully and passionately wrought in accordance with Hopkins' own aesthetic; two of its chief tenets are presented in the selections below, a note on "inscape" and the preface to his poetic manuscript. By "inscape" he means the "outward reflection of the *inner* nature of a thing," a conception he developed by analogy from the *haeccitus* ("this-ness") in the philosophy of Duns Scotus. "Sprung Rhythm" reflects his interest in Welsh and Anglo-Saxon poetry and anticipates, on entirely different grounds, the effort of Pound and Eliot to free the metrics of English verse from the mechanical regularity of late nineteenth-century practice.

BIBLIOGRAPHY. *Poems,* ed. W. H. Gardner, 3rd edition (New York and London, 1948); *The Letters of Gerard Manley Hopkins to Robert*

Bridges, ed. C. C. Abbott, 2 vols. (2nd ed., New York and London, 1955); *The Journals and Papers of Gerard Manley Hopkins*, ed. Humphrey House (New York and London, 1959).
W. H. Gardner, *Gerard Manley Hopkins*, 2 vols. (New Haven, 1948–49); The Kenyon Critics, *Gerard Manley Hopkins* (New York, 1945); W. A. M. Peters, *Gerard Manley Hopkins: A Critical Essay* (Oxford, 1948); John Pick, *Gerard Manley Hopkins, Priest and Poet* (London, 1942); Norman Weyand, ed., *Immortal Diamond: Studies in Gerard Manley Hopkins* (New York, 1949).

TEXT. *Journals and Papers; Poems* (Oxford, 1930).

LECTURE NOTES ON POETRY AND VERSE *

[1873–1874]

Is ALL VERSE POETRY or all poetry verse?—Depends on definitions of both. Poetry is speech framed for contemplation of the mind by the way of hearing or speech framed to be heard for its own sake and interest even over and above its interest of meaning. Some matter and meaning is essential to it but only as an element necessary to support and employ the shape which is contemplated for its own sake. (Poetry is in fact speech only employed to carry the inscape of speech for the inscape's sake—and therefore the inscape must be dwelt on. Now if this can be done without repeating it *once* of the inscape will be enough for art and beauty and poetry but then at least the inscape must be understood as so standing by itself that it could be copied and repeated. If not repetition, *oftening, over-and-overing, aftering* of the inscape must take place in order to detach it to the mind and in this light poetry is speech which afters and oftens its inscape, speech couched in a repeating figure and verse is spoken sound having a repeating figure.) Verse is (inscape of spoken sound, not spoken words, or speech employed to carry the inscape of spoken sound—

* "Preface" from *Poems of Gerard Manley Hopkins* (Copyright 1918, 1930) and "Lecture Notes on Poetry and Verse" from *Journals and Papers of Gerard Manley Hopkins* (Copyright 1959), reprinted by permission of the Oxford University Press.

or in the usual words) speech wholly or partially repeating the same figure of sound. Now there is speech which wholly or partially repeats the same figure of grammar and this may be framed to be heard for its own sake and interest over and above its interest of meaning. Poetry then may be couched in this, and therefore all poetry is not verse but all poetry is either verse or falls under this or some still further development of what verse is, speech wholly or partially repeating some kind of figure which is over and above meaning, at least the grammatical, historical, and logical meaning.

But is all verse poetry?—Verse may be applied for use, e.g. to help the memory, and then is useful art, not μουσική [inspired song] ('Thirty days hath September' and 'Propria quae maribus' or Livy's *horrendum carmen*) and so is not poetry. Or it might be composed without meaning (as nonsense verse and choruses—'Hey nonny nonny' or 'Wille wau wau wau' etc.) and then *alone* it would not be poetry but might be part of a poem. But if it has a meaning and is meant to be heard for its own sake it will be poetry if you take poetry to be a kind of composition and not the virtue or success or excellence of that kind, as eloquence is the virtue of oratory and not oratory only and beauty the virtue of inscape and not inscape only. In this way poetry may be high or low, good or bad, and doggrel will be poor or low poetry but not merely verse, for it aims at interest or amusement. But if poetry is the virtue of its own kind of composition then all verse even composed for its own interest's sake is not poetry.

preface to

POEMS

[1883]

THE POEMS IN THIS BOOK are written some in Running Rhythm, the common rhythm in English use, some in Sprung Rhythm, and some in a mixture of the two. And those in the common rhythm are some counterpointed, some not.

Common English rhythm, called Running Rhythm above, is measured by feet of either two or three syllables and (putting aside the imperfect feet at the beginning and end of lines and also some unusual measures, in which feet seem to be paired together and double or composite feet to arise) never more or less.

Every foot has one principal stress or accent, and this or the syllable it falls on may be called the Stress of the foot and the other part, the one or two unaccented syllables, the Slack. Feet (and the rhythms made out of them) in which the stress comes first are called Falling Feet and Falling Rhythms, feet and rhythms in which the slack comes first are called Rising Feet and Rhythms, and if the stress is between two slacks there will be Rocking Feet and Rhythms. These distinctions are real and true to nature; but for purposes of scanning it is a great convenience to follow the example of music and take the stress always first, as the accent of the chief accent always comes first in a musical bar. If this is done there will be in common English verse only two possible feet—the so-called accentual Trochee and Dactyl, and correspondingly only two possible uniform rhythms, the so-called Trochaic and Dactylic. But they may be mixed and then what the Greeks called a Logaoedic Rhythm arises. These are the facts and according to these the scanning of ordinary regularly-written English verse is very simple indeed and to bring in other principles is here unnecessary.

But because verse written strictly in these feet and by these principles will become same and tame the poets have brought in licences and departures from rule to give variety, and especially when the natural rhythm is rising, as in the common ten-syllable or five-foot verse, rhymed or blank. These irregularities are chiefly Reversed Feet and Reversed or Counterpoint Rhythm, which two things are two steps or degrees of licence in the same kind. By a reversed foot I mean the putting the stress where, to judge by the rest of the measure, the slack should be and the slack where the stress, and this is done freely at the beginning of a line and, in the course of a line, after a pause; only scarcely ever in the second foot or place and never in the last, unless when the poet designs some extraordinary effect; for these places are characteristic and sensitive and cannot well be touched. But the reversal of the first foot and of some middle foot after a strong pause is a thing so natural that our poets have generally done it, from Chaucer down, without remark and it commonly passes unnoticed and cannot be said to amount to a formal change of rhythm, but rather is that irregularity which all natural growth and motion shews. If however the reversal is repeated in two feet running, especially so as to include the sensitive second foot, it must be due either to great want of ear or else is a calculated effect, the superinducing or *mounting* of a new rhythm upon the old; and since the new or mounted rhythm is actually heard and at the same time the mind naturally supplies the natural or standard foregoing rhythm, for we do not forget what the rhythm is that by rights we should be hearing, two rhythms are in some manner running at once and we have something answerable to counterpoint in music, which is two or more strains of tune going on together, and this is Counterpoint Rhythm. Of this kind of verse Milton is the great master and the choruses of *Samson Agonistes* are written throughout in it—but with the disadvantage that he does not let the reader clearly know what the ground-rhythm is meant to be and so they have struck most readers as merely irregular. And in fact if you counterpoint throughout, since one only of the counter rhythms is actually heard, the other is really destroyed or cannot come to exist, and what is written is one rhythm only and probably Sprung Rhythm, of which I now speak.

Sprung Rhythm, as used in this book, is measured by feet of from one to four syllables, regularly, and for particular effects any number of weak or slack syllables may be used. It has one stress, which falls on the only syllable, if there is only one, or, if there are more, then scanning as above, on the first, and so gives rise to four sorts of feet, a monosyllable and the so-called accentual Trochee, Dactyl, and the First Paeon. And there will be four corresponding natural rhythms; but nominally the feet are mixed and any one may follow any other. And hence Sprung Rhythm differs from Running Rhythm in having or being only one nominal rhythm, a mixed or "logaoedic" one, instead of three, but on the other hand in having twice the flexibility of foot, so that any two stresses may either follow one another running or be divided by one, two, or three slack syllables. But strict Sprung Rhythm cannot be counterpointed. In Sprung Rhythm, as in logaoedic rhythm generally, the feet are assumed to be equally long or strong and their seeming inequality is made up by pause or stressing.

Remark also that it is natural in Sprung Rhythm for the lines to be *rove over,* that is for the scanning of each line immediately to take up that of the one before, so that if the first has one or more syllables at its end the other must have so many the less at its beginning; and in fact the scanning runs on without break from the beginning, say, of a stanza to the end and all the stanza is one long strain, though written in lines asunder.

Two licences are natural to Sprung Rhythm. The one is rests, as in music; but of this an example is scarcely to be found in this book, unless in the *Echoes,* second line. The other is *hangers* or *outrides,* that is one, two, or three slack syllables added to a foot and not counting in the nominal scanning. They are so called because they seem to hang below the line or ride forward or backward from it in another dimension than the line itself, according to a principle needless to explain here. These outriding half feet or hangers are marked by a loop underneath them, and plenty of them will be found.

The other marks are easily understood, namely accents, where the reader might be in doubt which syllable should have the stress; slurs, that is loops *over* syllables, to tie them together into the time of one; little loops at the end of a line to shew that the rhyme goes on to the first letter of the next line; what in music are called pauses ⌢, to shew that the syllable should be dwelt on; and twirls ∼, to mark reversed or counterpointed rhythm.

Note on the nature and history of Sprung Rhythm—Sprung Rhythm is the most natural of things. For (1) it is the rhythm of common speech and of written prose, when rhythm is perceived in them. (2) It is the rhythm of all but the most monotonously regular music, so that in the words of choruses and refrains and in songs written closely to music it arises. (3) It is found in nursery rhymes, weather saws, and so on; because, however these may have been once made in running rhythm, the terminations having dropped off by the change of language, the stresses come together and so the rhythm is sprung. (4) It arises in common verse when reversed or counterpointed, for the same reason.

But nevertheless in spite of all this and though Greek and

Latin lyric verse, which is well known, and the old English verse seen in "Pierce Ploughman" are in sprung rhythm, it has in fact ceased to be used since the Elizabethan age, Greene being the last writer who can be said to have recognized it. For perhaps there was not, down to our days, a single, even short, poem in English in which sprung rhythm is employed—not for single effects or in fixed places—but as the governing principle of the scansion. I say this because the contrary has been asserted: if it is otherwise the poem should be cited.

Some of the sonnets in this book are in five-foot, some in six-foot or Alexandrine lines.

Nos. 13 and 22 are Curtal-Sonnets, that is they are constructed in proportions resembling those of the sonnet proper, namely, 6+4 instead of 8+6, with however a halfline tail-piece (so that the equation is rather $12/2 + 9/2 = 21/2 = 10\frac{1}{2}$).

Walter Pater

[1839-1894]

◆◆◆

PATER WAS A QUIET semi-recluse whose life was most noteworthy for its total uneventfulness. From his nineteenth year until his death he lived at Oxford, as a student and then as a tutor and Fellow of Brasenose College. His first book, *Studies in the History of the Renaissance* (1873), was popular with the younger generation, but its doctrine of sensation sought for its own sake so offended some of Pater's contemporaries that in the second edition he suppressed the "Conclusion" of the book, with its famous exhortation to "burn with a hard, gem-like flame," restoring it to later editions only in a modified version. Other books were *Marius the Epicurean* (1885), *Imaginary Portraits* (1887), *Appreciations* (1889), *Plato and Platonism* (1893), and two posthumous collections, *Greek Studies* and *Miscellaneous Studies* (both 1895).

The Renaissance came at a time of reaction against the militant moralism of the High Victorians, and Pater was taken up as the prophet of Aestheticism and Decadence in a way which must have been highly distasteful to him. It is true that his criticism is impressionistic and aesthetic (two terms which were, for Pater, interchangeable), and that one does not find in his writing the Victorian critical vocabulary—Truth, Reality and Morality have given way to Curiosity, Strangeness, and Beauty. Still, art-for-art's sake did not mean for Pater what it meant for Wilde; Pater had concluded that, in the absence of absolutes, one must limit one's aspirations after knowledge to direct sensation, but this meant, as he explained in *Marius*, "Not pleasure, but a general completeness of life," and the mode of living which he presented is best described by a word which recurs throughout the book—*decorous*.

Pater's aesthetic impressionism meant, in critical practice, the abandonment of historical or other objective methods of description and judgment: *classical* and *romantic* become eternal elements rather than historical movements, and subjective recreation of the aesthetic experience replaces argued evaluation. As a result, the criticism itself

281

becomes a work of art; just as *Marius* is on the borderline between
fiction and philosophy, so Pater's essays lie between formal criticism
and poetic prose (a point demonstrated by Yeats when he chose a
passage from *The Renaissance* as the first "poem" in his *Oxford Book
of Modern Verse*).

Nevertheless, Pater's method does not imply an abandonment of
values: like Arnold, he was concerned to secure the highest products
of the human mind from the degradations of the Philistines, and thus
to preserve the moral worth of art. Arnold chose to do so by insisting
that art be a "criticism of life"; Pater, more indirectly, urged that the
love of art for its own sake gives a significance to "your moments as
they pass" which is itself a kind of moral knowledge, and a defence
against stupidity and vulgarity.

BIBLIOGRAPHY. *Works,* 10 vols. (London, 1910).

Ruth C. Child, *The Aesthetic of Walter Pater* (New York, 1940);
T. S. Eliot, "Arnold and Pater," in *Selected Essays* (New York, 1932);
Graham Hough, *The Last Romantics* (London, 1949); Helen Hawthorne Young, *The Writings of Walter Pater* (Bryn Mawr, Penna.,
1933).

TEXT. *Studies in the History of the Renaissance* (London, 1873).

from preface to

STUDIES IN THE HISTORY OF THE RENAISSANCE

[1873]

MANY ATTEMPTS HAVE BEEN MADE by writers on art and poetry
to define beauty in the abstract, to express it in the most general
terms, to find a universal formula for it. The value of such attempts has most often been in the suggestive and penetrating
things said by the way. Such discussions help us very little to
enjoy what has been well done in art or poetry, to discriminate
between what is more and what is less excellent in them, or to
use words like beauty, excellence, art, poetry, with more meaning

than they would otherwise have. Beauty, like all other qualities presented to human experience, is relative; and the definition of it becomes unmeaning and useless in proportion to its abstractness. To define beauty not in the most abstract, but in the most concrete terms possible, not to find a universal formula for it, but the formula which expresses most adequately this or that special manifestation of it, is the aim of the true student of aesthetics.

'To see the object as in itself it really is,' has been justly said to be the aim of all true criticism whatever; and in aesthetic criticism the first step towards seeing one's object as it really is, is to know one's own impression as it really is, to discriminate it, to realize it distinctly. The objects with which aesthetic criticism deals, music, poetry, artistic and accomplished forms of human life, are indeed receptacles of so many powers or forces; they possess, like natural elements, so many virtues or qualities. What is this song or picture, this engaging personality presented in life or in a book, to *me*? What effect does it really produce on me? Does it give me pleasure? and if so, what sort or degree of pleasure? How is my nature modified by its presence and under its influence? The answers to these questions are the original facts with which the aesthetic critic has to do; and, as in the study of light, of morals, of number, one must realize such primary data for oneself or not at all. And he who experiences these impressions strongly, and drives directly at the analysis and discrimination of them, need not trouble himself with the abstract question what beauty is in itself, or its exact relation to truth or experience,— metaphysical questions, as unprofitable as metaphysical questions elsewhere. He may pass them all by as being, answerable or not, of no interest to him.

The aesthetic critic, then, regards all the objects with which he has to do, all works of art and the fairer forms of nature and human life, as powers or forces, producing pleasurable sensations, each of a more or less peculiar and unique kind. This influence he feels and wishes to explain, analyzing it, and reducing it to its elements. To him, the picture, the landscape, the engaging personality in life or in a book, La Gioconda, the hills of Carrara, Pico of Mirandula, are valuable for their virtues, as we say in speaking of a herb, a wine, a gem; for the property each has of affecting one with a special, unique impression of pleasure. Education grows in proportion as one's susceptibility to these impressions increases in depth and variety. And the function of the aesthetic critic is to distinguish, analyze, and separate from its adjuncts, the virtue by which a picture, a landscape, a fair personality in life or in a book, produces this special impression of beauty or pleasure, to indicate what the source of that impression is, and under what conditions it is experienced. His end is reached when he has disengaged that virtue, and noted it, as a chemist notes some natural element, for himself and others; and the rule for those who would reach this end is stated with great exactness in the words of a recent critic of Sainte-Beuve: 'De se borner à connaître de près les belles choses, et à s'en nourrir en exquis amateurs, en humanistes accomplis' [To devote oneself to knowing intimately the finer things of life, and to nourish oneself with such things, as an expert connoisseur, an accomplished humanist].

What is important, then, is not that the critic should possess a correct abstract definition of beauty for the intellect, but a certain kind of temperament, the power of being deeply moved by the presence of beautiful objects. He will remember always that beauty exists in many forms. To him all periods, types, schools of taste, are in themselves equal. In all ages there have been some excellent workmen and some excellent work done. The question he asks is always, In whom did the stir, the genius, the sentiment of the period find itself? who was the receptacle of its refinement, its elevation, its taste? 'The ages are all equal,' says William Blake, 'but genius is always above its age.'

Often it will require great nicety to disengage this virtue from the commoner elements with which it may be found in combination. Few artists, not Goethe or Byron even, work quite cleanly, casting off all debris, and leaving us only what the heat of their imagination has wholly fused and transformed. Take for instance the writings of Wordsworth. The heat of his genius, entering into the substance of his work, has crystallized a part, but only a part, of it; and in that great mass of verse there is much which might well be forgotten. But scattered up and down it, sometimes fusing and transforming entire compositions, like the Stanzas on 'Resolution and Independence' and the Ode on the 'Recollections of

Childhood,' sometimes, as if at random, turning a fine crystal here and there, in a matter it does not wholly search through and transform, we trace the action of his unique incommunicable faculty, that strange mystical sense of a life in natural things, and of man's life as a part of nature, drawing strength and color and character from local influences, from the hills and streams and natural sights and sounds. Well! that is the *virtue*, the active principle in Wordsworth's poetry; and then the function of the critic of Wordsworth is to trace that active principle, to disengage it, to mark the degree in which it penetrates his verse. . . .

conclusion to

STUDIES IN THE HISTORY OF THE RENAISSANCE

[1873]

Λέγει που Ἡράκλειτος ὅτι πάντα χωρεῖ καὶ οὐδὲν μένει.
[Heraclitus says somewhere that everything moves and nothing abides.]

To REGARD ALL THINGS and principles of things as inconstant modes or fashions has more and more become the tendency of modern thought. Let us begin with that which is without—our physical life. Fix upon it in one of its more exquisite intervals, the moment, for instance, of delicious recoil from the flood of water in summer heat. What is the whole physical life in that moment but a combination of natural elements to which science gives their names? But these elements, phosphorus and lime and delicate fibres, are present not in the human body alone: we detect them in places most remote from it. Our physical life is a perpetual motion of them—the passage of the blood, the wasting and repairing of the lenses of the eye, the modification of the tissues of the brain by every ray of light and sound—processes which science reduces to simpler and more elementary forces. Like the elements of which we are composed, the action of these forces extends beyond us; it rusts iron and ripens corn. Far out on every side of us these elements are broadcast, driven by many forces; and birth and gesture and death and the springing of violets from the grave are but a few out of ten thousand resulting combinations. That clear perpetual outline of face and limb is but an image of ours under which we group them—a design in a web, the actual threads of which pass out beyond it. This at least of flame-like our life has, that it is but the concurrence, renewed from moment to moment, of forces parting sooner or later on their ways.

Or if we begin with the inward world of thought and feeling, the whirlpool is still more rapid, the flame more eager and devouring. There it is no longer the gradual darkening of the eye and fading of color from the wall,—the movement of the shore side, where the water flows down indeed, though in apparent rest,—but the race of the midstream, a drift of momentary acts of sight and passion and thought. At first sight experience seems to bury us under a flood of external objects, pressing upon us with a sharp importunate reality, calling us out of ourselves in a thousand forms of action. But when reflection begins to act upon those objects they are dissipated under its influence; the cohesive force is suspended like a trick of magic; each object is loosed into a group of impressions,—color, odor, texture,—in the mind of the observer. And if we continue to dwell on this world, not of objects in the solidity with which language invests them, but of impressions unstable, flickering, inconsistent, which burn and are extinguished with our consciousness of them, it contracts still further; the whole scope of observation is dwarfed to the narrow chamber of the individual mind. Experience, already reduced to a swarm of impressions, is ringed round for each one of us by that thick wall of personality through which no real voice has ever pierced on its way to us, or from us to that which we can only conjecture to be without. Every one of those impressions is the impression of the individual in his isolation, each mind keeping as a solitary prisoner its own dream of a world.

Analysis goes a step further still, and tells us that those impressions of the individual to which, for each one of us, experience dwindles down, are in perpetual flight; that each of them is limited by time, and that as time is infinitely divisible, each of them is infinitely divisible also; all that is actual in it being a single moment, gone while we try to apprehend it, of which it may ever be more truly said that it has ceased to be than that it is. To such a tremulous wisp constantly reforming itself on the stream, to a single sharp impression, with a sense in it, a relic more or less fleeting, of such moments gone by, what is real in our life fines itself down. It is with the movement, the passage and dissolution of impressions, images, sensations, that analysis leaves off,—that continual vanishing away, that strange perpetual weaving and unweaving of ourselves.

Philosophiren, says Novalis, *ist dephlegmatisiren, vivificiren.* [Philosophizing is dephlegmatizing, inspiriting.] The service of philosophy, and of religion and culture as well, to the human spirit, is to startle it into a sharp and eager observation. Every moment some form grows perfect in hand or face; some tone on the hills or sea is choicer than the rest; some mood of passion or insight or intellectual excitement is irresistibly real and attractive for us,—for that moment only. Not the fruit of experience, but experience itself is the end. A counted number of pulses only is given to us of a variegated, dramatic life. How may we see in them all that is to be seen in them by the finest senses? How can we pass most swiftly from point to point, and be present always at the focus where the greatest number of vital forces unite in their purest energy?

To burn always with this hard gem-like flame, to maintain this ecstasy, is success in life. Failure is to form habits; for habit is relative to a stereotyped world; meantime it is only the roughness of the eye that makes any two persons, things, situations, seem alike. While all melts under our feet, we may well catch at any exquisite passion, or any contribution to knowledge that seems, by a lifted horizon, to set the spirit free for a moment, or any stirring of the senses, strange dyes, strange flowers, and curious odors, or work of the artist's hands, or the face of one's friend. Not to discriminate every moment some passionate attitude in those about us, and in the brilliance of their gifts some tragic dividing of forces on their ways is, on this short day of frost and sun, to sleep before evening. With this sense of the splendor of our experience and of its awful brevity, gathering all we are into one desperate effort to see and touch, we shall hardly have time to make theories about the things we see and touch. What we have to do is to be for ever curiously testing new opinions and courting new impressions, never acquiescing in a facile orthodoxy of Comte or of Hegel, or of our own. Theories, religious or philosophical ideas, as points of view, instruments of criticism, may help us to gather up what might otherwise pass unregarded by us. *La philosophie, c'est la microscope de la pensée.* [Philosophy is the microscope of thought.] The theory, or idea, or system, which requires of us the sacrifice of any part of this experience, in consideration of some interest into which we cannot enter, or some abstract morality we have not identified with ourselves, or what is only conventional, has no real claim upon us.

One of the most beautiful places in the writings of Rousseau is that in the sixth book of the 'Confessions,' where he describes the awakening in him of the literary sense. An undefinable taint of death had always clung about him, and now in early manhood he believed himself stricken by mortal disease. He asked himself how he might make as much as possible of the interval that remained; and he was not biassed by anything in his previous life when he decided that it must be by intellectual excitement, which he found in the clear, fresh writings of Voltaire. Well, we are all *condamnés,* as Victor Hugo says: *les hommes sont tous condamnés a morte avec des sursis indéfinis* [all men are condemned to death by indefinite delays]: we have an interval, and then our place knows us no more. Some spend this interval in listlessness, some in high passions, the wisest in art and song. For our one chance is in expanding that interval, in getting as many pulsations as possible into the given time. High passions give one this quickened sense of life, ecstasy and sorrow of love, political or religious enthusiasm, or the 'enthusiasm of humanity.' Only, be sure it is passion, that it does yield you this fruit of a quickened, multiplied consciousness. Of this wisdom, the poetic passion, the desire of beauty, the love of art for art's sake has most; for art comes to you professing frankly to give nothing but the highest quality to your moments as they pass, and simply for those moments' sake.

Henry James

[1843–1916]

HENRY JAMES WAS BORN IN New York City and was educated in Europe and at Harvard. His father was a transcendental philosopher and friend of Emerson and Carlyle; his brother, William, was a distinguished psychologist. James' literary career began at the age of 22 when his first story appeared in the *Atlantic Monthly*; four years later he moved to Europe and lived there, in London, Paris, and Italy, until his death, with only intermittent trips to the United States. In 1916, the year of his death, he became a British citizen as a protest against America's policy of non-intervention in the First World War. In all, James wrote almost 80 books, including novels, volumes of stories and of travel observations, plays, autobiography, biography, and criticism.

James wrote more about the art of the novel—both his own and other writers'—than any other novelist. His prefaces to the New York Edition of his fiction (1907–1917) are brilliantly illuminating examples of a master craftsman explaining how it was done. In his numerous essays and reviews of other writers' work he is still the craftsman, but he is also the high priest of fiction, insisting that the novel is "a sacred office," and condemning novelists (like Trollope) who are content to tell a good story, to "make believe."

James, more than any other writer in English, is responsible for the present status of the novel as an art form. When he first appeared on the scene, the English novel had, as he says in this essay (first published in 1884), "no air of having a theory, a conviction, a consciousness of itself behind it." It was regarded as either an entertainment for the young and idle, or as a mode of moral instruction, and was subject to severe restrictions of subject and treatment. James abandoned neither the idea of entertainment ("the only obligation to which in advance we may hold a novel . . . is that it be interesting") nor the idea of morality. But he saw the moral value of a novel as a function of its truth to reality, and insisted therefore that there must be "freedom to feel and say" what truth demanded. What we judge, in the end, is not the subject but the execution of the subject, and this will

289

be determined by the quality of mind of the artist. "In proportion as that intelligence is fine will the novel, the picture, the statue partake of the substance of beauty and truth." In this sentence, the gap between Art and Morality, which has run through Victorian criticism, is bridged.

BIBLIOGRAPHY. *French Poets and Novelists* (London, 1878); *Hawthorne* (London, 1879); *Partial Portraits* (London and New York, 1888); *Views and Reviews* (Boston, 1908); *Notes on Novelists* (London, 1914); *Notes and Reviews* (Cambridge, Mass., 1921); *The Art of the Novel: Critical Prefaces,* ed. R. P. Blackmur (New York, 1934); *The American Essays,* ed. Leon Edel (New York, 1956); *Literary Reviews and Essays,* ed. Albert Mordell (New York, 1957).

Leon Edel, *Prefaces of Henry James* (Paris, 1931); F. W. Dupee, ed., *The Question of Henry James* (New York, 1945); R. P. Blackmur, "Henry James," in *Literary History of the United States,* vol. II, ed. R. E. Spiller *et al.* (New York, 1949).

TEXT. *Partial Portraits* (1888).

THE ART OF FICTION

[1888]

I SHOULD NOT HAVE AFFIXED so comprehensive a title to these few remarks, necessarily wanting in any completeness upon a subject the full consideration of which would carry us far, did I not seem to discover a pretext for my temerity in the interesting pamphlet lately published under this name by Mr. Walter Besant. Mr. Besant's lecture at the Royal Institution [1]—the original form of his pamphlet—appears to indicate that many persons are interested in the art of fiction, and are not indifferent to such remarks, as those who practice it may attempt to make about it. I am therefore anxious not to lose the benefit of this favourable association, and to edge in a few words under cover of the attention which Mr. Besant is sure to have excited. There is something

[1] Walter Besant (1836–1901), British novelist. The lecture was given in April, 1884.

very encouraging in his having put into form certain of his ideas on the mystery of story-telling.

It is a proof of life and curiosity—curiosity on the part of the brotherhood of novelists as well as on the part of their readers. Only a short time ago it might have been supposed that the English novel was not what the French call *discutable*. It had no air of having a theory, a conviction, a consciousness of itself behind it—of being the expression of an artistic faith, the result of choice and comparison. I do not say it was necessarily the worse for that: it would take much more courage than I possess to intimate that the form of the novel as Dickens and Thackery (for instance) saw it had any taint of incompleteness. It was, however, *naïf* (if I may help myself out with another French word); and evidently if it be destined to suffer in any way for having lost its *naïveté* it has now an idea of making sure of the corresponding advantages. During the period I have alluded to there was a comfortable, good-humoured feeling abroad that a novel is a novel, as a pudding is a pudding, and that our only business with it could be to swallow it. But within a year or two, for some reason or other, there have been signs of returning animation—the era of discussion would appear to have been to a certain extent opened. Art lives upon discussion, upon experiment, upon curiosity, upon variety of attempt, upon the exchange of views and the comparison of standpoints; and there is a presumption that those times when no one has anything particular to say about it, and has no reason to give for practice or preference, though they may be times of honour, are not times of development—are times, possibly even, a little of dulness. The successful application of any art is a delightful spectacle, but the theory too is interesting; and though there is a great deal of the latter without the former I suspect there has never been a genuine success that has not had a latent core of conviction. Discussion, suggestion, formulation, these things are fertilizing when they are frank and sincere. Mr. Besant has set an excellent example in saying what he thinks, for his part, about the way in which fiction should be written, as well as about the way in which it should be published; for his view of the "art," carried on into an appendix, covers that too. Other labourers in the same field will doubtless take up the argument, they will give it the light of their experience, and the effect will surely be to make our interest in the novel a little more what it had for some time threatened to fail to be—a serious, active, inquiring interest, under protection of which this delightful study may, in moments of confidence, venture to say a little more what it thinks of itself.

It must take itself seriously for the public to take it so. The old superstition about fiction being "wicked" has doubtless died out in England; but the spirit of it lingers in a certain oblique regard directed toward any story which does not more or less admit that it is only a joke. Even the most jocular novel feels in some degree the weight of the proscription that was formerly directed against literary levity: the jocularity does not always succeed in passing for orthodoxy. It is still expected, though perhaps people are shamed to say it, that a production which is after all only a "make-believe" (for what else is a "story"?) shall be in some degree apologetic—shall renounce the pretension of attempting really to represent life. This, of course, any sensible, wide-awake story declines to do, for it quickly perceives that the tolerance granted to it on such a condition is only an attempt to stifle it disguised in the form of generosity. The old evangelical hostility to the novel, which was as explicit as it was narrow, and which regarded it as little less favourable to our immortal part than a stage-play, was in reality far less insulting. The only reason for the existence of a novel is that it does attempt to represent life. When it relinquishes this attempt, the same attempt that we see on the canvas of the painter, it will have arrived at a very strange pass. It is not expected of the picture that it will make itself humble in order to be forgiven; and the analogy between the art of the painter and the art of the novelist is, so far as I am able to see, complete. Their inspiration is the same, their process (allowing for the different quality of the vehicle) is the same, their success is the same. They may learn from each other, they may explain and sustain each other. Their cause is the same, and the honour of one is the honour of another. The Mohametans think a picture an unholy thing, but it is a long time since any Christian did, and it is therefore the more odd that in the Christian mind the traces (dissimulated though they may be) of a suspicion of the sister art should linger to this day. The only effectual way to lay it to rest is to emphasize the analogy to which I just alluded—to insist on the fact that as the picture is reality, so the novel is history. That is the only general description (which does it justice) that we may give of the novel. But history also is allowed to represent life; it is not, any more than painting, expected to apologize. The subject-matter of fiction is stored up likewise in documents and records, and if it will not give itself away, as they say in California, it must speak with assurance, with the tone of the historian. Certain accomplished novelists have a habit of giving themselves away which must often bring tears to the eyes of people who take their fiction seriously. I was lately struck, in reading over many pages of Anthony Trollope, with his want of discretion in this particular. In a digression, a parenthesis or an aside, he concedes to the reader that he and this trusting friend are only "making believe." He admits that the events he narrates have not really happened, and that he can give his narrative any turn the reader may like best. Such a betrayal of a sacred office seems to me, I confess, a terrible crime; it is what I mean by the attitude of apology, and it shocks me every whit as much in Trollope as it would have shocked me in Gibbon or Macaulay. It implies that the novelist is less occupied in looking for the truth (the truth, of course I mean, that he assumes, the premises that we must grant him, whatever they may be) than the historian, and in doing so it deprives him at a stroke of all his standing-room. To represent and illustrate the past, the actions of men, is the task of either writer, and the only difference that I can see is, in proportion as he succeeds, to the honour of the novelist, consisting as it does in his having more difficulty in collecting his evidence, which is so far from being purely literary. It seems to me to give him a great character, the fact that he has at once so much in common with the philosopher and the painter; this double analogy is a magnificent heritage.

It is of all this evidently that Mr. Besant is full when he insists upon the fact that fiction is one of the *fine* arts, deserving in its turn of all the honours and emoluments that have hitherto been reserved for the successful profession of music, poetry, painting, architecture. It is impossible to insist too much on so important a truth, and the place that Mr. Besant demands for the work of the novelist may be represented, a trifle less abstractly, by saying that he demands not only that it shall be reputed artistic, but that it shall be reputed very artistic indeed. It is excellent that he should have struck this note, for his doing so indicates that there was need of it, that his proposition may be to many people a novelty. One rubs one's eyes at the thought; but the rest of Mr. Besant's essay confirms the revelation. I suspect in truth that it would be possible to confirm it still further, and that one would not be far wrong in saying that in addition to the people to whom it has never occurred that a novel ought to be artistic, there are a great many others who, if this principle were urged upon them, would be filled with an indefinable mistrust. They would find it difficult to explain their repugnance, but it would operate strongly to put them on their guard. "Art," in our Protestant communities, where so many things have got so strangely twisted about, is supposed in certain circles to have some vaguely injurious effect upon those who make it an important consideration, who let it weigh in the balance. It is supposed to be opposed in some mysterious manner to morality, to amusement, to instruction. When it is embodied in the work of the painter (the sculptor is another affair!) you know what it is: it stands there before you, in the honesty of pink and green and a gilt frame; you can see the worst of it at a glance, and you can be on your guard. But when it is introduced into literature it becomes more insidious—there is danger of its hurting you before you know it. Literature should be either instructive or amusing, and there is in many minds an impression that these artistic preoccupations, the search for form, contribute to neither end, interfere indeed with both. They are too frivolous to be edifying, and too serious to be diverting; and they are moreover priggish and paradoxical and superfluous. That, I think, represents the manner in which the latent thought of many people who read novels as an exercise in skipping would explain itself if it were to become articulate. They would argue, of course, that a novel ought to be "good," but they would interpret this term in a fashion of their own, which indeed would vary considerably from one critic to another. One would say that being good means representing virtuous and aspiring characters, placed in prominent positions; another would say that it depends on a "happy ending," on a distribution at the last of prizes, pensions, husbands, wives, babies, millions, appended paragraphs, and cheerful remarks. Another still would say that it means being full of incident and movement, so that we shall wish to jump ahead, to see who was the mysterious stranger, and if the stolen will was ever found, and shall not be distracted from this pleasure by any tiresome analysis or "description." But they would all agree that the "artistic" idea would spoil some of their fun. One would hold it accountable for all the description, another would see it revealed in the absence of sympathy. Its hostility to a happy ending would be evident, and it might even in some cases render any ending at all impossible. The "ending" of a novel is, for many persons, like that of a good dinner, a course of dessert and ices, and the artist in fiction is regarded as a sort of meddlesome doctor who forbids agreeable aftertastes. It is therefore true that this conception of Mr. Besant's of the novel as a superior form encounters not only a negative but a positive indifference. It matters little that as a work of art it should really be as little or as much of its essence to supply happy endings, sympathetic characters, and an objective tone, as if it were a work of mechanics; the association of ideas, however incongruous, might easily be too much for it if an eloquent voice were not sometimes raised to call attention to the fact that it is at once as free and as serious a branch of literature as any other.

Certainly this might sometimes be doubted in presence of the enormous number of works of fiction that appeal to the credulity of our generation, for it might easily seem that there could be no great character in a commodity so quickly and easily produced. It must be admitted that good novels are much compromised by bad ones, and that the field at large suffers discredit from overcrowding. I think, however, that this injury is only superficial, and that the superabundance of written fiction proves nothing against the principle itself. It has been vulgarized, like all other kinds of literature, like everything else to-day, and it has proved more than some kinds accessible to vulgarization. But there is as much difference as there ever was between a good novel and a bad one: the bad is swept with all the daubed canvases and spoiled marble into some unvisited limbo, or infinite rubbish-yard beneath the back-windows of the world, and the good subsists and emits its light and stimulates our desire for perfection. As I shall take the liberty of making but a single criticism of Mr. Besant, whose tone is so full of the love of his art, I may as well have done with it at once. He seems to me to mistake in attempting to say so definitely beforehand what sort of an affair the good novel will be. To indicate the danger of such an error as that has been the purpose of these few pages; to suggest that certain traditions on the subject, applied *a priori,* have already had much to answer for, and that the good health of an art which undertakes so immediately to reproduce life must demand that it be perfectly free. It lives upon exercise, and the very meaning of exercise is freedom. The only obligation to which in advance we may hold a novel, without incurring the accusation of being arbitrary, is that it be interesting. That general responsibility rests upon it, but it is the only one I can think of. The ways in which it is at liberty to accomplish this result (of interesting us) strike me as innumerable, and such as can only suffer from being marked out or fenced in by prescription. They are as various as the temperament of man, and they are successful in proportion as they reveal a particular mind, different from others. A novel is in its broadest definition a personal, a direct impression of life: that, to begin with, constitutes its value, which is greater or less according to the intensity of the impression. But there will be no intensity at all, and therefore no value, unless there is freedom to feel and say. The tracing of a line to be followed, of a tone to be taken, of a form to be filled out, is a limitation of that freedom and a suppression of the very thing that we are most curious about. The form, it seems to me, is to be appreciated after the fact: then the author's choice has been made, his standard has been indicated; then we can follow lines and directions and compare tones and resemblances. Then in a word we can enjoy one of the most charming of pleasures, we can estimate quality, we can apply the test of execution. The execution belongs to the author alone; it is what is most personal to him, and we measure him by that. The advantage, the luxury, as well as the torment and responsibility of the novelist, is that there is no limit to what he may attempt as an executant—no limit to his possible experiments, efforts, discoveries, successes. Here it is especially that he works, step by step, like his brother of the brush, of whom we may always say that he has painted his picture in a manner best known to himself. His manner is his secret, not necessarily a jealous one. He cannot disclose it as a general thing if he would; he would be at a loss to teach it to others. I say this with a due recollection of having insisted on the community of method of the artist who paints a picture and the artist who writes a novel. The painter *is* able to teach the rudiments of his practice, and it is possible, from the study of good work (granted the aptitude), both to learn how to paint and to learn how to write. Yet it remains true, without injury to the *rapprochement*, that the literary artist would be obliged to say to his pupil much more than the other, "Ah, well, you must do it as you can!" It is a question of degree, a matter of delicacy. If there are exact sciences, there are also exact arts, and the grammar of painting is so much more definite that it makes the difference.

I ought to add, however, that if Mr. Besant says at the beginning of his essay that the "laws of fiction may be laid down and taught with as much precision and exactness as the laws of harmony, perspective, and proportion," he mitigates what might appear to be an extravagance by applying his remark to "general" laws, and by expressing most of these rules in a manner with which it would certainly be unaccommodating to disagree. That the novelist must write from his experience, that his "characters must be real and such as might be met with in actual life"; that "a young lady brought up in a quiet country village should avoid descriptions of garrison life," and "a writer whose friends and personal experience belong to the lower middle-class should carefully avoid introducing his characters into society"; that one should enter one's notes in a common-place book; that one's figures should be clear in outline; that making them clear by some trick of speech or of carriage is a bad method, and "describing them at length" is a worse one; that English Fiction should have a "conscious moral purpose"; that "it is almost impossible to estimate too highly the value of careful workmanship—that is, of style"; that "the most important point of all is the story," that "the story is everything"; these are principles with most of which it is surely impossible not to sympathize. That remark about the lower middle-class writer and his knowing his place is perhaps rather chilling; but for the rest I should find it difficult to dissent from any one of these recommendations. At the same time, I should find it difficult positively to assent to them, with the exception, perhaps, of the injunction as to entering one's notes in a common-place book. They scarcely seem to me to have the quality that Mr. Besant attributes to the rules of the novelist—the "precision and exactness" of "the laws of harmony, perspective, and proportion." They are suggestive, they are even inspiring, but they are not exact, though they are doubtless as much so as the case admits of: which is a proof of that liberty of interpretation for which I just contended. For the value of these different injunctions—so beautiful and so vague—is wholly in the meaning one attaches to them. The characters, the situation, which strike one as real will be those that touch and interest one most, but the measure of reality is very difficult to fix. The reality of Don Quixote or of Mr. Micawber is a very delicate shade; it is a reality so coloured by the author's vision that, vivid as it may be, one would hesitate to propose it as a model: one would expose one's self to some very embarrassing questions on the part of a pupil. It goes without saying that you will not write a good novel unless you possess the sense of reality; but it will be difficult to give you a recipe for calling that sense into being. Humanity is immense, and reality has a myriad forms; the most one can affirm is that some of the flowers of fiction have the odour of it, and others have not; as for telling you in advance how your nosegay should be composed, that is another affair. It is equally excellent and inconclusive to say that one must write from experience; to our supposititious aspirant such a declaration might savour of mockery. What kind of experience is intended, and where does it begin and end? Experience is never limited, and it is never complete; it is an immense sensibility, a kind of huge spiderweb of the finest silken threads suspended in the chamber of consciousness, and catching every airborne particle in its tissue. It is the very atmosphere of the mind; and when the mind is imaginative—much more when it happens to be that of a man of genius—it takes to itself the faintest hints of life, it converts the very pulses of the air into revelations. The young lady living in a village has only to be a damsel upon whom nothing is lost to make it quite unfair (as it seems to me) to declare to her that she shall have nothing to say about the military. Greater miracles have been seen than that, imagination assisting, she should speak the truth about some of these gentlemen. I remember an English novelist, a woman of genius, telling me that she was much commended for the impression she had managed to give in one of her tales of the nature and way of life of the French Protestant youth. She had been asked where she learned so much about this recondite being, she had been congratulated on her peculiar opportunities. These opportunities consisted in her having once, in Paris, as she ascended a staircase, passed an open door where, in the household of a *pasteur,* some of the young Protestants were seated at table round a finished meal. The glimpse made a picture; it lasted only a moment, but that moment was experience. She had got her direct personal impression, and she turned out her type. She knew what youth was, and what Protestantism; she also had the advantage of having seen what it was to be French, so that she converted these ideas into a concrete image and produced a reality. Above all, however, she was blessed with the faculty which when you give it an inch takes an ell, and which for the artist is a much greater source of strength than any accident of residence or of place in the social scale. The power to guess the unseen from the seen, to trace the implication of things, to judge the whole piece by the pattern, the condition of feeling life in general so completely that you are well on your way to knowing any particular corner of it—this cluster of gifts may almost be said to constitute experience, and they occur in country and in town, and in the most differing stages of education. If experience consists of impressions, it may be said that impressions *are* experience, just as (have we not seen it?) they are the very air we breathe. Therefore, if I should certainly say to a novice, "Write from experience and experience only," I should feel that this was rather a tantalizing monition if I were not careful immediately to add, "Try to be one of the people on whom nothing is lost!"

I am far from intending by this to minimize the importance of exactness—of truth of detail. One can speak best from one's own taste, and I may therefore venture to say that the air of reality (solidity of specification) seems to me to be the supreme virtue of a novel—the merit on which all its other merits (including that conscious moral purpose of which Mr. Besant

speaks) helplessly and submissively depend. If it be not there
they are all as nothing, and if these be there, they owe their
effect to the success with which the author has produced the
illusion of life. The cultivation of this success, the study of this
exquisite process, form, to my taste, the beginning and the end of
the art of the novelist. They are his inspiration, his despair, his
reward, his torment, his delight. It is here in very truth that he
competes with life; it is here that he competes with his brother the
painter in *his* attempt to render the look of things, the look that
conveys their meaning, to catch the colour, the relief, the expression, the surface, the substance of the human spectacle. It is in
regard to this that Mr. Besant is well inspired when he bids him
take notes. He cannot possibly take too many, he cannot possibly
take enough. All life solicits him, and to "render" the simplest surface, to produce the most momentary illusion, is a very compli-
cated business. His case would be easier, and the rule would be
more exact, if Mr. Besant had been able to tell him what notes to
take. But this, I fear, he can never learn in any manual; it is the
business of his life. He has to take a great many in order to
select a few, he has to work them up as he can, and even the
guides and philosophers who might have most to say to him
must leave him alone when it comes to the application of precepts, as we leave the painter in communion with his palette.
That his characters "must be clear in outline," as Mr. Besant
says—he feels that down to his boots; but how he shall make
them so is a secret between his good angel and himself. It
would be absurdly simple if he could be taught that a great deal
of "description" would make them so, or that on the contrary
the absence of description and the cultivation of dialogue, or
the absence of dialogue and the multiplication of "incident,"
would rescue him from his difficulties. Nothing, for instance, is
more possible than that he be of a turn of mind for which this
odd, literal opposition of description and dialogue, incident and
description, has little meaning and light. People often talk of
these things as if they had a kind of internecine distinctness,
instead of melting into each other at every breath, and being
intimately associated parts of one general effort of expression.
I cannot imagine composition existing in a series of blocks, nor
conceive, in any novel worth discussing at all, of a passage of

description that is not in its intention narrative, a passage of
dialogue that is not in its intention descriptive, a touch of truth
of any sort that does not partake of the nature of incident, or
an incident that derives its interest from any other source than
the general and only source of the success of a work of art—
that of being illustrative. A novel is a living thing, all one and
continuous, like any other organism, and in proportion as it lives
will it be found, I think, that in each of the parts there is something of each of the other parts. The critic who over the close
texture of a finished work shall pretend to trace a geography of
items will mark some frontiers as artificial, I fear, as any that
have been known to history. There is an old-fashioned distinction between the novel of character and the novel of incident
which must have cost many a smile to the intending fabulist
who was keen about his work. It appears to me as little to the
point as the equally celebrated distinction between the novel
and the romance—to answer as little to any reality. There are
bad novels and good novels, as there are bad pictures and good
pictures; but that is the only distinction in which I see any
meaning, and I can as little imagine speaking of a novel of character as I can imagine speaking of a picture of character. When
one says picture one says of character, when one says novel one
says of incident, and the terms may be transposed at will. What
is character but the determination of incident? What is incident but the illustration of character? What is either a picture
or a novel that is not of character? What else do we seek in it
and find in it? It is an incident for a woman to stand up with
her hand resting on a table and look out at you in a certain way;
or if it be not an incident I think it will be hard to say what it
is. At the same time it is an expression of character. If you say
you don't see it (character in *that—allons donc!*), this is exactly
what the artist who has reasons of his own for thinking he *does*
see it undertakes to show you. When a young man makes up his
mind that he has not faith enough after all to enter the church
as he intended, that is an incident, though you may not hurry
to the end of the chapter to see whether perhaps he doesn't
change once more. I do not say that these are extraordinary or
startling incidents. I do not pretend to estimate the degree of
interest proceeding from them, for this will depend upon the

skill of the painter. It sounds almost puerile to say that some
incidents are intrinsically much more important than others,
and I need not take this precaution after having professed my
sympathy for the major ones in remarking that the only classification of the novel that I can understand is into that which
has life and that which has it not.

The novel and the romance, the novel of incident and that
of character—these clumsy separations appear to me to have
been made by critics and readers for their own convenience,
and to help them out of some of their occasional queer pre-
dicaments, but to have little reality or interest for the producer, from whose point of view it is of course that we are attempting to consider the art of fiction. The case is the same
with another shadowy category which Mr. Besant apparently
is disposed to set up—that of the "modern English novel";
unless indeed it be that in this matter he has fallen into an
accidental confusion of standpoints. It is not quite clear
whether he intends the remarks in which he alludes to it to be
didactic or historical. It is as difficult to suppose a person intending to write a modern English as to suppose him writing
an ancient English novel: that is a label which begs the question. One writes the novel, one paints the picture, of one's
language and of one's time, and calling it modern English will
not, alas! make the difficult task any easier. No more, unfortunately, will calling this or that work of one's fellow-artist a
romance—unless it be, of course, simply for the pleasantness
of the thing, as for instance when Hawthorne gave his head-
ing to his story of *Blithedale*. The French, who have brought
the theory of fiction to remarkable completeness, have but
one name for the novel, and have not attempted smaller things
in it, that I can see, for that. I can think of no obligation to
which the "romancer" would not be held equally with the novelist; the standard of execution is equally high for each. Of course
it is of execution that we are talking—that being the only point
of a novel that is open to contention. This is perhaps too often
lost sight of, only to produce interminable confusions and cross-
purposes. We must grant the artist his subject, his idea, his
donnée: our criticism is applied only to what he makes of it.
Naturally I do not mean that we are bound to like it or find it

interesting: in case we do not our course is perfectly simple— to let it alone. We may believe that of a certain idea even the most sincere novelist can make nothing at all, and the event may perfectly justify our belief; but the failure will have been a failure to execute, and it is in the execution that the fatal weakness is recorded. If we pretend to respect the artist at all, we must allow him his freedom of choice, in the face, in particular cases, of innumerable presumptions that the choice will not fructify. Art derives a considerable part of its beneficial exercise from flying in the face of presumptions, and some of the most interesting experiments of which it is capable are hidden in the bosom of common things. Gustave Flaubert has written a story about the devotion of a servant-girl to a parrot,[2] and the production, highly finished as it is, cannot on the whole be called a success. We are perfectly free to find it flat, but I think it might have been interesting; and I, for my part, am extremely glad he should have written it; it is a contribution to our knowledge of what can be done—or what cannot. Ivan Turgénieff has written a tale about a deaf and dumb serf and a lap-dog,[3] and the thing is touching, loving, a little masterpiece. He struck the note of life where Gustave Flaubert missed it—he flew in the face of a presumption and achieved a victory. Nothing, of course, will ever take the place of the good old fashion of "liking" a work of art or not liking it: the most improved criticism will not abolish that primitive, that ultimate test. I mention this to guard myself from the accusation of intimating that the idea, the subject, of a novel or a picture, does not matter. It matters, to my sense, in the highest degree, and if I might put up a prayer it would be that artists should select none but the richest. Some, as I have already hastened to admit, are much more remunerative than others, and it would be a world happily arranged in which persons intending to treat them should be exempt from confusions and mistakes. This fortunate condition will arrive only, I fear, on the same day that critics become purged from error. Meanwhile, I repeat, we do not judge the artist with fairness unless we say to him,

2 *Un coeur simple*
3 *Mumu*

"Oh, I grant you your starting-point, because if I did not I should seem to prescribe to you, and heaven forbid I should take that responsibility. If I pretend to tell you what you must not take, you will call upon me to tell you then what you must take; in which case I shall be prettily caught. Moreover, it isn't till I have accepted your data that I can begin to measure you. I have the standard, the pitch; I have no right to tamper with your flute and then criticize your music. Of course I may not like your idea at all; I may think it silly, or stale, or unclean; in which case I wash my hands of you altogether. I may content myself with believing that you will not have succeeded in being interesting, but I shall, of course, not attempt to demonstrate it, and you will be as indifferent to me as I am to you. I needn't remind you that there are all sorts of tastes: who can know it better? Some people, for excellent reasons, don't like to read about carpenters; others, for reasons even better, don't like to read about courtesans. Many object to Americans. Others (I believe they are mainly editors and publishers) won't look at Italians. Some readers don't like quiet subjects; others don't like bustling ones. Some enjoy a complete illusion, others the consciousness of large concessions. They choose their novels accordingly, and if they don't care about your idea they won't, *a fortiori*, care about your treatment."

So that it comes back very quickly, as I have said, to the liking: in spite of M. Zola, who reasons less powerfully than he represents, and who will not reconcile himself to this absoluteness of taste, thinking that there are certain things that people ought to like, and that they can be made to like. I am quite at a loss to imagine anything (at any rate in this matter of fiction) that people *ought* to like or to dislike. Selection will be sure to take care of itself, for it has a constant motive behind it. That motive is simply experience. As people feel life, so they will feel the art that is most closely related to it. This closeness of relation is what we should never forget in talking of the effort of the novel. Many people speak of it as a factitious, artificial form, a product of ingenuity, the business of which is to alter and arrange the things that surround us, to translate them into conventional, traditional moulds. This, however, is a view of the matter which carries us

but a very short way, condemns the art to an eternal repetition of
a few familiar *clichés,* cuts short its development, and leads us
straight up to a dead wall. Catching the very note and trick, the
strange irregular rhythm of life, that is the attempt whose strenu-
ous force keeps Fiction upon her feet. In proportion as in what
she offers us we see life *without* rearrangement do we feel that
we are touching the truth; in proportion as we see it *with* rearrangement do we feel that we are being put off with a substitute,
a compromise and convention. It is not uncommon to hear an
extraordinary assurance of remark in regard to this matter of
rearranging, which is often spoken of as if it were the last word
of art. Mr. Besant seems to me in danger of falling into the great
error with his rather unguarded talk about "selection." Art is
essentially selection, but it is a selection whose main care is to be
typical, to be inclusive. For many people art means rose-coloured
windowpanes, and selection means picking a bouquet for Mrs.
Grundy. They will tell you glibly that artistic considerations have
nothing to do with the disagreeable, with the ugly; they will rattle off shallow commonplaces about the province of art and the
limits of art till you are moved to some wonder in return as to
the province and the limits of ignorance. It appears to me that
no one can ever have made a seriously artistic attempt without
becoming conscious of an immense increase—a kind of revelation
—of freedom. One perceives in that case—by the light of a heavenly ray—that the province of art is all life, all feeling, all observation, all vision. As Mr. Besant so justly intimates, it is all
experience. That is a sufficient answer to those who maintain
that it must not touch the sad things of life, who stick into its
divine unconscious bosom little prohibitory inscriptions on the
end of sticks, such as we see in public gardens—"It is forbidden
to walk on the grass; it is forbidden to touch the flowers; it is
not allowed to introduce dogs or to remain after dark; it is re-
quested to keep to the right." The young aspirant in the line of
fiction whom we continue to imagine will do nothing without
taste, for in that case his freedom would be of little use to him;
but the first advantage of his taste will be to reveal to him the
absurdity of the little sticks and tickets. If he have taste, I must
add, of course he will have ingenuity, and my disrespectful

reference to that quality just now was not meant to imply that
it is useless in fiction. But it is only a secondary aid; the first is a
capacity for receiving straight impressions.

Mr. Besant has some remarks on the question of "the story"
which I shall not attempt to criticize, though they seem to me
to contain a singular ambiguity, because I do not think I understand them. I cannot see what is meant by talking as if
there were a part of a novel which is the story and part of it
which for mystical reasons is not—unless indeed the distinction be made in a sense in which it is difficult to suppose that
any one should attempt to convey anything. "The story," if it
represents anything, represents the subject, the idea, the *donnée* of the novel; and there is surely no "school"—Mr. Besant
speaks of a school—which urges that a novel should be all
treatment and no subject. There must assuredly be something
to treat; every school is intimately conscious of that. This
sense of the story being the idea, the starting-point, of the
novel, is the only one that I see in which it can be spoken of
as something different from its organic whole; and since in
proportion as the work is successful the idea permeates and
penetrates it, informs and animates it, so that every word and
every punctuation-point contribute directly to the expression,
in that proportion do we lose our sense of the story being a
blade which may be drawn more or less out of its sheath. The
story and the novel, the idea and the form, are the needle
and thread, and I never heard of a guild of tailors who recommended the use of the thread without the needle, or the needle without the thread. Mr. Besant is not the only critic who
may be observed to have spoken as if there were certain things
in life which constitute stories, and certain others which do
not. I find the same odd implication in an entertaining article
in the *Pall Mall Gazette,* devoted, as it happens, to Mr. Besant's lecture. "The story is the thing!" says this graceful
writer, as if with a tone of opposition to some other idea. I
should think it was, as every painter who, as the time for
"sending in" his picture looms in the distance, finds himself
still in quest of a subject—as every belated artist not fixed
about his theme will heartily agree. There are some subjects
which speak to us and others which do not, but he would be a

clever man who should undertake to give a rule—an *index expurgatorius*—by which the story and the no-story should be known apart. It is impossible (to me at least) to imagine any such rule which shall not be altogether arbitrary. The writer in the *Pall Mall* opposes the delightful (as I suppose) novel of *Margot la Balafrée* to certain tales in which "Bostonian nymphs" appear to have "rejected English dukes for psychological reasons." [4] I am not acquainted with the romance just designated, and can scarcely forgive the *Pall Mall* critic for not mentioning the name of the author, but the title appears to refer to a lady who may have received a scar in some heroic adventure. I am inconsolable at not being acquainted with this episode, but am utterly at a loss to see why it is a story when the rejection (or acceptance) of a duke is not, and why a reason, psychological or other, is not a subject when a cicatrix is. They are all particles of the multitudinous life with which the novel deals, and surely no dogma which pretends to make it lawful to touch the one and unlawful to touch the other will stand for a moment on its feet. It is the special picture that must stand or fall, according as it seems to possess truth or to lack it. Mr. Besant does not, to my sense, light up the subject by intimating that a story must, under penalty of not being a story, consist of "adventures." Why of adventures more than of green spectacles? He mentions a category of impossible things, and among them he places "fiction without adventure." Why without adventure, more than without matrimony, or celibacy, or parturition, or cholera, or hydropathy, or Jansenism? This seems to me to bring the novel back to the hapless little *rôle* of being an artificial, ingenious thing—bring it down from its large, free character of an immense and exquisite correspondence with life. And what *is* adventure, when it comes to that, and by what sign is the listening pupil to recognize it? It is an adventure—an immense one—for me to write this little article; and for a Bostonian nymph to reject an English duke is an adventure only less stirring, I should say, than for an English duke to be rejected by a Bostonian nymph. I see dramas within dramas in that, and innumerable points of

[4] The "romance" is obviously James' *An International Episode* (1879).

view. A psychological reason is, to my imagination, an object
adorably pictorial; to catch the tint of its complexion—I feel
as if that idea might inspire one to Titianesque efforts. There
are few things more exciting to me, in short, than a psychological reason, and yet, I protest, the novel seems to me the
most magnificent form of art. I have just been reading, at the
same time, the delightful story of *Treasure Island,* by Mr.
Robert Louis Stevenson, and, in a manner less consecutive, the
last tale from M. Edmond de Goncourt, which is entitled
Chérie. One of these works treats of murders, mysteries, islands
of dreadful renown, hairbreadth escapes, miraculous coincidences
and buried doubloons. The other treats of a little French girl
who lived in a fine house in Paris, and died of wounded sensibility
because no one would marry her. I call *Treasure Island* delightful, because it appears to me to have succeeded wonderfully
in what it attempts; and I venture to bestow no epithet upon
Chérie, which strikes me as having failed deplorably in what it
attempts—that is, in tracing the development of the moral consciousness of a child. But one of these productions strikes me
as exactly as much of a novel as the other, and as having a
"story" quite as much. The moral consciousness of a child is
as much a part of life as the islands of the Spanish Main, and
the one sort of geography seems to me to have those "surprises"
of which Mr. Besant speaks quite as much as the other. For myself (since it comes back in the last resort, as I say, to the
preference of the individual), the picture of the child's experience has the advantage that I can at successive steps (an
immense luxury, near to the "sensual pleasure" of which Mr.
Besant's critic in the *Pall Mall* speaks) say Yes or No, as it
may be, to what the artist puts before me. I have been a child
in fact, but I have been on a quest for a buried treasure only in
supposition, and it is a simple accident that with M. de Goncourt
I should have for the most part to say No. With George Eliot,
when she painted that country with a far other intelligence, I
always said Yes.

The most interesting part of Mr. Besant's lecture is unfortunately the briefest passage—his very cursory allusion to the
"conscious moral purpose" of the novel. Here again it is not
very clear whether he be recording a fact or laying down a

principle; it is a great pity that in the latter case he should not
have developed his idea. This branch of the subject is of immense importance, and Mr. Besant's few words point to considerations of the widest reach, not to be lightly disposed of.
He will have treated the art of fiction but superficially who is
not prepared to go every inch of the way that these considerations will carry him. It is for this reason that at the beginning
of these remarks I was careful to notify the reader that my reflections on so large a theme have no pretension to be exhaus-
tive. Like Mr. Besant, I have left the question of the morality
of the novel till the last, and at the last I find I have used up
my space. It is a question surrounded with difficulties, as witness the very first that meets us, in the form of a definite question, on the threshold. Vagueness, in such a discussion, is fatal,
and what is the meaning of your morality and your conscious
moral purpose? Will you not define your terms and explain
how (a novel being a picture) a picture can be either moral
or immoral? You wish to paint a moral picture or carve a
moral statue: will you not tell us how you would set about it?
We are discussing the Art of Fiction; questions of art are
questions (in the widest sense) of execution; questions of
morality are quite another affair, and will you not let us see
how it is that you find it so easy to mix them up? These things
are so clear to Mr. Besant that he has deduced from them a
law which he sees embodied in English Fiction, and which is
"a truly admirable thing and a great cause for congratulation."
It is a great cause for congratulation indeed when such thorny
problems become as smooth as silk. I may add that in so far as
Mr. Besant perceives that in point of fact English Fiction has
addressed itself preponderantly to these delicate questions he
will appear to many people to have made a vain discovery.
They will have been positively struck, on the contrary, with
the moral timidity of the usual English novelist; with his (or
with her) aversion to face the difficulties with which on every
side the treatment of reality bristles. He is apt to be extremely
shy (whereas the picture that Mr. Besant draws is a picture
of boldness), and the sign of his work, for the most part, is a
cautious silence on certain subjects. In the English novel (by
which of course I mean the American as well), more than in

any other, there is a traditional difference between that which people know and that which they agree to admit that they know, that which they see and that which they speak of, that which they feel to be a part of life and that which they allow to enter into literature. There is the great difference, in short, between what they talk of in conversation and what they talk of in print. The essence of moral energy is to survey the whole field, and I should directly reverse Mr. Besant's remark and say not that the English novel has a purpose, but that it has a diffidence. To what degree a purpose in a work of art is a source of corruption I shall not attempt to inquire; the one that seems to me least dangerous is the purpose of making a perfect work. As for our novel, I may say lastly on this score that as we find it in England to-day it strikes me as addressed in a large degree to "young people," and that this in itself constitutes a presumption that it will be rather shy. There are certain things which it is generally agreed not to discuss, not even to mention, before young people. That is very well, but the absence of discussion is not a symptom of the moral passion. The purpose of the English novel—"a truly admirable thing, and a great cause for congratulation"—strikes me therefore as rather negative.

There is one point at which the moral sense and the artistic sense lie very near together; that is in the light of the very obvious truth that the deepest quality of a work of art will always be the quality of the mind of the producer. In proportion as that intelligence is fine will the novel, the picture, the statue partake of the substance of beauty and truth. To be constituted of such elements is, to my vision, to have purpose enough. No good novel will ever proceed from a superficial mind; that seems to me an axiom which, for the artist in fiction, will cover all needful moral ground: if the youthful aspirant take it to heart it will illuminate for him many of the mysteries of "purpose." There are many other useful things that might be said to him, but I have come to the end of my article, and can only touch them as I pass. The critic in the *Pall Mall Gazette,* whom I have already quoted, draws attention to the danger, in speaking of the art of fiction, of generalizing. The danger that he has in mind is rather, I imagine, that of

particularizing, for there are some comprehensive remarks
which, in addition to those embodied in Mr. Besant's suggestive lecture, might without fear of misleading him be addressed to the ingenuous student. I should remind him first of
the magnificence of the form that is open to him, which offers
to sight so few restrictions and such innumerable opportunities. The other arts, in comparison, appear confined and ham-
pered; the various conditions under which they are exercised
are so rigid and definite. But the only condition that I can
think of attaching to the composition of the novel is, as I have
already said, that it be sincere. This freedom is a splendid
privilege, and the first lesson of the young novelist is to learn to
be worthy of it. "Enjoy it as it deserves [I should say to him];
take possession of it, explore it to its utmost extent, publish
it, rejoice in it. All life belongs to you, and do not listen either
to those who would shut you up into corners of it and tell you
that it is only here and there that art inhabits, or to those who
would persuade you that this heavenly messenger wings her
way outside of life altogether, breathing a superfine air, and
turning away her head from the truth of things. There is no
impression of life, no manner of seeing it and feeling it, to
which the plan of the novelist may not offer a place; you have
only to remember that talents so dissimilar as those of Alex-
andre Dumas and Jane Austen, Charles Dickens and Gustave
Flaubert have worked in this field with equal glory. Do not
think too much about optimism and pessimism; try and catch
the colour of life itself. In France to-day we see a prodigious
effort (that of Émile Zola, to whose solid and serious work no
explorer of the capacity of the novel can allude without respect), we see an extraordinary effort vitiated by a spirit of
pessimism on a narrow basis. M. Zola is magnificent, but he
strikes an English reader as ignorant; he has an air of working
in the dark; if he had as much light as energy, his results
would be of the highest value. As for the aberrations of a shallow optimism, the ground (of English fiction especially) is
strewn with their brittle particles as with broken glass. If you
must indulge in conclusions, let them have the taste of a wide
knowledge. Remember that your first duty is to be as complete as possible—to make as perfect a work. Be generous and
delicate and pursue the prize."

William Butler Yeats

[1865–1939]

❦

YEATS WAS BORN IN Ireland, the son of the Anglo-Irish painter, John Butler Yeats. His education included a year at art school, but before he was 21 he committed himself to a career as a poet, a dedication from which he never swerved. His life touched many currents of thought and action of his time—theosophy and spiritualism, Irish nationalism, the Irish theater, politics—but in all his activities he resolutely played the role of Poet (sometimes to the annoyance of his associates, who would have preferred a Politician or a Stage Manager). He was appointed to the Irish Senate in 1922 in recognition of his services to his country; two years later he received the Nobel Prize for literature.

Of the writers in this volume, Yeats is the only one who was born after Darwin published *On the Origin of Species*. This fact is worth noting because it was important to Yeats: in his own mind he was definitely "post-Darwinian." Yeats grew up convinced that "scientific opinion" had deprived him of traditional beliefs, without providing in their place any beliefs which a poet could use (brooding over scientific opinion had, he thought, "extinguished the central flame in Tennyson"); his life was spent in a search for beliefs that would be poetically valid, and his work is a record of that search. This explains Yeats' involvement in such movements as The Hermetic Students of the Golden Dawn, as well as his interest in William Blake and in the French symbolists. For all these interests have this in common—all assumed that through symbols a kind of truth could be discovered and communicated which was not accessible to the methods of science.

In the nineteenth century, as in the twentieth, a hostility to science meant a hostility to the dominant values of society. A significant aspect of the symbolist movement is its assumption that the artist is, and must be, isolated from and hostile toward the society in which he lives. This assumption is not peculiar to the Symbolists; it can be found in Shelley and Byron, and is perhaps an inevitable result of the spread of

312

industrialism and middle-class material prosperity. For as materialism grew, the place of art, with its non-material values, seemed to shrink; to many artists it seemed that science and materialism had together created a world from which art was necessarily and eternally excluded.

Yeats expresses this view in his hostility to "journalists and their readers," and in his contemptuous use of the word *popular*. He is in the symbolist tradition in abandoning the idea of a general audience, and also in urging "a casting out of descriptions of nature for the sake of nature, of the moral law for the sake of the moral law, a casting out of all anecdotes and of that brooding over scientific opinion. . . ." The result, he says, will be a "return to imagination"; but it is also, as he does not say, a withdrawal from areas which had traditionally been the subjects of poetry—from physical nature, from morality, from history, from the realm of ideas and the realm of facts. For symbolism, as Yeats describes it, is a subjective event (one of his favorite words at this period was *dream*), and its truths and realities are not of this world.

Yeats later saw that this view of poetry gave up too much, and he devoted his theory and practice in the next two decades to restoring the actual, the physical, and the human to his poems. But that is a matter for the critic of twentieth-century theory.

BIBLIOGRAPHY. *Essays and Introductions* (New York, 1961); *Explorations* (London, 1962); *Letters*, ed. Allen Wade (New York, 1955).

Richard Ellmann, *Yeats, the Man and the Masks* (New York, 1948); Frank Kermode, *Romantic Image* (London, 1957); T. R. Henn, *The Lonely Tower* (New York, 1952).

TEXT. *Ideas of Good and Evil* (New York, 1903).

THE SYMBOLISM OF POETRY *

[1900]

"SYMBOLISM, AS SEEN IN the writers of our day, would have no value if it were not seen also, under one disguise or another, in every great imaginative writer," writes Mr. Arthur Symons in *The*

* "The Symbolism of Poetry" from *Ideas of Good and Evil* (Copyright 1904), reprinted by permission of The Macmillan Company of Canada, Ltd., and Mrs. W. B. Yeats.

Symbolist Movement in Literature, a subtle book which I cannot praise as I would, because it has been dedicated to me; and he goes on to show how many profound writers have in the last few years sought for a philosophy of poetry in the doctrine of symbolism, and how even in countries where it is almost scandalous to seek for any philosophy of poetry, new writers are following them in their search. We do not know what the writers of ancient times talked of among themselves, and one bull is all that remains of Shakespeare's talk, who was on the edge of modern times; and the journalist is convinced, it seems, that they talked of wine and women and politics, but never about their art, or never quite seriously about their art. He is certain that no one, who had a philosophy of his art or a theory of how he should write, has ever made a work of art, that people have no imagination who do not write without forethought and after-thought as he writes his own articles. He says this with en-thusiasm, because he has heard it at so many comfortable dinner-tables, where someone has mentioned through carelessness, or foolish zeal, a book whose difficulty has offered indolence, or a man who had not forgotten that beauty is an accusation. Those formulas and generalisations, in which a hidden sergeant has drilled the ideas of journalists and through them the ideas of all but all the modern world, have created in their turn a forget-fulness like that of soldiers in battle, so that journalists and their readers have forgotten, among many like events, that Wagner spent seven years arranging and explaining his ideas before he began his most characteristic music; that opera, and with it modern music, arose from certain talks at the house of one Giovanni Bardi of Florence; and that the Pliade laid the founda-tions of modern French literature with a pamphlet. Goethe has said, "a poet needs all philosophy, but he must keep it out of his work," though that is not always necessary; and certainly he cannot know too much, whether about his own work, or about the procreant waters of the soul where the breath first moved, or about the waters under the earth that are the life of passing things; and almost certainly no great art, outside England, where journalists are more powerful and ideas less plentiful than elsewhere, has arisen without a great criticism, for its herald or its interpreter and protector, and it is perhaps for this reason that great art, now that vulgarity has armed itself and multiplied itself, is perhaps dead in England.

All writers, all artists of any kind, in so far as they have had any philosophical or critical power, perhaps just in so far as they have been deliberate artists at all, have had some philosophy, some criticism of their art; and it has often been this philosophy, or this criticism, that has evoked their most startling inspiration, calling into outer life some portion of the divine life, of the buried reality, which could alone extinguish in the emotions what their philosophy or their criticism would extinguish in the intellect. They have sought for no new thing, it may be, but only to understand and to copy the pure inspiration of early times, but because the divine life wars upon our outer life, and must needs change its weapons and its movements as we change ours, inspiration has come to them in beautiful startling shapes. The scientific movement brought with it a literature, which was always tending to lose itself in externalities of all kinds, in opinion, in declamation, in picturesque writing, in word-painting, in what Mr. Symons has called an attempt "to build in brick and mortar inside the covers of a book"; and now writers have begun to dwell upon the element of evocation, of suggestion, upon what we call the symbolism in great writers.

II

In "Symbolism in Painting" I tried to describe the element of symbolism that is in pictures and sculpture, and described a little the symbolism in poetry, but did not describe at all the continuous indefinable symbolism which is the substance of all style.

There are no lines with more melancholy beauty than these by Burns—

> 'The white moon is setting behind the white wave,
> And Time is setting with me, O!' [1]

and these lines are perfectly symbolical. Take from them the whiteness of the moon and of the wave, whose relation to

[1] From "Open the Door to Me, O"; Burns' first line reads, "The wan moon sets behind the white wave."

the setting of Time is too subtle for the intellect, and you take from them their beauty. But, when all are together, moon and wave and whiteness and setting Time and the last melancholy cry, they evoke an emotion which cannot be evoked by any other arrangement of colors and sounds and forms. We may call this metaphorical writing, but it is better to call it symbolical writing, because metaphors are not profound enough to be moving, when they are not symbols, and when they are symbols they are the most perfect, because the most subtle, outside of pure sound, and through them one can the best find out what symbols are. If one begins the reverie with any beautiful lines that one can remember, one finds they are all like those of Burns. Begin with this line by Blake—

The gay fishes on the wave when the moon sucks up the dew;[2]

or these lines by Nash—

> Brightness falls from the air,
> Queens have died young and fair,
> Dust hath closed Helen's eye;' [3]

or these lines by Shakespeare—

> 'Timon hath made his everlasting mansion
> Upon the beached verge of the salt flood;
> Who once a day with his embossed froth
> The turbulent surge shall cover;' [4]

or take some line that is quite simple, that gets its beauty from its place in a story, and see how it flickers with the light of the many symbols that have given the story its beauty, as a sword-blade may flicker with the light of burning towers.

All sounds, all colours, all forms, either because of their pre-ordained energies or because of long association, evoke indefinable and yet precise emotions, or, as I prefer to think, call down among us certain disembodied powers, whose footsteps

---

[2] From "Europe," Blake, *Complete Writings*, ed. Keynes (1957), p. 243.
[3] Thomas Nashe (1567–1601), "In Time of Pestilence."
[4] *Timon of Athens*, Act V, scene i, ll. 216–219.

over our hearts we call emotions; and when sound, and colour, and form are in a musical relation, a beautiful relation to one another, they become as it were one sound, one colour, one form, and evoke an emotion that is made out of their distinct evocations and yet is one emotion. The same relation exists between all portions of every work of art, whether it be an epic or a song, and the more perfect it is, and the more various and numerous the elements that have flowed into its perfection, the more powerful will be the emotion, the power, the god it calls among us. Because an emotion does not exist, or does not become perceptible and active among us, till it has found its expression, in colour, in sound or in form, or in all of these, and because no two modulations or arrangements of these evoke the same emotion, poets and painters and musicians, and in a less degree because their effects are momentary, day and night and cloud and shadow, are continually making and un-making mankind. It is indeed only those things which seem useless or very feeble that have any power, and all those things that seem useful or strong, armies, moving wheels, modes of architecture, modes of government, speculations of the reason, would have been a little different if some mind long ago had not given itself to some emotion, as a woman gives herself to her lover, and shaped sounds or colours or forms, or all of these, into a musical relation, that their emotion might live in other minds. A little lyric evokes an emotion, and this emotion gathers others about it and melts into their being in the making of some great epic; and at last, needing an always less delicate body, or symbol, as it grows more powerful, it flows out, with all it has gathered, among the blind instincts of daily life, where it moves a power within powers, as one sees ring within ring in the stem of an old tree. This is maybe what Arthur O'Shaughnessy meant when he made his poets say they had built Nineveh with their sighing; and I am certainly never certain, when I hear of some war, or of some religious excitement, or of some new manufacture, or of anything else that fills the ear of the world, that it has not all happened because of something that a boy piped in Thessaly. I remember once asking a seer to ask one among the gods who, as she believed, were standing about her in their symbolic bodies, what would come of a charming but seeming trivial labour of a friend, and the form answering,

"the devastation of peoples and the overwhelming of cities." I
doubt indeed if the crude circumstance of the world, which seems
to create all our emotions, does more than reflect, as in multiply-
ing mirrors, the emotions that have come to solitary men in
moments of poetical contemplation; or that love itself would
be more than an animal hunger but for the poet and his shadow
the priest, for unless we believe that outer things are the reality,
we must believe that the gross is the shadow of the subtle, that
things are wise before they become foolish, and secret before they
cry out in the market-place. Solitary men in moments of contemplation receive, as I think, the creative impulse from the
lowest of the Nine Hierarchies, and so make and unmake mankind, and even the world itself, for does not "the eye altering
alter all"?

> Our towns are copied fragments from our breast;
> And all man's Babylons strive but to impart
> The grandeurs of his Babylonian heart.

III

The purpose of rhythm, it has always seemed to me, is to
prolong the moment of contemplation, the moment when we are
both asleep and awake, which is the one moment of creation, by
hushing us with an alluring monotony, while it holds us waking
by variety, to keep us in that state of perhaps real trance, in which
the mind liberated from the pressure of the will is unfolded in
symbols. If certain sensitive persons listen persistently to the
ticking of a watch, or gaze persistently on the monotonous flash-
ing of a light, they fall into the hypnotic trance; and rhythm is
but the ticking of a watch made softer, that one must needs
listen, and various that one may not be swept beyond memory
or grow weary of listening; while the patterns of the artist are
but the monotonous flash woven to take the eyes in a subtler
enchantment. I have heard in meditation voices that were forgotten the moment they had spoken; and I have been swept,
when in more profound meditation, beyond all memory but of
those things that came from beyond the threshold of waking
life. I was writing once at a very symbolical and abstract poem,
when my pen fell on the ground; and as I stooped to pick it up,

I remembered some phantastic adventure that yet did not seem phantastic, and then another like adventure, and when I asked myself when these things had happened, I found that I was remembering my dreams for many nights. I tried to remember what I had done the day before, and then what I had done that morning; but all my waking life had perished from me, and it was only after a struggle that I came to remember it again, and as I did so that more powerful and startling life perished in its turn. Had my pen not fallen on the ground and so made me turn from the images that I was weaving into verse, I would never have known that meditation had become trance, for I would have been like one who does not know that he is passing through a wood because his eyes are on the pathway. So I think that in the making and in the understanding of a work of art, and the more easily if it is full of patterns and symbols and music, we are lured to the threshold of sleep, and it may be far beyond it, without knowing that we have ever set our feet upon the steps of horn or of ivory.

IV

Besides emotional symbols, symbols that evoke emotions alone, —and in this sense all alluring or hateful things are symbols, although their relations with one another are too subtle to delight us fully, away from rhythm and pattern,—there are intellectual symbols, symbols that evoke ideas alone, or ideas mingled with emotions; and outside the very definite traditions of mysticism and the less definite criticism of certain modern poets, these alone are called symbols. Most things belong to one or another kind, according to the way we speak of them and the companions we give them, for symbols, associated with ideas that are more than fragments of the shadows thrown upon the intellect by the emotions they evoke, are the playthings of the allegorist or the pedant, and soon pass away. If I say "white" or "purple" in an ordinary line of poetry, they evoke emotions so exclusively that I cannot say why they move me; but if I say them in the same mood, in the same breath with such obvious intellectual symbols as a cross or a crown of thorns, I think of purity and sovereignty; while innumerable other meanings, which are held to one another by bondage of subtle suggestion, and alike in the emotions and in the intellect, move visibly through my mind, and move invisibly beyond the threshold of sleep, casting lights and shadows of an indefinable wisdom on what had seemed before, it may be, but sterility and noisy violence. It is the intellect that decides where the reader shall ponder over the procession of the symbols, and if the symbols are merely emotional, he gazes from amid the accidents and destinies of the world; but if the symbols are intellectual too, he becomes himself a part of pure intellect, and he is himself mingled with the procession. If I watch a rushy pool in the moonlight, my emotion at its beauty is mixed with memories of the man that I have seen ploughing by its margin, or of the lovers I saw there a night ago; but if I look at the moon herself and remember any of her ancient names and meanings, I move among divine people, and things that have shaken off our mortality, the tower of ivory, the queen of waters, the shining stag among enchanted woods, the white hare sitting upon the hill top, the fool of faery with his shining cup full of dreams, and it may be "make a friend of one of those images of wonder," and "meet the Lord in the air." [5] So, too, if one is moved by Shakespeare, who is content with emotional symbols that he may come nearer to our sympathy, one is mixed with the whole spectacle of the world; while if one is moved by Dante, or by the myth of Demeter, one is mixed into the shadow of God or of a goddess. So too one is furthest from symbols when one is busy doing this or that, but the soul moves among symbols and unfolds in symbols when trance, or madness, or deep meditation has withdrawn it from every impulse but its own. "I then saw," wrote Gerard De Nerval [6] of his madness, "vaguely drifting into form, plastic images of antiquity, which outlined themselves, became definite, and seemed to represent symbols of which I only seized the idea with difficulty." In an earlier time he would have been of that multitude, whose souls austerity withdrew, even more perfectly than madness could withdraw his soul, from hope and memory, from desire and regret, that they might reveal those processions of symbols that men bow to before altars, and woo

---

[5] Blake, "A Vision of the Last Judgment," *Works* (N. Y., 1957), p. 611.
[6] French poet (1808–1855), precursor of the symbolists.

with incense and offerings. But being of our time, he has been like Maeterlinck,[7] like Villiers De L'Isle Adam in *Axël*,[8] like all who are preoccupied with intellectual symbols in our time, a fore-shadower of the new sacred book, of which all the arts, as some-body has said, are begging to dream, and because, as I think, they cannot overcome the slow dying of men's hearts that we call the progress of the world, and lay their hands upon men's heart-strings again, without becoming the garment of religion as in old times.

V

If people were to accept the theory that poetry moves us be-cause of its symbolism, what change should one look for in the manner of our poetry? A return to the way of our fathers, a casting out of descriptions of nature for the sake of nature, of the moral law for the sake of the moral law, a casting out of all anecdotes and of that brooding over scientific opinion that so often extinguished the central flame in Tennyson, and of that vehemence that would make us do or not do certain things; or, in other words, we should come to understand that the beryl stone was enchanted by our fathers that it might unfold the pictures in its heart, and not to mirror our own excited faces, or the boughs waving outside the window. With this change of substance, this return to imagination, this understanding that the laws of art, which are the hidden laws of the world, can alone bind the imagination, would come a change of style, and we would cast out of serious poetry those energetic rhythms, as of a man running, which are the inventions of the will with its eyes always on some-thing to be done or undone; and we would seek out those waver-ing, meditative, organic rhythms, which are the embodiment of the imagination, that neither desires nor hates, because it has done with time, and only wishes to gaze upon some reality, some beauty; nor would it be any longer possible, for anybody to deny the im-portance of form, in all its kinds, for although you can expound an opinion, or describe a thing when your words are not quite

[7] Maurice Maeterlinck (1862–1949), Belgian dramatist and poet.
[8] *Axël*, a Rosicrucian play by Villiers De L'Isle Adam (1833–1889), French symbolist, impressed Yeats.

well chosen, you cannot give a body to something that moves
beyond the senses, unless your words are as subtle, as complex,
as full of mysterious life, as the body of a flower or of a woman.
The form of sincere poetry, unlike the form of the popular poetry,
may indeed be sometimes obscure, or ungrammatical as in some
of the best of the Songs of Innocence and Experience, but it must
have the perfections that escape analysis, the subtleties that have
a new meaning every day, and it must have all this whether it be
but a little song made out of a moment of dreamy indolence, or
some great epic made out of the dreams of one poet and of a
hundred generations whose hands were never weary of the sword.